Praise

A GREEN ⎯⎯⎯⎯ ⎯ ⎯ ⎯⎯ W ⎯⎯⎯ Y

"When I read...Patrick O'Sullivan's memoir, I was by turns amused, entranced, saddened, and astounded by his fortitude in coming through a childhood so fraught with obstacles yet so leavened with love. His portraits of his family and friends, mentors and nemeses, loves and lovers...ring so true, and drew me so effortlessly into the story, that I despaired, hoped, and rejoiced with him at each step along his path.

This is a wonderful...triumphant story, written by someone who can turn a phrase and coin a perfect neologism with the best of them, and Mr. O'Sullivan is one of those rare beings whose healing spirit embraces, with grace, humor, and joy, the hardships he endured."

A.D. Reed
author of *Reed's Homophones: a comprehensive book of sound-alike words*

"This book is a poignant, courageous and colorful exploration of what it takes for a boy to become a man. And it turns out that the man can tell a great story. I don't know whether there's another book in Patrick O'Sullivan's future, but I bet I'm not the only one who hopes the answer is yes."

John D. Gates
author of *The duPont Family* and an award-winning editor and columnist

A Green One *for*

WOODY

Pisgah Press

Pisgah Press was established in 2011 to publish and promote works of quality offering original ideas and insight into the human condition, the realm of knowledge, and the world around us.

Printed in the United States of America

Published by Pisgah Press, LLC
PO Box 1427, Candler, NC 28715
www.pisgahpress.com

Cover: artwork by Lois Williams and adapted by John Walker

pp. 57–58: *Light My Fire,* The Doors © Warner/Chappell Music, Inc.
p. 84: *I Feel Like I'm Fixin' To Die,*
Country Joe McDonald © Alkatraz Corner Music, BMI

Library of Congress Cataloging-in-Publication Data
D. Patrick O'Sullivan
A Green One for Woody/O'Sullivan

Library of Congress Control Number: 2012955414

ISBN-13: 978-0985387549
Biography/Autobiography

First Edition
Third Printing
July 2013

David & Rebekah,
Merry Christmas 2015

Patrick O

A GREEN ONE FOR WOODY

A memoir by
Patrick O'Sullivan

Pisgah Press, LLC
Candler, NC

Dedication

Brian,

I wish I'd been a better brother. Oh, well.

And hang in there, bro'. Your comeback will be absolute and fulfilling. We're cheering for you.

Love,
Rocky

CONTENTS

Contents

One

Bessie's Box

(Summer 1979)

UNCLE EMMETT'S DEMISE was premature and unexpected. He was only forty-three when he took his own life.

An expert marksman and a decorated Army sniper during World War II, Emmett served in the southwest Pacific theater. He was assigned to search out and extinguish Japanese snipers. Guys like him. Emmett returned home a different, damaged man. He suffered chronic headaches and drank excessively, and he acquired a quick temper and suffered occasional amnesia. But just after the war he enjoyed a worthy occupation working for the state of Michigan, plus he hosted a weekly radio show in Jackson, offering advice to veterans, and listeners would call in. He was well known and admired. A local hero.

On an evening when my aunt Frieda, his wife, sent cousins Michael and Phyllis to the movies, Uncle Emmett descended to the cellar. Alone, he sat in a straight-backed chair. One can only imagine the nightmares he suffered. Closing his eyes at bedtime. Only to see, in his mind's eye — and through the telescopic sight of his assassin's rifle — the exploded and disfigured faces of his quarry. Emmett raised his firearm and took precise aim across his lair. He shot his own, pale reflection in a framed, beveled mirror. When Aunt Frieda scrambled down the steps to investigate, he ordered her out of the kill zone. As she retreated to the top of the staircase, another shot rang out, and Uncle Emmett's head no longer had to battle his demons. It had been distributed throughout the room. Not even the police or undertaker could stomach the scene he'd left. So haunted he was by the evil that lurked within that he was compelled to shoot himself twice. And bear witness, the first time.

Emmett was loved and revered and respected. But the family was humiliated and ashamed by his unholy act. Whether selfish or selfless, he killed more than one soul that day when he swallowed his gun. His deliberate act further sullied an already tarnished family name. It wasn't the first time that we'd been embarrassed and disgraced by a member of our clan. Nor would it be the last.

Emmett's mother was my great-grandma Bessie O'Sullivan. Bessie turned ninety-seven on February 4, 1979. But she died an awkward death in June the same year, near her home in Jackson. Bessie was born in 1882 in Grand Isle, Nebraska, and married Patrick Henry O'Sullivan on December 7, 1903, in Grand Rapids, Michigan.

Unless an unexpected tragedy befell one of my ancestors, they often lived to be long in the tooth. This trait was exemplified by William H. Cottrell, Bessie's grandfather and my great-great-great-grandfather. Remarkably, William passed away in 1903 at the age of eighty-seven, when the life expectancy of a man was forty years his junior.

Bessie had four children: Donall O'Sullivan, my grandfather, who we called Bompi; Louise, my aunt who married Charlie Dunigan; Emmett, who committed suicide; and Robert, about whom I knew practically nothing until a few days after Bessie died. Then a box of treasures divulged a bounty of truths, previously untold.

Another untimely death, and a mystery of great curiosity to me, was the loss of Great-grandpa Patrick Henry O'Sullivan, Bessie's husband. He'd been dead forty years by the time she passed away. I could never get a straight answer out of anyone as to how or why he died. Only Uncle Charlie, Aunt Louise's husband, would offer a clue. Charlie used to say to me, "Sonofabitch got drunk and fell in a ditch."

In the 1920s, Patrick and Bessie moved into a wooden bungalow at 312 East High Street in Jackson. For decades, she held court in a small, narrow sunroom off the back of her house where she read the newspaper, listened to the Tigers and watched Johnny Carson host *The Tonight Show*.

Bessie's skin was crinkled and creased, but velvet to the touch. She was beautiful and beguiling in her flowered dresses and chunky jewelry and smelled of sugary perfume that lingered after a loving hug. Her silver hair was always tidy and coiffed high on her head. It was impossible to think of Great-grandma Bessie as old. But it was easy to think of her as great, because she was.

Bessie was bright and articulate, and she had a point of view and was eager to share it. She told salacious jokes and racy tales. We'd sit and she'd talk, and during her storytelling she'd grasp my right hand with hers and the left hand would clutch my right forearm and she wouldn't let go, and I didn't want her to. She told me about toiling for years at the Standard Underwear Company with her sister Leila, who, she said, "died too young," and later in her life at a business that made coils and springs during World War I. She recalled the Great Depression and spoke of the many colorful characters in our family and her unfettered love for life. She was a treasure. A family icon. A modern woman ahead of her time. Strong and confident and real. Honest and good to the bone.

We buried our matriarch beneath the green grass of St. John's Cemetery. Much to the surprise of fellow pallbearers and my numerous Catholic relatives in attendance, I participated in the celebration of Holy Communion. One of my cousins leaned my way and hissed, "I didn't know you were Catholic." I whispered back, but loud enough for the priest and those nearby to hear, "I didn't know you were gay."

Bessie had fallen and broken her hip and had been recovering in a nursing home, called Medical Care, when a trip to the loo and a reluctant bowel movement resulted in a stroke. A nurse found her listing to starboard and dead, slumped on the pot in her room.

My stricken father had been moved to Medical Care as well, mitigating my grandfather Bompi's burdensome visitation schedule. Ironically, Bessie and Daddy were neighbors when she died. A fact that she knew, but he didn't.

After the service and interment there was a boozy, smoky reception at Aunt Louise's cottage on Clarklake thirty minutes south of Jackson. Bompi and I briefly attended the wake, but he insisted I see my dad, since I was in town, and he said, "There's a box that we need to get. Some stuff that Momma wanted me to have."

He drove and I rode along in silence. After we arrived at the nursing home, I sat outside on a long, gray bench that was punctuated, at each end, with ashtrays on pedestals and filled with wet sand and smelling of dirty butts. Just like inside.

I'd decided on the drive that I'd go in only if Bompi insisted. He had

not, so I sat alone and felt guilty and selfish and relieved that I didn't have
to see my dad. I knew Bompi was patting Daddy's arm and calling him
"Bub" and telling him that he was going to be all right. Bompi would kneel
and pray for him and then rub his feet and legs and arms and then he'd
wash his face and fluff his curly hair. Then he'd pat him on the arm again
and say, "Goodbye, Bub. I love you."

Doctors told us he was brain dead when hospitalized in March. But
instead of letting him go, we held onto him. He regained the ability to
breathe on his own, but otherwise lingered in a coma. Unaware of us
or himself.

Bompi emerged from the building twenty minutes later, shuffling his
shoes as he approached me and looking only at the ground in front of his
toes. He was mute and so was I. He'd just buried his mother and visited his
only son and the burdens of the day crushed his spirit and weighed heavy
in his heart. I couldn't wrap myself around my own amorphous feelings.
I loved my dad. And I missed him, too. But he'd tortured me for years.
There was hope near the end. But his sudden rally fell short in late innings,
though by no fault of his own, maybe. It was agonizing to see him limp,
but sometimes twitching, and always unresponsive. To me, he was already
gone. To Bompi, hope sprang eternal. His trust in God sustained him. My
faith waned and wavered with each passing day.

At Bessie's old house, we entered through the sunroom where she and
I used to sit. The door was unlocked. We proceeded to the kitchen and
into the dining room where, on a table covered in doilies crocheted of
Irish linen, there was a corrugated container—a hatbox—with the name
"Donall" written on the side. I snatched the carton. It was neither heavy
nor light and seemed to be filled with papers, which shifted slightly as I
tilted the box to and fro.

"Do you want to go through it?"

"Not now," he said.

"May I?"

"Sure," he said. "But not here, please. Take it to Muskegon with you.
Bring it back in a month. The next time you visit your dad."

"Okay. That sounds good. I will."

———◦◦◦———

IN MUSKEGON, a hundred and fifty miles north of Jackson, at home on Bear Lake Road and behind my closed bedroom door, I put Bessie's box on my bed and opened it and spread the musty contents over an old, colorful quilt comforter.

It was the summer between my junior and senior years of college. The prior ten months had delivered a disastrous sequence of unforeseen tragedies. My dad's coma and Bessie's death were merely chapters in an epic book of woe. Bessie's box offered a distraction and perhaps answers to some of what plagued me.

I was most intrigued by a small, dog-eared journal, its binding all but disintegrated. An inch thick, five-and-a-half inches wide and eight inches tall, it was intended to be a log of "sources, subject points and authors." There were hundreds of entries, sometimes methodical and sometimes haphazard and sometimes chronological, but all reflected fragments of Bessie's early life from the 1890s through 1939. There were newspaper clippings from as far back as 1913. And notations about marriages and births and deaths of friends and relatives, about many of whom I was unaware.

I found a receipt in impeccable condition. It was from Jackson, Michigan, and Desnoyer Funeral Home where, ironically, Bompi worked late in his career, until 1978. The deceased was Miss Leila B. Cothrell, Bessie's younger sister. The one with whom she worked spinning yarn. It was dated August 11, 1917. The charge for her "lavender casket" was $125.00 and the "taxi for priest" was $3.00. The total funeral cost was $184.00. Leila's obituary, yellowed and ragged, was taped inside the first page of the journal. She worked thirteen years at Standard Underwear and "six girls from the...factory" were her pallbearers. She was just thirty years old when she died. And hospitalized for only six days, suffering from the bacterial disease tetanus or, as the newspaper said, "lockjaw."

There were two tattered obituaries, from 1913, for Catherine Sullivan, my great-great grandmother, who emigrated from Ireland in 1868 with her husband. One said she died at sixty-nine years old and the other said she was sixty. Both obituaries listed three sons: Patrick, George and Alexander. There was no mention of her deceased husband, also named George.

According to family lore, when George, Catherine's son, passed away there was a reception at his brother Alex's house in Grand Rapids. It was a beautiful day, and the brothers and uncles and cousins were all drinking heavily—as they're supposed to at a wake. A family disagreement escalated into a fistfight, which turned into a full-fledged donnybrook. Chairs were tossed and tables broken, but no one was arrested or hospitalized. It was a bloody and loving and memorable day for all involved. A perfect Irish funeral.

Catherine's son, Patrick, was my great-grandfather Patrick Henry O'Sullivan, Bessie's husband. I found other records in the journal indicating that Patrick used the surname "Sullivan" early in his life, like his father and mother. But he and his brother Emmett went by "O'Sullivan" in later years. The reason for the change was a mystery.

Five years before Bessie and Patrick were married, there was a journal entry from May 24, 1898, that said, "heard from him at Tampa, Florida" and then on July 3, "at Fernandina, Florida—taken sick." And then a series of notes indicating Patrick was getting better. From October 14, 1898, a memo said, "home" from the Spanish-American War.

There were more obituaries and newspaper articles on various military conflicts and stories about things to which I knew of no obvious connection. And I found additional funeral home receipts for dead relatives, some stuck between pages and others taped or glued inside. There were faded notations memorializing the birth of my grandfather, Bompi, and his brother Emmett and sister Louise.

I discovered an entry regarding mysterious "Uncle" Robert. In some family obituaries, Robert had been listed as "brother" to Bompi and Emmett and Louise. Bessie's journal indicated that she gave birth to Robert in 1902: "Robert Arthur McInnis was born...Wednesday November 12th...Dr. Wright attending." I took a deep breath and reread the note to make certain I hadn't misinterpreted the surname or date. I had not. The date "1902" was written neatly and clearly, in Great-grandma Bessie's own hand. Robert was born to Bessie thirteen months before she and Patrick were married, while she was corresponding with Patrick as he served overseas in the Philippine-American war. They'd been engaged. But, obviously, she had an affair of sorts, and apparently with a man with the last name McInnis.

What a bombshell. I was shocked. Who knew? Robert Arthur McInnis was Bessie's first child and half-brother to Bompi and Emmett and Louise. Bessie and Patrick weren't married until 1903, but they'd been a couple since the late 1890s. Searching the hatbox, I found a single picture of towheaded Robert, in military uniform but without a date or other reference. He looked nothing like my great-grandfather or any other O'Sullivan that I knew. And it all made sense, perhaps. I'd heard family members talk of a McInnis tribe, from Toledo, but I'd always been told they were "distant cousins" of the O'Sullivan clan. But apparently they weren't distant at all, genetically speaking. Cousin Phyllis, Uncle Emmett's daughter, once told me about a McInnis that had been killed by a runaway horse in the early 1900s. He must have been Bessie's lover and Robert's father, the source of a bastard seed and the cause of a century-old secret.

I kept turning pages. A few were blank. Some were filled with recipes, and others contained additional newspaper articles and more obituaries. Near the back of the journal, smartly folded, was a newspaper story that looked as though it had been undisturbed for decades.

The clipping was from *The Detroit Times* and was published with a Detroit dateline, but from the "Jackson Edition." It was dated Friday, February 24, 1939. The banner indicated the paper had "32 PAGES" and cost "THREE CENTS."

The headline shouted, "Probe Death in Sewer Trench." The subhead said, "War Veteran, Ball Player Fatally Hurt."

The story stated that there would be an autopsy "today" (February 24, 1939) with respect to the death of Patrick Henry O'Sullivan, "the former minor league baseball player, coach and veteran of three wars."

Great-grandpa Patrick served in the Spanish-American War, the Philippine-American War and the "World War." The article said that Patrick:

...came to Jackson in 1908 to play with the Jaxon All-Stars, then one of the best semi-pro teams in this section of the country. He had been playing with the Grand Rapids team in the Michigan-Ontario league.

There was further backstory on my great-grandfather. But the journalist also detailed the events that, as they were reported, led to his death at age fifty-eight.

Uncle Charlie used to say, "Sonofabitch got drunk and fell in a ditch." The article, based on interviews and police reports, suggested that Uncle Charlie may have had it right:

O'Sullivan fell into a sewer trench being dug at Railroad and Perrine streets. Willard Hamilton, foreman of the night crew working on the job, told officers he warned O'Sullivan twice not to approach the edge of the excavation and that it was a third approach to the trench which caused the fatal accident.

There were no additional entries in Bessie's journal after Great-grandpa Patrick's passing. No more articles or obituaries or funeral home receipts, though I did find the invoice for Patrick's funeral, still in its original envelope and postmarked March 6, 1939. It was from Denoyer Funeral Home. The cost to bury Patrick Henry O'Sullivan was $358.80, with the footnote that "you may deduct $10.50 as a discount, providing payment in full is mailed on or before March 24, 1939."

Was it a drunken accident or a drunken suicide? He served in three wars as a medic and nurse. He pieced bloody bodies back together. Dozens may have died in his arms. What battle horrors did Patrick see when he closed his eyes at night?

In Bessie's journal, I found a newspaper article from 1916 concerning long-dead Cousin Hortense Dozeman. The Dozemans were of Cottrell lineage and Bessie was close-knit with them. The story said Hortense's father, John Dozeman, perished a year earlier in a freak accident on the first night of his new job working as a night watchman at a construction site near a gravel pit in Grand Rapids. One of his responsibilities was to tend the fire in the big steam shovel at the site. He evidently lost his footing while retrieving kindling from the top of a boxcar and fell to his death in the pit next to the railroad bed. Hortense's grief was debilitating and devastating. Her mom was already dead. Hortense's love for her father was profound and unconditional. While living with her grandmother, Hortense left the following message:

My home was so unpleasant since Dad was killed I have come to the conclusion to end it all. After he went I had no one to care for, to really love. Say goodbye to everybody for me. I think God will forgive me, at least I have that feeling. –Hortense

After finishing the note, Hortense sat and drank a tall glass of sweet, clear carbolic acid. Neighbors heard breaking glass and a body thumping to the floor. But there was no saving her from a wretched and painful death.

"Sonofabitch got drunk and fell in a ditch."

Cousin Hortense jumped. Uncle Emmett jumped. After three wars and too much booze, maybe Great-grandpa Patrick jumped, too?

And then there was my dad. Once a victor himself. Unconscious and perpetually oblivious. He lifted a whiskey bottle to his head and pulled the trigger.

Did he fall or did he jump?

Two

Living With The Dead
(Early 1960s)

I SAW MY first dead person when I was just three years old.

My grandfather used to pick me up so that I could peer inside each casket. He'd hold me, suspended, and I'd rest my hands on the satin surface, hovering over each face. I'd study their noses. Dangling in his arms, I'd search for the slightest flare in their nostrils. I'd watch their chests to be certain they weren't holding their breath. They never were. "Look, but don't touch," he'd say. And I didn't. I saw a thousand lifeless bodies before he retired. And since Bompi and Gigi made their bed in a funeral home, living with the dead was part of my life.

My mom and dad and my brother, Brian, and I lived in Jackson, Michigan, in the early 1960s. Part of that time, in '63 and '64, we stayed in a small white rental house on Michigan Avenue downtown, in the same block as McComb's Funeral Home, where Bompi and Gigi lived and my grandfather worked. Our home was not nice and Michigan Avenue was a busy street. We didn't have money, not much anyway. And my parents couldn't resist the convenience of being able to unload my brother and me at a moment's notice, so we spent almost every weekend at the funeral home. And not at ours.

There would always be at least one body on display at McComb's. Regardless, I would call my grandfather and ask, "Bompi, got any bodies?" The more the merrier. I was never disappointed unless there were dead babies or dead kids. I didn't like that.

By the time we were dropped off, family visitation would have ended. The corpses would lie cold and alone. Out of guilt or love, the bodies would be surrounded with yellow and lavender gladiolus. The flowers were stacked beside and behind the caskets. On occasion, there would be a blanket of red roses or amethyst or angel's breath draped across and over where legs lay still underneath.

Torchiere lamps, with gaudy stained glass designs, flanked the flowers. At night the lamps threw complicated colors across the already cluttered scene and the sweet, syrupy scent from the flowers seemed to intensify. I was happy for that because I didn't want to smell the dead. Bompi assured me that he'd already fixed the corpses so that they wouldn't stink. They did that work in the basement where there was an embalming suite.

I never wanted to see dead babies or little kids. Their coffins looked like jewel boxes, especially the newborns. Thankfully they were, without fail, closed. Seeing older dead people seemed okay. Somehow natural. Their bodies looked natural, too. Dressed for church, but not going. Their hair was perfect and their lips had color. Even the men had rouge on their cheeks and powdered faces and necks. Reposed on a quilted and pillowy mattress, the people looked relaxed and asleep, belying the fact that they were stiffer than boards and forever dead.

In the back of the funeral home were several offices. The one closest to the parking lot was where the magnetic flags were kept. The flags were used to identify cars in the funeral parade. They'd lock down the casket on a gurney and roll it outside and load it into a hearse. Family members would crawl into a black Cadillac limousine that would follow the body to a church or cemetery. Bompi would stick flags on all the cars that would queue up behind the Caddy. Then they would deliver the dead person, inside, to his or her final resting place, outside.

Behind the funeral home there was a four-stall garage with a storage area above for extra casket inventory. The opposite end of the lot, that went through the entire block, was where the owners John and Mimi McComb lived. They had a small, nice, red brick home with a flower garden. Their house faced the street behind the funeral home.

On the east side of the property, there was a sizable steel dumpster that served as my jungle gym, until I sliced open my arm from elbow to shoulder. It took more than two dozen stitches to close the chasm. I wasn't very good at following doctor's orders. I returned to Foote Hospital twice after re-opening my stitches. My mom told me I'd have an ugly scar if I didn't take better care of myself. When the gash finally healed, I had an awful, ugly scar.

Upstairs, above the parlors of dead, was where Bompi and Gigi lived. Their apartment was tiny, with a small space above a porte-cochère that served as the family room. It was adjacent to where Mom Mason "convalesced," as they used to say. In fact, she was stuck in bed with no hope of getting better.

Mom Mason was Gigi's mother and one of my great-grandmothers. Everyone called her Mom Mason. I wasn't sure why. They told me to call her Mom Mason, too. So I did.

Mom Mason was much like the dead people downstairs, except she wasn't dead quite yet. When she did die, conveniently, they just wheeled her body into an ancient elevator and lowered her to the basement to embalm her, and then they stuck her in a casket and carted her off to the cemetery. Then there was no more Mom Mason.

Disconnected from the family room, the apartment's kitchen and bath were near the lift and next to an area where they displayed caskets for sale: "the showroom." That meant we had to keep the door to the family room closed so that some grieving family wouldn't walk by and see Mom Mason lying in her poop. To complicate matters, we were instructed to keep the kitchen and bathroom doors shut as well. Bompi told me that when people shopped for caskets or visited their dead friends or relatives, they didn't want to smell poop or food. And that was another reason to have all those gladiolus, too.

Bompi and Gigi's refrigerator was practically empty because of all the restrictions and Gigi's aversion to cooking. But if you liked whole wheat bread and turkey and cheese and mayo and soft, chewy Archway cookies, then you could find something to eat. The absence of cooking was not alarming. When we stayed with Bompi and Gigi, we usually went out to eat. We often dined down the street at Loomis Park Grill.

At the grill I ordered bowls of bean soup. I liked the salty taste and the comfort of the warm beans. For dessert I'd have mushy rice pudding drowned in cream and sprinkled with cinnamon. There was an A & W Root Beer stand nearby where we'd get juicy burgers and hot fries and large root beers in cold, frosty mugs. Pretty girls would come out to our car and wait on us. We'd pull our food from a tray that hung on the window. At Paka Plaza we'd visit the Coney Island stand and buy hot dogs with chili and chopped white onions piled high on top and mustard and relish, too. They made a huge mess, which upset Gigi. She was "anal," according to my mom. And there was the Taffy Wagon. And my favorite, The Dome. The Dome looked like a mosque, but with carhop service. They served junior-sized cheeseburgers. I'd insist on the regular ones because I was big enough. They had amazing ice cream sundae concoctions that would freeze my head when I ate them too fast. Sometimes drinking water wouldn't help. I'd have to lie on the floor of the car until my head thawed.

I slept above the porte-cochère on a couch that folded out into a bed by the television. I'd stay up late and watch black-and-white cowboy movies and pray that Mom Mason didn't wake up and moan and beg for the bed pan. If she did, I'd pretend to be asleep and hope that Bompi or Gigi would hear her. Or that she'd fall back asleep. Without pooping on herself.

Each night, before I got ready for bed, my grandfather would go through his close-up routine. When I wasn't there, he would go downstairs and turn off all the lights and check the doors to make sure they were locked. When I spent the night, though, I turned out the lights. First Bompi would go downstairs and lock the doors. Then he would come upstairs and tell me that it was okay for me to "close up." I'd go downstairs among the dead. Starting with the casket in the parlor furthest from the stairs, I'd turn off the torchieres and proceed to the next room, until all the lights were out. Except for the last one. Next to the casket nearest the stairway.

A funeral parlor at night is the quietest place on earth. When I grew tall enough, I'd study the face on the last cadaver. And check again for the slightest movement of the lips. A flare of a nostril. The rise or fall of the chest. The smell of the gladiolas hung thick and sweet. The closer I came to turning off the last light, the faster my heart would beat. The excitement heightened my senses to the stillness and the smells and the fear of being stuck, in the dark, with rooms full of death.

I'd whisper "goodnight" to the final corpse—the one in front of me—then I'd take a deep breath, turn off the switch of the last torchiere and run like hell, up the stairs, into Bompi's loving arms.

Three

Dead Stiff
(Early 1963)

NO ONE KNEW I'd snuck into the basement, outside the embalming room, while some lady was being drained of her blood and flushed of unwanted fluids and reconstituted with formaldehyde and ethanol.

A lift ran from the basement to the casket showroom on the second floor. There was a scissor-style grate door on the elevator and a wooden deck. After throwing the black metal grate shut, a large switch had to be toggled before the noisy gears would engage and move the lift up or down. The ride was loud and jarring. Starts and stops were jerky and abrupt. But the longest possible trip was only two floors up or down. The lift worked just fine for that.

The previous day Bompi had taken me for a ride to show me the embalming room, but with no dead people present. I saw wall posters that diagrammed the human venous system and cabinets neat with brightly colored fluids in glass jars. There were sinks and tanks and hoses and pumps and a huge, slanted stainless steel table that had drain holes that connected to more hoses that led somewhere down, underneath the floor. Something that resembled a round, white ceramic bathtub sat in the center of the room.

Acrid smells filled the air, similar to cleaning fluids but more pungent. I couldn't help but think it would be better to smell food in the parlors of dead people. But Bompi assured me the odors of the embalming fluids never left the basement, and the only thing we'd ever smell upstairs would be flowers.

I learned early on that in the embalming suite dead people went through a transformation that preserved them, temporarily, and made them present-able to the public. It was where the magic happened. Bompi promised me that no dead person whom he embalmed would ever stink up the funeral home. I was happy for that because that was my primary concern.

There was a sit-down hair dryer in the corner of the suite, just like the ones I'd seen at my grandma's beauty parlor. A big, cone-shaped hood pivoted on a column above a chair. Gigi's hairdresser would guide her to the chair, position the massive cone over her head, lower it and flick a switch. The machine made whirring sounds as though readying for take-off. But, of course, the dryer didn't move. Instead, Gigi and the other grandmothers would sit for what seemed like forever, covered in bland gowns and sucking on cigarettes with ashtrays balanced on their laps, as they impatiently smoked and thumbed *Life* magazines. I imagined a dead woman under the dryer, in a gown, but without the cigarette and magazine and strapped into place, to stay upright, as the machine whirred above a head that could no longer hear.

Mounted on the wall was a pegboard where huge needles of different shapes and sizes were stored. And there was thread, too. Bompi told me they used the needles and thread to "set the person's features," sew up incisions and tie down uncooperative body parts. They were essential tools of the mortician. He was proud of their work.

The next day I was goofing around the funeral home, exploring different rooms and closets, and I found a back stairway that led to the basement. I heard someone down there. I didn't want to disturb them if for some reason they were going about important business. And I knew I was some-where that I shouldn't have been. But I went on anyway.

Off the back stairway, the basement was a maze of discarded lamps and chairs and tables as well as other furnishings, broken or out of fashion. I inched toward a light that glowed in the embalming area. I could see move-ment, but I couldn't see what they were doing. Until I got too close. And then I saw everything.

My grandfather and another man were conducting an awkward dance with a partially covered dead woman. They were in the process of moving the lady from a table where she'd lain with her head on a block. They tried to move her, without the benefit of a stretcher, and her body didn't cooperate. Her arms and legs were stiff, pointing in different directions. She was white-skinned and white-headed and bony and wrinkled and brittle. In their attempt to place her in the ceramic tub, they dropped her. She thumped and crunched to the floor. The man with Bompi cursed. They lifted her up enough to get a white sheet underneath. The three-way dance turned into a wrestling match and, without grace, they plopped her down into the tub. Her limbs hung over the sides and her head fell back. I thought it might snap off. But they slid her down, so her head was in a more comfortable position. Of course that was ridiculous. She was dead and couldn't be comfortable or uncomfortable. But that's what I was thinking.

My heart was in my throat. I was fascinated. I wanted to see more. But I had an inkling that I was somewhere I wasn't supposed to be. I silently picked my way back through the maze of dated lamps and chairs and tables.

I found the stairway and sneaked quietly back to the apartment upstairs, with an image of the stiff, leggy dead lady in a tub forever stuck in my head.

Four

Chief Rocky

(September 1963)

THE KINDERGARTEN TEACHER was holding a clipboard, from which she was reading names aloud.

"When I read your name, you should stand. Stay standing until all the names have been read."

In unison, we nodded our little heads.

When she said, "Patrick O'Sullivan," I didn't move. She read the name again. No one stood, including me. So she kept going. After exhausting the names on the list, she read the name one more time, "Patrick O'Sullivan." I was the only kid still sitting on the floor except for the one next to me. Whose name she didn't call, either.

We'd been sitting in a big circle. Fifteen of us. We were scared and fidgety. The kid next to me smelled like pee and Chocks Vitamins. The teacher approached me and said, "I met your mommy this morning. I'm certain she said your name was Patrick."

"Nope. My name is Rocky."

Pee-boy, still next to me, scooted closer, sitting his smelly, wet corduroys on my hand. I jerked my hand out from under him, singeing the skin. He looked at me like I was a freak. My hand was damp. And red. I slid it under my own leg so the kid couldn't get it any wetter.

"Well, it says here your name is Patrick."

"Mommy and Daddy and Bompi and Gigi call me Rocky."

She told everyone else to "sit back down, please." I scooted further away from pee-boy. The teacher passed out Indian headdresses made of colored construction paper, and we sat in a circle again and pretended to be warrior chiefs. We chanted, sitting with our legs crossed, "Indian style," she said. We folded our arms across our chests. She directed us to say, "How." The kid next to me still smelled like pee and vitamins. I thought I'd rather have been home watching *Howdy Doody* or *Our Gang* or *Superman* or *The Lone Ranger* on television. Or, better yet, checking out the new dead people at the funeral home.

After school, the teacher sent me home with a note detailing the disruption I'd caused. My mom apologized to me. She explained that the only name I ever remembered being called was not my name at all. Not legally, anyway. She told me that when I came home from the hospital, after my birth on November 19, 1957, I had my fists clenched tightly and tucked under my chin. My dad decided, at that moment, my name would change. No longer Patrick, I became Rocky.

One of my dad's heroes was 1950s middleweight champion Rocky Graziano, whose name was really Thomas Barbella. Daddy was also a fan of Rocky Colavito, a handsome Cleveland Indian in 1957. My dad loved the Indians, and our home state team, the Detroit Tigers. Given the circumstances of the day, I decided that I didn't like the Cleveland Indians. And I didn't care if my dad did.

Then, a week after school started, Bompie told me my first name was not Patrick, as I'd come to understand. It was really Donall. When he heard about the confusion with Rocky and Patrick, he thought that he should tell me the real truth. That just made things even more confusing.

He emphasized that my name was not Donald. It was Donall, with two "l's" on the end. Donall was Bompi's first name, too. And I learned that my dad's name was not David, as I'd been told, but Donall as well. His middle name was David. So I'd understood my new name was Patrick O'Sullivan. But I learned it was really Donall Patrick O'Sullivan. At school, I was to go by Patrick. At home, I would be Rocky. I wouldn't be called Donall at all, just like my dad, and not like my grandfather, Bompi, whose name was Donall Patrick O'Sullivan, like me, but everyone called him Don, except for those of us that called him Bompi, and my cousins, who called him Uncle Donkey.

Sure as sugar, it was all kind of confusing.

My mom's family, the Sweetlands, would still know me as Patrick. Not Donall or Rocky. The Sweetlands hated my dad's guts. It was better that they not learn my dad had changed my name. That was just another reason not to like him.

I rarely had to see the Sweetlands, anyway. That was just as well. I was taught to fear them, so I did.

Five

The First Family

MOMMY, Daddy and friends would gather at our rental house on Michigan Avenue, just down the street from McComb's Funeral Home. They'd listen to a record album called *The First Family*. While the disc spun, they'd drink adult beverages and laugh out loud and chain smoke cigarettes. Then they'd drink more and laugh even louder.

The album cover showed the first family. But not really. They looked similar to the Kennedy clan, gathered on the White House lawn. There was a look-a-like to Caroline's pony. Plus water skis, a butler and a nurse. And what might have been the real White House, in the background.

I didn't understand the parody. But my parents thought the impersonation of President Kennedy's New England accent was hysterical, and so did I. The skits seemed harmless. The actors poked fun at the real first family, but the intent didn't seem mean-spirited. We'd listen to the skits over and over, and no one thought any less of the Kennedy's. It was all in good fun. Everyone roared. It made me so happy that I would dance around the room and kick up my heels. And I'd laugh, too.

The album was made in front of a live audience. Their guffaws launched Mommy and Daddy into a comic tizzy. The performer did sound like President Kennedy. I'd listened to the President talk on television on numerous occasions. At least once during the Cuban Missile crisis. And other times, too. He was treated more like a movie star than a politician. On the news,

I saw Marilyn Monroe sing "Happy Birthday" to the President.

In November of 1963, I attended kindergarten class in the morning. You were either a morning student or an afternoon student. Kindergarteners went to school for half a day. And that was still too long.

On November 22, just after noon, I noticed older kids walking home from school, consoling one another. They didn't typically leave school until after three o'clock. My mom was home. I asked her why the kids were crying. About the same time, she received a phone call from Bompi. He asked her if she'd heard the news. She said, "What news?" Then she turned on the television.

A very sad man sat hunched behind a desk. He was talking in the most serious of tones, reporting that JFK had been shot dead in Dallas, Texas.

Later in the afternoon, we learned that Lee Harvey Oswald had been arrested for assassinating the President.

Just two days later, I was watching live television with my dad when Jack Ruby stepped out from a gathering of cops and journalists and photographers and shot Lee Harvey Oswald with a snub-nosed Colt Cobra. At first it was hard for me to process what I'd seen. But the media replayed the scene over and over and over. Ruby simply stepped out of the crowd. He stuck a gun in the gut of the President's killer. Then he pulled the trigger. Just like that.

It was easy.

President Kennedy's funeral was the day after Oswald's murder. On television, we watched, in silence, as a horse-drawn caisson carried the flag-draped casket. The clacking hooves cut through the stillness all the way to St. Matthew's Cathedral. An enormous, coal-black quarter horse marched alone, without a rider but with boots reversed in the stirrups.

"That's in honor of the President," my dad said.

Outside the Cathedral, John, Jr., three years old and three years my junior, offered his dead dad an official-looking salute. The gesture was purposeful, but peculiar in that he was wearing a double-breasted coat, shorts and white bobby socks. Dressed curiously to look like a girl on a cool November day.

The pomp and circumstance made a huge impression. The significance of the moment, if not obvious from how friends and family reacted, was driven home by the sober events so well documented by television. I sat as close to the tube as my mom would allow.

My dad and I set up a tent in the family room. He said he fancied camping. But he and I never did so outside. We used encyclopedias to hold down the floor corners. He tied off the top to doors and the stairwell. We gathered a pile of pillows and blankets and camped for two nights. The canvas smelled of damp, cut grass. It felt like being outside. But safe from madmen with guns. Or whatever kind of evil lurked behind bookshelves or grassy knolls. Or in the sewers on the street.

We created a womb of invincibility. It helped me through a few troubling days. Before long I began to forget how horrible things were. Time fogged my memory. Soon other thoughts would occupy my time and mind.

We didn't play *The First Family* album after President Kennedy was gone. The parodied Harvard accents were no longer humorous. The record cover's image of the faux first family seemed suddenly disrespectful. Instead of harmless fun. One day, I discovered the album. I walked it over to the big metal dumpster behind the funeral home. The same one on which I sliced my arm. I scaled the beast, then lowered myself into its belly. I buried the record deep inside.

I didn't want anyone, anywhere, to ever listen to it again.

Six

Oh, Brother

GRANDMA GIGI OFTEN complained about her urgent need for a bowel movement. To get things moving along, she'd eat chocolate Ex-Lax tablets.

Gigi gobbled Ex-Lax like it was candy. She'd make Mom Mason eat them, too. Mom would lie across her bed pan and fuss about not being able to go. Gigi would share her not-so-secret weapon. Mom Mason would gum the medicine until she could swallow it. Then Gigi would hold a glass of water in front of Mom's face with a straw so that Mom could wash it down. There was always Ex-Lax next to Mom Mason's bed. And Gigi kept a supply in her purse, too. I'm not sure where Brian—who was thirteen months younger than I—found the medicine, but there was no shortage in the apartment.

Brian and I were at the funeral home while my mom and dad were away. Bompi was downstairs. Gigi was at work. Mom Mason was confined to her bed. I was counting pennies and didn't notice when Brian started to eat the Ex-Lax. I found him on the floor, at the foot of Mom Mason's bed. I yelled for Bompi. When he saw what had happened he shouted, "Shit." I immediately took two steps back. If "shit" meant that Brian might explode, I was certain the stink would be worse than when Mom Mason pooped in her pan. And, for sure, I didn't want any of it sprayed on me.

We were at the hospital minutes later, in the emergency room. It was familiar to me because I'd ended up there the previous year on multiple occasions. My last visit was after my red flying saucer crashed into a tree at the bottom of the hill at Loomis Park, across the street from our rental. I hit the oak at full speed, sliding backwards. I fractured my skull. There didn't appear to be any permanent damage at the time.

I remembered the dingy green walls and how cold and awful the place was. I didn't like the doctors or nurses. They lectured me about sliding down the snowy hill into the trees and how dangerous it was. I said, "I didn't crash on purpose."

Brian's condition was of grave concern, based on the long faces of Mommy and Bompi. Gigi appeared later. She said she was sorry about what had happened. She wasn't sure if Brian took the Ex-Lax out of her purse or off the nightstand or "from somewhere else." The doctor met us in the waiting room. They were going to "pump Brian's stomach." I wasn't positive what that meant, but I knew it was something I didn't want to befall me.

They emptied his gut and sucked out all the Ex-Lax and his breakfast and lunch and dinner, and maybe some lipstick or whatever else Brian found and ate out of Gigi's purse. Or off the nightstand.

———————◆❧◆———————

BRIAN AND I didn't get along. And the first chance he had to make me the scapegoat for something he did, he took advantage—to my detriment.

I was already in hot water. While my mom was running errands, I dismantled a wooden trellis in our backyard. The structure was old and scabby, with peeling white paint. A number of segments were broken. Nails were in the process of reversing their intended direction, exposing their heads. The previous week, Bompi had shown me how to pull a nail with the claw of a hammer. He was doing handyman work at the funeral home. I was his helper. When I used two hands, I could yank out a nail as well as he could.

I found a hammer in the garage and marched to the backyard, determined to demonstrate my nail-removal skill on the rotting arbor. When my mom confronted me, weapon in hand and the trellis in a hundred pieces on the grass, I told her that the structure had been attacked by a giant, large woodpecker. I showed her, with my hands spread far apart, how big the woodpecker was.

She belly-laughed and applauded my creativity. But I could tell she was also disappointed. And she admonished me.

My brother wasn't quite as inventive a week later. My mom and dad had gone somewhere. Brian and I were left to fend for ourselves. He found my mom's red nail polish and concluded that the dining room walls would be a terrific place to demonstrate his emerging graffiti skills. I was unaware of his deed, but alerted to a concern when my mom screamed "Rocky!" and demanded "your ass" in the dining room.

My brother had written "roc," the first three letters of my nickname, on the wall. He attempted to camouflage his artistry by sliding a dining room chair in front of his handiwork.

"I suppose a giant, large woodpecker wrote your name on my dining room wall?" my mom asked sarcastically.

I unconvincingly made my case. Brian played dumb and dumber. I was grounded for two days. And perpetually pissed at my brother.

Seven

Daddy

(Winter/Spring 1964)

MY DAD HAD forewarned me. "We're going ice fishing." I wasn't sure what to expect. I'd never fished through the ice before.

When I was five, the previous summer, we had vacationed with Bompi and Gigi and rented a cabin on Otsego Lake. We caught perch and bluegill. Some of them were the size of my dad's hands, which were pretty big. My mom and brother didn't go because he couldn't be trusted and didn't like to fish. Gigi didn't fish, either. But she came along anyway and sat on the shore with a scarf protecting the big bump of hair on her head. She passed time picking lint off her slacks and smoking cigarettes, while Bompi and my dad and I fished from a wooden boat that we rowed offshore. Just past the drop-off.

My dad woke me on a Saturday morning in January, before sunrise. He helped me dress, putting a snowsuit on over my clothes. Before we left for the lake, we walked down the street to the funeral home. Daddy threw snowballs at Bompi and Gigi's second floor bedroom window. He asked me to throw, too. I had on the bulky snowsuit and couldn't toss a snowball out of my shadow. Finally Bompi came to the window. My dad signaled for him to join us. Bompi waved to me and smiled. Then he shook his head back and forth, while looking at my dad. Daddy said, "Come on." We walked back to our place.

I climbed into his frozen car and we rode out Michigan Avenue. It was dark and cold. The road was white with snow. Most people were still in bed except kids waking up early, in anticipation of Saturday cartoons. Not me. I was going ice fishing with my dad.

We picked up donuts and hot chocolate for me. My dad smoked cigarettes and drank coffee while he drove. I ate a donut that was a foot long. I told my dad that Bompi called the donut a "long john." Daddy said it was a "Bismarck." I didn't care what it was called because it was covered in powdered sugar. When I bit into it I got a burst of red jelly. Eating the donut was better than watching silly cartoons.

We finally reached a lake in the country. But it looked like a field covered with snow. I knew it was a lake because of the land sloping up from the edges of the flat, white surface. In some areas there were tall grasses surrounding the frozen water, bent heavy with snow. The sky was gray and low. They weren't clouds, really. Just one great, gauzy gray blanket that covered everything above us. Out of the blanket an occasional flurry of snow would wiggle down from the sky. And fall at our feet.

My dad opened the car trunk. I was surprised to see my sled. There were also two buckets, a tackle box and a Styrofoam cooler that squeaked uncomfortably when my dad picked it up and strapped it to the toboggan with the other gear. He dragged our cargo by woven rope and carried a big, steel auger. We trudged onto the lake. As we walked along, the crunch of the snow and ice rang loudly in my ears. But there was no one else to hear.

Daddy punched a hole in the ice. Then he sat me on an upside-down pail and put a tiny wax worm on a tinier hook on a fishing pole and line that looked more like a toy than the kind we used the previous summer. The pole was only two feet long. I thought that was great because it was just my size. He showed me how to lower the line into the hole and jig the wax worm up and down. "Before long," he said, "we'll be catching fish."

He punched his own hole and sat on his own bucket. We jigged our lines, anticipating scaly rewards. Daddy opened the cooler and grabbed a beer. We sat in the cold and nothing happened for a long time. He showed me how to take a ladle and scoop the crust of ice that formed on the water in my hole. It was fun for a time or two. I began to get bored and my dad was piling up empty cans of beer. I asked him if I could walk on the lake. He said, "Sure. But be careful."

As long as I could see my dad, I felt safe. I walked but there wasn't much else to see. It was more about listening than looking. With each step I made a slightly different crunching sound. I listened to myself crunch, crunch,

crunch. Each crunch sounded different, and the same, but different. I could still see my dad when I arrived near a section of the shoreline that was less elevated. There was a narrow river, either feeding into the lake or away from it. I walked closer to see better. The ice went from snow-covered to mushy and gray. I stomped on it. That was not the smart thing to do. I punched through with my leg. Like my dad did with the auger.

The water underneath was not still. It was rushing away from the lake toward the river. My leg was being dragged in the same direction. The ice began to break and slope down. Water rose around me and I clawed at the mushy snow with my mittens. My dad was a football field away. I didn't bother to yell for him because I was solely focused on getting out of the water. But I was slipping the wrong way. My leg was cold and my snowsuit and pants were saturated. My boot had filled with water. I was clawing at the mush in a frantic panic. I feared the end of me if my second leg found the lake. After what seemed like minutes, but was probably just seconds, I clawed myself to safety and crawled on my hands and knees away from the hole. I didn't stop until the ice was covered with white snow again. And not mushy and gray.

I knew my dad would be furious. I'd seen him angry before and I didn't want that. My snowsuit was soaked. My boot was full of water and my teeth were chattering. I made my way toward him and his bucket and heap of cans. Halfway back I stopped because water was sloshing up my leg with each step. When I pulled off my boot my sock went with it. My foot was so red it was purple. I couldn't feel my toes or foot. I put my sock and boot back on. When I arrived at our fish camp my dad said, "I'm out of beer. Time to go."

He turned his back to me and unzipped his trousers. He peed into his ice fishing hole.

Then we left.

⁕──────⁕❦⁕──────⁕

NOT LONG AFTER we went ice fishing, Daddy brought home a black German shepherd puppy and proclaimed his name Night Train.

Dick "Night Train" Lane was one of my dad's favorite football players. Lane joined the Detroit Lions in 1960. He was born in Austin, Texas, and played junior college ball at Western Nebraska and then the Los Angeles Rams and Chicago Cardinals before he was traded to Detroit. My dad told me Night Train's mom was a hooker and his dad was a pimp. He was the most feared tackler in football because of his propensity to rip ball carriers to the turf by snaring their heads or necks.

Night Train the dog was as black as Night Train the Lion. And equally intimidating. The puppy grew quickly and, before long, he was big and lean and beautiful. White teeth gleamed against red gums, and his royal blackness often bared his teeth when things didn't go his way.

Since I'd dismantled the trellis and my brother had painted fingernail polish on the dining room walls and we had a size-ten German shepherd in a size-seven house, my mom and dad came to the logical conclusion that we should move. So we did.

We relocated to another small, white rental a half-hour drive south of town, across the street from a public beach on Clarklake and not far from Uncle Charlie and Aunt Louise's cottage on the same lake. Our house was perched on a hill and had a bigger yard and less car traffic. It was a good place for little kids and a dog.

The great irony of the Night Train's namesake was that he learned how to hike a football. My dad told friends that Night Train taught himself. I didn't know if that was true or not. The dog would straddle a football with his paws properly positioned. Then, on the command—"hike!"—he would jettison the ball between his hind legs. We'd pick sides to play in the back-yard. Night Train played center for each team. That was fine because that's what Night Train wanted to do. And he wasn't good for much else. Except scaring people. And biting them.

Night Train's first victim was my cousin Clancey. We were running around the backyard at the Clarklake rental. Clancey was provoking Night Train to jump into the air. While descending from one of his fabulous leaps, he was able to sink his canines into Clancey's already fat lower lip. Night Train didn't let go. The result was a bloody mess, another trip to the hospital and a visit by a sheriff's deputy, who had heard about the huge, black German Shepherd. The deputy sat at our picnic table. As he talked to my dad, he drew his .38 revolver. He stuck it under Night Train's nose and let him sniff it. The deputy boasted that sometimes he shot dogs that bit people.

I was more frightened of the sheriff than Night Train. Regardless, the episode was embarrassing and dangerous. My dad excused it all away. Night Train was "still a puppy, after all."

And he blamed it on Clancey, nobody's favorite cousin.

Eight

Mommy

MY MOM WAS born a preacher's kid.

As the daughter of the Reverend Albert Sweetland and his wife, Carrie, she told me early on that there were two kinds of preachers' kids. Those who acted like preachers expected their kids to act. And those who didn't. She said she was the latter, not the former.

According to Clarklake lore, late in the summer of 1957 Mommy asked Uncle Charlie to pull her with a powerboat, on one water ski, while she was seven months pregnant with me. Holding the rope handle in one hand, a can of Stroh's in her free hand and a cigarette dangling from her lips, she slalomed back and forth across the lake, alternating the beer with the cigarette. She did it for the entertainment pleasure of our boozing family and the rowdy crowd that had gathered on the beach.

She was a darling. A favorite of the folks on my dad's side of the family. She seemed a better fit for the O'Sullivans than the Sweetlands. I figured that was part of what attracted my mom to my dad and to the rest of our clan. An act of defiance in the face of her fundamentalist Baptist upbringing. She found uncommon comfort in being welcomed into the bosom of a family that was more suitable to her than her own.

She was funny, bright, attractive and engaging. She found little benefit in the addition of lipstick or rouge. She was real and natural, and without pretense in every regard. With her there was nothing to hide, except the contempt she had for some of her own family that had teased and berated and belittled her as a little girl. But she prevailed. She would live a life in a direction of her own choosing. Defying her parents and their One-Way Baptist Church.

Mommy was the pride of Greenville, Michigan—the high school's 1954 football season homecoming queen and the target of desire for any man that met her. She was every bit as beautiful as she was witty and charming and loving. A little boy couldn't have had a better mom.

At Clarklake, our small rental was across the street from a public park that featured a tidy beach adjacent to an area with reeds and weeds that sported turtles and frogs and snakes. I'd wade through the marshy water and catch whatever I could with my hands. I learned that if you grabbed snakes they sometimes returned the favor with their razor-sharp mouths.

On a warm, pretty day during the summer of 1964, Mommy asked if I wanted to play in the water in front of Uncle Charlie and Aunt Louise's cottage. I said, "Sure." I didn't want to go back to where the snakes grabbed me. She asked me to change into my swimsuit. I did. I waited patiently for her in the family room where my dad was playing with my brother, Brian, and Night Train.

My mom was gone for a long time. Finally, from the top of the stairs, in beauty pageant mode, the former Miss Greenville proudly announced herself and requested attention. She said, "I'm about to model the latest in one-piece swimwear."

First a foot appeared. Then disappeared. Then it was back again. The second time, I noticed her foot was wrapped in an open-toed, high-heeled shoe. Soon I could see both feet. And part of Mommy's legs. She began making exaggerated kicks as she descended the stairs. Before long she was showing off all of her pretty, brown bare legs. Then I noticed she had on a tiny, green bikini bottom. As she revealed more, I could see she had two of my dad's green paisley ties tucked into the front of her bikini, crossing in the middle of her chest and thrown over each shoulder. As she spun around while continuing to descend, I noticed that the ties were tucked into the back of her bikini, too. When she spun around again, I finally saw that the ties framed her naked, white boobs. Bouncing up and down. As she finished her decent.

Too quickly, she was done. She gave a final beauty queen wave and pose with her left hand on her hip. The radiant smile on her face could have shined light around a corner. She was very happy with herself. And gorgeous as well.

I said, "Mommy, you can't go to Uncle Charlie and Aunt Louise's wearing that. No, you can't."

Nine

Face of the Winds

OUR STAY AT the rental at Clarklake was brief—just a few months. My dad announced we were moving again, the fifth time for me.

He told us he'd been hired as a social worker in Muskegon, Michigan. He said it involved helping other people. I thought that sounded generous and good. My dad moved before the rest of us to start his new job and find a place to live. He returned a month later and informed us that we were moving to White Lake, near the village of Whitehall, twenty miles north of Muskegon, next to a resort and Lake Michigan. "There was no prettier place anywhere." He was animated when he claimed our new home was magnificent and stately. He said that the cottage even had its own name— Face of the Winds. Daddy promised that the house sat on the lakeshore. He was over the moon with pride.

We moved during a scorching weekend in late August of 1964. Bompi and Gigi took time from their jobs to lend a hand. With a U-Haul trailer and three cars, we loaded our belongings and began our adventure. Gigi wasn't enamored with the idea of us moving one hundred and fifty miles from Jackson. My dad was her only child. And he was uprooting his wife and grandkids, taking us across the state and further north. I rode with Bompi and Gigi on the trip "up north." She sat in the front seat with a scarf tied tightly over the massive bun of hair on her head. It was stifling and suffocating in the car. Gigi insisted we crack the windows "only a tiny little bit," so as not to mess her hair. The entire trip she grumbled and complained about the move, while she and Bompi sucked cigarettes. Bompi told her the change was important to my dad, and that "everything will work out just fine." But I could tell she was agitated and unhappy.

My eyes almost jumped out of my head when we approached White-hall. As we cruised serpentine South Shore Drive, overlooking White Lake, I spied dozens of sailboats tacking across the water. The scene was a dream come true. We passed the White Lake Golf Club and then we arrived at an intersection with Murray Road. We could no longer see White Lake, but Bompi said the signs on the road suggested that over the huge, wooded sand dunes in front of us was Lake Michigan, just hundreds of feet away. We turned right and began a steep, tense descent along a question mark-shaped curve. We advanced haltingly down the grade. Bompi pumped the car's brakes the entire downward climb. Gigi's hair bun bounced back to front to back with each jab of the peddle. She admonished him to "be more careful," as we were only a few feet behind the U-Haul that my dad was pulling. The instant we safely made the bottom of the hill, Gigi fumbled through her purse, searching for cigarettes. When she found them, her hands shook nervously as she flicked her lighter under the Salem that bobbed in her lips.

To our left and right were long, unpaved driveways leading some-times to nowhere obvious, and other times to homes and cottages. Our surroundings had turned to green and brown and beige. We were among massive sand dunes to our west and little bumps of dunes to the east and big stretches of sand surrounding us, dotted with clumps of dune grass and trees and bushes. Bompi explained that we were on a spit of land pinched between White Lake and, still unseen, Lake Michigan. I thought it was strange and magnificent. Nothing like what I'd expected. I wanted to get out of the car, right then, to explore.

A mile down Murray Road, we passed a white wooden sign painted with fancy black letters. Bompi announced that we'd arrived in Waba-ningo. Another sign said we were at Sylvan Beach. I was delighted but confused by unfamiliar names.

My dad stopped his car and the U-Haul and he walked back to our car and he said we'd gone too far. I was disappointed until I heard him tell Bompi that "we passed the place—just a little bit back behind us." That was great relief because everything was so beautiful.

Bompi turned the car, following my dad and, just down the road, we made a left turn onto a two-track, dirt driveway with a sign near the mail box that read, "Face of the Winds." The house had a name, just like my dad said it would. That pleased Bompi. For a minute, Gigi stopped grousing.

We bounced down the rutted road. Three hundred feet later we parked behind two large homes. An old man dressed head to toe in tan canvas — cap, trousers and shirt — stood at the end of the drive. He acted as though he expected us, but he didn't greet us warmly. The stranger was accompanied by a black and brown German shepherd that looked like Rin Tin Tin. Night Train barked his disapproval. My dad introduced us to Mr. Spikelmeyer, our newest landlord. Daddy told us Mr. Spikelmeyer owned both big houses. We were renting the one on the lake and Mr. Spikelmeyer and his wife and Rin Tin Tin lived in the other house that sat beside and slightly behind ours.

Our new home was two stories tall and grand and sat on a bluff. Daddy gave us a tour and explained that around the point to the left was the White River channel that ran from White Lake, past the light station and into Lake Michigan. A half mile to the right was the White Lake Yacht Club. Miles down the lake were the sister villages of Whitehall and Montague. The place was spacious. An enclosed porch fronted the entire house. The views were precious. Standing on the porch, I felt as close to the water as I did at the end of the dock at Uncle Charlie and Aunt Louise's cottage on Clarklake. We stepped off the porch and onto the bluff. The true blue lake stretched out before us. The wind whipped up white cat's paws on the water. It was everything my dad said it would be. I was giddy. My mom was happy. Gigi battened down her scarf because of breeze off the lake. Bompi slapped my dad's back in approval. Night Train foamed at the mouth. And Brian slept peacefully in the back of my mom's car.

August quickly turned to September. After Labor Day, many of our neighbors and all the kids vanished. Daddy explained that most of the people who lived in Wabaningo and Sylvan Beach did so only in the summertime. Before you could say "Mr. Spikelmeyer" we began to experience our first Northern Michigan winter. My mom and dad had a difficult twenty-two mile commute to Muskegon, where they both had jobs. Even in agreeable weather, the drive was cumbersome, up and down winding, two-lane roads. And when the days got shorter and the weather turned foul, the trip became longer and darker and even more dangerous.

To complicate matters, since we were remote, childcare was elusive and expensive. My mom finally did hire a babysitter. She was mean and obese. When she accidentally stepped on one of my mom's new baby kittens and killed the poor thing, I told my mom the next babysitter had to be skinny like she was.

Snow began to fall in abundance, and with regularity, after my seventh birthday in late November. The hazardous hill on Murray road was often impassable. More than once, I made the long walk down the driveway to the school bus stop and I waited and waited, but the bus didn't show. When I was finally too numb to endure any longer, I'd trudge back down the driveway to join my brother and the cat-killer babysitter to freeze in the house together.

To heat the great cottage we used coal. In the cellar there was a stubby black door near the ceiling, at ground level. A chute led down into the cellar. A big truck came one day and unloaded the coal through the opening, down the chute and into the basement.

The coal pieces were big and irregular. My dad taught me how to take a shovel that had a flat head twice as wide as any other shovel I'd ever seen and scrape the floor at the edge of the pile and scoop up the coal and dump the chunks into the mouth that was created when the furnace door was open. The coal smoldered slowly and rhythmically, with its own heartbeat, and made a ticking sound when burning and smelled like oil. Shoveling was dirty and hard work. I hated our coal furnace. My mom and dad fought about how much money we spent to heat the house. No matter the quantity of coal we piled into the furnace, inside the house they called Face of the Winds we were never warm in the winter. When the gales blew outside, they blew inside, too. While the house was grand, it was also a sieve. With ancient windows and uninsulated walls and doors that didn't seal. I longed to be someplace cozy and warm.

By the middle of January, titanic drifts of snow blocked our driveway. Mr. Spikelmeyer had a plow blade attached to the front of his truck and he kept the driveway open for both families, but sometimes he had to plow and scrape several times a day. We had last seen the sun in November. It snowed every day because the frigid air from Wisconsin would cross Lake Michigan, pumping the clouds full of moisture, to be deposited as snow along the frozen shore. Face of the Winds was Mother Nature's first stop. Winter's grip seemed endless and cold. So cold. So bitterly cold.

Our relationship with Mr. Spikelmeyer and Rin Tin Tin was not warm, either. The Spikelmeyer canine was well tutored and, for the most part, obedient. Mr. Spikelmeyer could control his dog with hand signals and voice commands. He behaved but also intimidated because he was big and a "police dog," as my dad sometimes called him. Night Train, on the other hand, while smart, was not trained in the traditional sense. He could hike a football, but he didn't always come when called. And he was intimidating, too. His white teeth and red tongue and gums were accentuated against his coal-black fur. But he didn't frighten Rin Tin Tin, and one day when Night Train was running wild and Mr. Spikelmeyer lost track of his dog, the two beasts tangled in a ferocious battle.

Blood and mayhem pervaded the scene. The dogs locked in a mad embrace with their jaws working at a frenetic pace and pieces of flesh and fur were tossed in the air as they spun in circles barking and biting and tearing at each other. I watched, paralyzed. Mr. Spikelmeyer ran to a brush pile and grabbed a long branch and rammed the impromptu spear into the sides of the spinning dogs. I screamed Night Train's name. Mr. Spikelmeyer kept stabbing. Finally the stick connected with the intersected heads of the dogs and they broke.

Both had gory patches of exposed skin on their faces. Neither claimed victory. They slinked away, in opposite directions, tails tucked between their legs. Mr. Spikelmeyer collared Rin Tin Tin. I chased Night Train back to the stairs of our porch and up and into the house.

Spring couldn't arrive quickly enough. As soon as I could play outside, Night Train and I built a fort out of driftwood and old boards and any other kind of scrap we could find. I borrowed a steak knife from our kitchen. As I was carving my name on the fort, the knife slipped. I sliced three inches of my thumb and hand. And I met more doctors and nurses at another hospital emergency room.

We spent only part of the summer at Face of the Winds. The move there was a colossal mistake. We couldn't afford the hulking house. The arduous, snowy commute wore on my mom and dad. I felt a million miles from Bompi and Gigi and the rest of our family in Jackson. Brian and I had no one to play with, except when the summer people came to stay at Wabaningo and Sylvan Beach.

Rin Tin Tin was pleased to see us go.

Ten

Sweetland

EARLY ON, my mom shared tales about her miserable childhood.

She told me she was bullied and teased by her brothers. Not allowed to play games on Sunday or — God forbid — she ever skip or dance or see a movie. There were happy times, too. But those were stories left untold.

She did show me pictures of cats that she cared for. She clothed the kitties in doll's attire and paraded them in baby carriages. My mom and I didn't dress our cats, but she did teach me how to put Scotch tape on all four feet. The cats would then dance a jig in a futile but entertaining attempt to be rid of the sticky stuff.

And she showed me a similar trick with wax paper.

We'd cut four-inch by four-inch squares and use rubber bands to secure the homemade booties onto each paw. The footwear was all but impossible to escape and, though the booties were benign, the cats would prance and spin, shaking their feet vigorously, in a desperate dance for freedom. After being sufficiently entertained, we'd remove the booties and the cats would be dispatched to do what cats did best — practically nothing.

Mommy was raised in bucolic Stanton and Greenville, Michigan, where her dad preached a hellfire-and-damnation message to fundamentalist Baptists in the state's Bible belt. Albert and Carrie Sweetland emigrated from Newfoundland. First they moved to Detroit, where Grandpa was a carpenter, just like Jesus. Then he embraced "a calling from God" to minister. He was tall and silver-haired and had strong, handsome features. She was sweet and petite and quiet and submissive—the perfect preacher's wife. Mommy had an older brother and two older sisters and two younger brothers, though one of them died from measles when he was just two years old.

She was closest to her older brother, John, and sister, Grace, who she called Gracie. My mom was more like her than anyone else in the Sweetland family. Gracie worked for the phone company and was divorced and lived near Detroit, in Royal Oak. She had a son named Mark whom Aunt Gracie called Marko. He was my age. My mom used to tell me that Aunt Gracie was wild and a renegade because she'd been baptized in "dirty water." I wasn't certain of the specific circumstances of my mom's own baptism, but water quality may have been an issue as well.

Sweetland life didn't always seem so sweet. Their rigid world revolved around church, seven days a week, and the associated restrictions that Grandpa Sweetland fixed under his absolute and sovereign rule, both at home and from the pulpit. The first time I saw Grandpa preach, I promptly learned that his God was a mean son-of-a-bitch, the Old Testament version: the unforgiving, unjust, bloodthirsty, homophobic, women-hating, control-freak God that would rather bully than nurture and love unconditionally. In the front pew, next to my mom, I shuddered in trepidation as Grandpa glared at us, the sinners, and bellowed about God's retribution and our eternal damnation. I didn't grasp everything he said, but he sure as sugar scared the Jesus out of me.

Grandpa and Grandma Sweetland loathed my dad. He got my mom pregnant while she was in nursing school and, worse than that, he descended from a clan of boozing Catholics. They attempted to elope in Angola, Indiana, just south of Jackson and the Michigan-Indiana state line. The city had "no waiting" marriage licenses, but my dad brought the wrong paperwork so the Justice of the Peace wouldn't consummate the deal. Ultimately they wed, with Grandpa Sweetland presiding, in the front yard of a relative's house in Jackson. I was alive in her belly, a fact that she and my dad knew but denied. Not long after, they moved into a raggedy-ass trailer park and started to build a life together. That would soon unravel.

I was seven the only time I recalled seeing Grandpa and Grandma Sweetland when my dad was also present. My brother and I were in the back of our blue Ford station wagon. Mom and Dad were in the front. As we barreled down country roads, they began to quarrel. The bickering made me anxious. I knew the argument was intensifying when my mom's voice first blared, then quivered. Then she began waving her arms. Her lit cigarette bumped the car ceiling upholstery and knocked ashes onto her shoulders and lap. That angered her even more. I couldn't follow their inflamed exchange. For a few moments, the tension eased. I relaxed. But then the fight resumed and escalated again.

Finally I figured out they were squabbling about.

The wrangle ended abruptly, when we pulled up to someone's house where Grandpa and Grandma Sweetland were guests. My mom took the cigarettes out of her purse and off the bench seat between her and my dad. Daddy handed her a pack that he extracted from his shirt pocket. She stuffed the sticks into the glove box and slammed the door shut. Then she turned to the back seat and looked at Brian and me, straight in the eyes, and said, "Don't you dare tell your Grandpa and Grandma Sweetland that Mommy and Daddy smoke."

"No shit," I thought.

Eleven

Muskegon
(1965-1967)

WE MOVED FROM Face of the Winds on the shores of White Lake and the quaint village of Wabaningo and the soaring dunes of Lake Michigan and our life in the country to a broken down rental on Hartford Avenue in dingy and dirty and decaying downtown Muskegon.

My dad's pipe dream of living in a grand cottage on a Northern Michigan lake was just that. The boondoggle was beyond our means and his ambition. A delusion based on the false pretense of affluence, and my dad's mystifying judgment—or lack thereof.

Long ago, the Muskegon area was home to Chippewa, then Ottawa and Patawatomi and Ojibwa. Eventually, the Indians were pushed west or minimized. In the early 1800s, the fur trade sustained the settlers. In 1825, the Erie Canal opened and the presence of the big ditch meant that corn, wheat, oats and the hides and furs from trappers, as well as lumber from the forests, could be harvested anywhere in the Midwest and flow through the Great Lakes and the canal east to Albany and then south to New York City and beyond.

Muskegon's heyday was likely the late 1800s, before the lumber barons denuded the forests that surrounded the long, languid Muskegon River, where they floated millions of feet of timber down the waterway and into deep Muskegon Lake and dozens of lakeside mills that sliced and diced the lumber that was then shipped by rail or on freighters through the

Muskegon Channel and into Lake Michigan and around the Midwest to fuel furnaces and build factories and houses and furniture. Lumber from Muskegon helped rebuild Chicago after the great fire of 1871. The wood built untold numbers of prairie towns in the West. Charles Hackley gave a fortune to the city. There was a park and a hospital and an art gallery and a library named for him. He was generous, but he also stripped the land bare. After the trees were gone and the lumber mills closed, Muskegon's industrial base grew up around gray iron and the burgeoning auto industry of the early- and mid-20th century. The sawmills that ringed the lake were replaced by foundries and scrap metal yards until the '50s and '60s. Then a dysfunctional auto industry lost its competitive edge. Stymied by unsustainable union demands and obsolete technology, Muskegon began to spiral down. The factories that made paper and cranes and tank treads and turbines and piston rings and camshafts and ball bearings and cable and wire and other mechanical parts and pieces began to shrink, relocate or close. Muskegon's most precious resource, the lakefront, was surrounded by vacant, hulking edifices that leached pollutants that sullied the water and view. This was our new hometown.

The rental on Hartford was two blocks from my dad's office at the county building. For a while, anyway. That gig didn't work out. He started another job at Muskegon Heights High School as a truant officer. The little dump was also near his favorite bar, the Tip Top Tap Room, where he spent much of his non-working time.

We had a small yard that backed up to an alley and a crumbling, abandoned red brick church. I explored the structure by prying loose a piece of plywood that covered a basement window. I went feet first through the opening and dropped into the lower level and what looked to be a Sunday school classroom. Outside the room, I found a darkened stairway, but without light I had to crawl on my hands and knees up the stairs. When I arrived near the top, I found the sun shining through stained glass. I could see again. Holes had been punched in the colored glass by rocks and bottles. The pews were untouched, but the sanctuary had been brutally vandalized. Crosses had been ripped from walls. There were sites for statues and monuments, but none remained. Envelopes, empty of offerings, were scattered on a damp, red carpet runner, spotted with black mold. I spooked pigeons roosting in the loft. They startled me. I prayed that someone would forgive me for my trespasses. I got the hell out of the church. And I never went back.

My dad's loyalty to Night Train was perplexing. We didn't have the resources or the space to properly care for the dog. My parents were both working when we lived on Hartford. When my brother and I came home from school, we were welcomed by piles of crap and rugs saturated with rancid pee. We were too small to walk the beast. And he was too dangerous to let run. So he soiled the house. I thought the filth was disgusting. I'd try to clean up behind the dog, but it was futile. My dad seemed oblivious to the mess. My mom somehow tolerated it. In addition to the dog, we had cats. Our living conditions were embarrassing. I hated it. I never brought home friends from school. I wished that Night Train would run away.

One evening on Hartford, my parents came home late at night and loaded on booze. As soon as the babysitter left, they began to bark angrily at each other. I ran upstairs and hid. My dad came looking for me. When he found me, he stood over me and screamed. The veins were popped out of his neck, which was red and sweaty, and he spit as he yelled. Full of fear, I started to crab walk backwards, away from him. He hovered over me again. I was afraid he would hurt me, so I scooted across the floor and slid down the wooden stairs. My mom screamed because she thought I'd hurt myself. But I slid down the stairs all the time when they weren't home. So I was okay, and I ran and stowed away in a cupboard. Where no one could find me.

Not many days after the night of the fight, my dad told me that "maybe" he and my mom wouldn't stay married much longer. He said there was no special reason why they might break up and that he loved my mom, but that things just weren't working out and that I shouldn't worry. Of course, starting that day, I was consumed with the thought of them breaking up. But we never discussed the topic again. And I didn't tell my mom what he said.

MRS. VADA E. FERGUSON was my second grade teacher at McLaughlin Elementary. She was patient and old and gentle and she played the piano and loved to sing, so we sang a lot. When we performed "She's a Grand Old Flag," we'd parade around the room with our knees up high. The marching made us sing louder and we slapped erasers together as though they were cymbals. Mrs. Ferguson was proud of us. She was a loving, caring person. Any kid that ever had her as a teacher was better for it.

On December 6, 1965, she wrote on my report card, "Patrick has made a fine adjustment to our room—is doing well in all areas." On May 2, 1966, she wrote, "We have all enjoyed having Patrick in our room." And she added, "Patrick has a fine voice—I think he will be a tenor some day." As wonderful as Vada E. Ferguson was, she was tone deaf, too.

I started third grade at McLaughlin with Mrs. Shaw. But my parents were not much for continuity, so we moved again. This time just over a mile away, to the corner of Southern and Park in the Nelson Elementary district. Another Muskegon neighborhood in inexorable decline. Daddy told me we bought the house, so that made it better than the rental on Hartford. It was across the street from a park with tennis courts. That was nice. And I was relieved that my dad decided that he and my mom would stay married.

Night Train moved with us to the house on Park. Without a fenced backyard, and still too big and strong and mean to be walked by a child, the dog was locked in the basement during the day.

After less than a year, my dad lost his job at the high school. Out of work again, he agreed to look after my brother and me and kids of some friends. There were six of us in the house, and in the yard, and in and out of the house. My dad was nowhere to be seen. I was pretty sure he was in his bedroom sleeping off a late night at the Tap Room.

Night Train was prone on the floor between the couch and a table, an attempt to avoid the mayhem. The dog's back was raw with open sores from a skin ailment that refused to heal. One of the kids my dad was supposed to be looking after was six-year-old Suzie Ghezzi.

Suzie was parked on the couch. She reached down and touched the black dog's back. Night Train cautioned her with a deep, vibrating growl. Someone told Suzie not to touch the dog. But she poked Night Train's back again. He growled and showed his teeth. The third time she touched him, he launched himself into her face and began to shred it, like he did Rin Tin Tin. Suzie was defenseless. The attack lasted seconds. But the damage was complete. Chaos ensued.

Kids scrambled in different directions, screaming "help!" and "no!" Suzie was on her back, still. Was she dead? Her hands were at her sides. She moaned. She was in shock. My dad appeared. We covered her face with towels.

I wished it had been me. The dog I hated had just ruined the pretty face of a little girl. The doctors said she'd be okay. But not the same. And not without numerous surgeries.

Night Train disappeared the next day. My mom and dad said he'd been taken to a farm to live out his life. I never believed that. Whatever his fate, dead or alive, Night Train was in a better place if he wasn't with us.

In December of 1967, less than a year after we'd moved to the house on Park and a couple months after Night Train chewed up Suzie Ghezzi's face, my mom ordered my dad from the house.

For Christmas that year, one last time we went to Jackson as a family. Even though we weren't a family any longer.

Christmas was what kept us connected to Jackson, and my mom to the O'Sullivans and the uncles and aunts and cousins that loved her so much. But that was to come to an end.

Things weren't going to be the same.

Twelve

Christmas Eve

(Until December 1971)

GROWING UP, I wanted every day to be like Christmas Eve at Aunt Hige's house.

Hige was Grandma Gigi's sister. She was married to Ralph Stewart. Uncle Ralph owned a gas station and a junkyard in Jackson and was always in a uniform of blue twill pants and a blue work shirt with "Ralph" embroidered over one breast pocket and "Stewart's Pure" over the other. Stuffed into his shirt pocket was a plastic sleeve filled with half a dozen pens and a tire-pressure gauge. He was not tall or particularly good looking. His hair was thin and disheveled and slick and his facial features were scrunched, shaded by furry eyebrows. He was quiet and kind and gentle. The kind of guy that sat in the back of the room, never yearning to be the center of attention. But always eager to lend a hand, if need beckoned.

Uncle Ralph was an early master of Polaroid camera technology. He marveled us with his proficiency in generating nearly instant photographs. He didn't speak in complete sentences but in mumbled and muffled bursts. He favored cigars and had one permanently engaged in the corner of his mouth. Ralph was sustained by pounds of grilled sausage sandwiches with mustard and hot peppers.

Hige and Ralph lived in a modest, one-level ranch home on a half-moon shaped lot on Albright Street in Jackson. The house was built in the '50s. It had low evergreen bushes in the front and a flower-flanked patio in the rear, and it was one of the nicest homes I'd visited. They had three bedrooms and a bathroom, a two-car garage and a basement that was a kid's delight.

The stairs to the basement were between the kitchen and garage, where Snuffles the brown-and-white Collie slept. On the wall, going down the stairs, hung a series of framed pictures of dogs smoking cigars and playing cards. Downstairs there was a large open room with a four-seat bar, to the right, that opened to a second, functional kitchen. Above the bar, a clock kept time backwards: the one in the position of the eleven, the two in the position of the ten and so on. Inside the kitchen was a commercial-style freezer where Ralph stored buckets of ice cream and meats, including venison and pheasant that he harvested on hunting trips "up north."

Adjacent to the kitchen and behind curtains was a laundry room that was never properly lit. Beyond the washer and dryer was a tiny, dank bedroom that shared space with a sump pump and water heater. The room was rarely used because it was damp, dark and noisy.

The centerpiece of the basement was a large fireplace with a towering deer head mounted above. The animal's rack impressively featured a dozen tines. The antlers provided utility. When my relatives played bridge on a card table, in front of the fireplace and underneath the deer, they would take completed score sheets and spear them onto an antler. After hours of bridge play, the mighty rack morphed into a papered crown. The royal deer's name was Rudolph and his nose was painted bright red, much to the delight of all my cousins and me.

For most of the 1960s, the Christmas Eve routine was relatively consistent, even after we moved upstate in 1964. Folks would begin to gather in the late afternoon or early evening. By the time everyone arrived—cousins, aunts, uncles and Bompi and Gigi, me and my brother and my dad and, for one last time, in 1967, my mom—there would be more than twenty of us.

Hige would announce that the buffet was "open for business." We would help ourselves to sliced ham and turkey and dinner rolls and warm potato salad and green beans with sliced almonds and delicious desserts, including my favorite, German chocolate cake.

After dinner, Hige would send off my cousins and Brian and me, with loaves of nutty brown bread wrapped in Christmas paper, to sing carols to neighbors. Afterwards, she would serve us hot chocolate and we'd snack on Christmas cookies and gather around the piano in the basement where

Gigi would play carols.

Gigi would sit proudly at the piano with her amazing hair bun perfectly arranged on the top of her head. She was taller than us, even sitting down. She couldn't read music and never had formal training, but she played with a ferociousness that entertained. Her fingernails were famously long. They would clickety-clack on the keys as she played. She wore charm bracelets, clogged with ornaments that banged along in rhythm. She was a one-woman band, with an unconventional percussion ensemble as support. We crooned loudly and chortled with pleasure and Gigi sang and laughed, too.

At some point in the evening, under the direction of Hige or Ralph, my dad would lead my brother and all my cousins and me in a "we want Santa Claus" march throughout the house. The parade signaled the time to gather in a series of concentric circles on the floor of the living room upstairs. The kids sat in the center circle and the younger adults in the next circle and the older adults in the back of the room, with Ralph floating about with his flash kit and Polaroid camera documenting the festivities.

The Christmas tree was in the basement. Gifts under the tree would be collected and relocated upstairs. Laundry baskets were used to haul the presents. With everyone helping, in short order, they would be piled high on the floor. Ready to open.

And then the fun would begin. One of the adults would be nominated Santa Claus. He or she would distribute the gifts. Presents were opened one at a time. The entire operation would take hours, but no one seemed to mind. Daddy and my cousin Judy's husband, Fred, would provide ongoing commentary about the suspect quality or inappropriateness of the gifts, or the lack of fashion sense of the gift-givers. On occasion, my dad's booze-infused sarcasm would cut too deeply, usually victimizing my brother or Gigi. But, more often than not, there were belly laughs galore. The banter was all in good fun. No one wanted the evening to end.

In June of 1972, Uncle Ralph succumbed to a sudden, massive coronary occlusion. And with him, our Christmas Eve tradition died as well.

Thirteen

Christmas Day

WHILE I SPENT Christmas Eve with Grandma Gigi's sister Hige and her family, Christmas Day meant a trip to Clarklake to be with Bompi's sister Louise and her merry clan.

The two events were disparate. I was a participant at Hige and Ralph's and an observer at Uncle Charlie and Aunt Louise's. That didn't mean that Christmas Day wasn't material; on the contrary, the day was rich and entertaining. I was certain to see Great-grandma Bessie and her sister Aunt Phrone. I cherished every minute I spent with the grand dames of the family. And I embraced the other characters: all the friends, cousins, uncles and aunts who were part of the colorful and compelling crowd.

Uncle Charlie and his brothers, Joe and Wilfred, started Dunigan Bros. in 1945. By all accounts, their company was a successful operation, specializing in water and sewer pipe excavation and installation. Around Southern Michigan, Dunigan Bros. trucks were distinctly visible due to their bright orange paint jobs. Because many water and sewer projects ran adjacent to major thoroughfares, their pumpkin-colored convoys were ubiquitous.

Uncle Charlie prospered working with his brothers and, in the mid-1950s, he and Aunt Louise built a second home, a cottage on Clarklake.

The cottage's great room had a soaring ceiling, knotty pine walls and a giant stone fireplace. With a lake view, the galley kitchen opened to a four-stool bar and served as the nerve-center for the house. Aunt Louise was permanently installed behind the bar, cooking food and mixing drinks and holding court. She was the consummate hostess and served the needs of friends and family and simultaneously directed traffic and chastised cousins and berated grandchildren and criticized Charlie. She did it all half-cocked, but with style and panache and in complete command of her domain.

There was a mélange of irresistible personalities at the cottage on Christmas Day.

My cousin Kevin, who studied law at the University of Michigan, spoke out of the side of his mouth, just above a whisper. He spent the late '60s and early '70s looking like Jesus Christ, right down to the leather sandals, flowing robe and long, wavy dark hair. The sight of Jesus leaning over a pool table with a cigarette bobbing in his lips never failed to illuminate my day.

My favorite cousin was P. Michael O'Sullivan. Michael was the son of Bompi's brother Emmett and his wife, Frieda. I never met Emmett, who shot himself in the head before I was born. Michael and his exotic and beautiful wife, Victoria, lived in Chicago. He was a photojournalist who enjoyed considerable success and recognition.

Michael worked on hundreds of assignments for publications around the world. His work covering the '60s race riots won him acclaim and, in 1967, one of his photos of the Detroit Riots was a cover for *Life Magazine*. He bravely and brilliantly captured the violence at the 1968 Democratic National Convention in Chicago and the riots in the same city after Martin Luther King's assassination.

In 1972, Michael published his photo essay *Patriot's Graves*. The book documented his year behind the lines and underground with the IRA in Northern Ireland, and the civil strife of her people. The same year he was an eyewitness to the Bloody Sunday attack by British soldiers on demonstrators in Londonderry. He photographed and interviewed Gerry Adams, future leader of Sinn Féin.

Michael's uniform was a black turtleneck and Levi's and boots. A mop of thick dark curls topped a square face featuring a mustache that looked like a push broom. Bedecked in a canvas jacket, outfitted with a dozen pockets for film and lenses, he looked as though he had been cast for the part he played. He performed his role with confidence and swagger, and he pursued the images of his craft with aggressiveness and zeal.

At the cottage, Michael was just another guy with a beer and a pool cue in his hand and a cigarette dangling from his lips. But he wasn't, either. He was different. He was special. An artist among drunks, wannabes and ditch diggers, Michael added flair and dimension that was sometimes invisible. But undeniably present. He was cool and real.

Though my dad tried not to show it, there was tension between Michael and him. It was revealed in Daddy's bravado during a game of eight-ball and the undeserved barbs tossed Michael's way and the not-so-subtle clenched fist at my dad's side. Michael was someone who became something from almost nothing. He wasn't a star athlete. His diminutive stature paled compared to my father's. But through innate talent and grit and hard work, and a little bit of luck, he became a man in full—at the top of his game in the prime of his life. I was sure my dad secretly hated his guts. But Michael was one of my heroes. I idolized him.

Uncle Charlie had none of Michael's cool, but he was great, too. Charlie was thick-bodied and tall. His face was big and pillowy and splotchy. His hair was thinning and he didn't talk, he muttered.

Charlie would sit me on a bar stool when I was a little kid, and he'd show me pictures of his fishing trips to Beaver Island, in Northern Michigan. He'd talk about his physician and friend Dr. Ludwig, who owned the Lodge on Beaver Island, and how they'd slay the fish, and that there was no better smallmouth bass fishery in the world. He promised he'd take me "up there, to Beaver Island, to fish someday." Talking about fishing got Charlie excited about it. He'd say, "Let's go fishin', Rock." And then we would.

In the summer, Charlie and I would grab a carton of leaf worms out of the refrigerator off the breezeway, or from the hole with the well pump outside where the air stayed cool underground. He'd take me into clear Clarklake on his pontoon boat. "Let's go to the sunken island," he'd say. Charlie had a silly captain's hat that he'd sometimes wear, slightly askew. He would motor us down the lake until he located his landmarks. Then he'd drop anchor and we'd fish.

I had a tough time understanding Uncle Charlie, but despite the garble of his muttering and mumbling he taught me how to bait a hook and when to set it and how to reel in a fish. He showed me how to navigate a boat and pump the bulb primer on the gas tank and how to steer and dock.

Belying his gruff exterior, Uncle Charlie was a tender, sweet man. He recognized that I needed someone like him to look up to and he wasn't shy about offering his worldly advice. When I was a thirteen-year-old, he paraded me over to a cousin sitting on the couch who was pregnant and unmarried. "See that?" Pointing to the basketball in my cousin's tummy. I told him that I did. "Well, keep your pecker in your pants or you'll end up with one of them. And you don't want that."

Charlie was a champ. He loved me and every grandkid and niece and nephew and cousin that swarmed his cottage and grounds. He just didn't want anyone to know it.

One Christmas Day, Charlie had removed the fireplace screen so that he could tend to a waning blaze. Youngsters were darting around the hearth as Charlie jabbed the logs with a fireplace poker. When he got them into just exactly the right position, he'd add another log to the fire.

From the kitchen and behind the bar, half shit-faced, Aunt Louise shouted with indignation that Charlie was putting children at risk by not having the fireplace screen in place.

Charlie responded with love, as only Charlie could. He said, "Jesus Christ, Louise, you'd think we were down to our last fuckin' kid."

Fourteen

The Safari Club

I WAS A DAZED and confused little man when the year started anew in January of 1968.

My dad's prediction that he and my mom might split came true. The break-up meant my mom and my brother and I were moving again. Back across Muskegon. Near the rental on Hartford Avenue. This time to a cramped, but cheap, apartment in a divided ramshackle house on Terrace Street.

We moved to the Muskegon area when I was seven. Now ten, we were on our fourth place to live in three years. If that was living.

My mom quit her job so that she could go back to nursing school. We were surviving on welfare, handouts from relatives and making the most of food stamps. Returning to McLaughlin Elementary School was comforting, to a degree. I found familiar faces from second and the first half of third grade. The teachers were welcoming. My new fourth grade teacher, Mrs. Nye, was what my dad called a "stone-killin' fox."

Mrs. Nye wore clothes that conformed nicely to her buxom backside. The hems of her skirts were more than the width of two palms—of a ten-year-old—above her knees. She sometimes wore fishnet stockings—though not often enough—and boots to her kneecaps, even when there wasn't snow on the ground. She was always sunshine on an otherwise cloudy day.

After Daddy left, things didn't go so well for him. But, of course, things hadn't gone well for some time. He seemed to drive a different, hobbled car each time I saw him. And, while he continued to live in Muskegon, I never saw his place. After he lost his job at the high school, he went to work in a foundry, as "a supervisor," he said. But that was short-lived. Then he tended bar at the Safari Club, off of Seaway Drive.

The club was down a side street in a mostly industrial area. A "Safari" sign hung vertically off the façade of the two-story building and was capped with a neon martini glass. The neighborhood had a decidedly blue-collar flavor with tiny, single-family hovels scattered among small light-manu-facturing plants. Mostly metal fabrication. The area was dirty and gritty and the smell of burnt sulfur often mixed with the sweet, putrid waft of the paper mill on Muskegon Lake. You didn't need a weatherman to know when the wind blew from the west.

Daddy picked me up one rare, sunny winter afternoon from the apart-ment on Terrace Street and took me to the club. The bright day was made more intense by the sun's reflection off the snow and ice. But the sun slammed her eyes shut when the big steel doors of the club collapsed behind us. At the far side of the black room, a bandstand stood large and was dominated by an unattended drum set. A pair of electric guitars leaned against speakers and acted as sentries over a vacant and scarred dance floor. Dozens of empty tables were scattered about the room. Dirty, black plastic ashtrays secured random stations on top of each table. I imagined, later that night, a thousand Marlboros being jabbed to death in the bottom of each vessel.

The room reeked of stale beer and pee and cigarettes. I could not have cared less. I went straight to the jukebox.

The machine gobbled up my nickels. With but a bit of indigestion, it began to whir and churn. A magic little arm reached into the organized plastic discs and, with a jerk and a flip, the arm haltingly but successfully laid the 45 onto the spinning turntable. I sat in silence listening with my heart as much as my ears as the song drew to an end. "...Come on baby, light my fire. Try to set the night on fire." Then a new light was born into that dark room.

A couple of months earlier, I'd seen Jim Morrison and The Doors on *The Ed Sullivan Show*. They performed "Light My Fire." And it lit my fire. Morrison had an ability to communicate that transcended the inferior audio of our black-and-white television.

I blasted the song five times on the jukebox and soaked up the energy and the passion. My dad grinned as he drank beers and washed cocktail glasses behind the bar. We were alone in that big, empty place, but we had company, too.

I had no idea what the song meant. But it was simple and raw and exposed and honest. Morrison left nothing in the bag. In leather from top to bottom, he performed without being subject to rule or convention. He flamboyantly sang and stalked and made love to his microphone with a two-fisted grip in a way that was freaky but sincere. Powerful and controlling, a head of shoulder-length curls a girl would yearn for framed a face that was handsome, enigmatic and mysterious.

As the fifth play ended, the club's entry door exploded open and sunshine crashed back into the bar. Four scruffy guys dressed in leather jackets and tees and jeans and pointy-toed Beatle boots entered loudly, dragging cases and bags and talking back and forth while sucking on Marlboros and spilling ashes as they made their way toward the bandstand.

An elfin, dark-haired band member yelled, "Hey, Sully!" to my dad. He noticed me and smiled and nodded his head and said, "Hey, kid."

For twenty minutes the band set up their equipment and executed sound checks. They drank Buds and smoked. I picked up three dimes from my dad and goofed around on the pool table, shooting balls but trying not to make any. I didn't want to feed the table again.

The same little guy spoke to us through his microphone. "Test, one, two. Test, one, two. Test. Test. Test." He said that he and his men had a new song they wanted to try out on us. I took a seat on chrome-legged bar stool. With a haunting keyboard leading the way, the four no-names laid into the song with the heart and soul of a generation.

You know that it would be untrue
You know that I would be a liar
If I was to say to you
Girl, we couldn't get much higher
Come on, baby, light my fire
Come on, baby, light my fire
Try to set the night on fire, yeah

When the band finished, the final refrain echoed in my head. Four wannabe rock stars had just rocked me. They'd sucked me into their performance and transported me to a place that I'd never been before. I wobbled as I stood. Then I checked the front of my pants to make sure I hadn't wet myself.

I whispered, "Dang, that was cool."

Fifteen

Thank God for the Tigers

MY MOM STUDIED a lot, especially that first winter back in nursing school. Brian and I tried to stay out of her way. On weekends, she'd sometimes treat us by buying a bag of Lay's potato chips and French onion dip. We'd camp out in the living room with our blankets and pillows and eat chips and dip and drink pop and watch *Mission: Impossible* or *I Spy* on television. It was great.

On April 4, my mom and I visited one of her girlfriends, Linda Wurtz. Linda and her husband lived in a tidy, compact apartment on the second floor of a partitioned old house, a mile from us down Terrace Street, on the other side of McLaughlin Elementary.

A framed poster hung on the wall of her living room. It said, "Visit Israel and See the Pyramids." It was designed to look like a vintage 1950s vacationland-style postcard. The kind with the waving, water-skiing lady and the headline "Visit Sunny Florida."

When Linda left the room to fetch a couple of drinks, I queried my mom about the poster.

"Oh, she's a Jew," she said.

Linda came back. She didn't leave for another thirty minutes, but when she did I said, "What does being a Jew have to do with it?" My mom explained that the poster was meant to be humorous. Israel fought, and won, a six-day war in 1967. They captured the Gaza Strip and the Sinai

Peninsula and the West Bank. "Israel is three times larger than it was," she said.

"Okay. Thanks, I guess."

Linda returned with fresh cocktails again. The phone rang. For a moment, she listened to whoever was on the other end. Then she said, "Oh, God, no," and switched on the radio. They didn't own a television.

The man on the radio reported that Martin Luther King, Jr. had been assassinated. He was agitated and spoke with nervous excitement, halting and stuttering. I knew of Dr. King because of the peaceful marches he'd led and his "I Have a Dream" speech. But some marches didn't have happy endings, and my mom and Linda spoke with grave concern because of what happened in Detroit, the previous summer, when blacks torched buildings and cars. And people were murdered in the streets.

I was unnerved. The news stories about the riots were terrifying. Late in 1967, on a visit to Aunt Gracie's in Royal Oak near Detroit, my aunt drove us the see the charred buildings and burned-out cars and the ghettos where the rioting occurred. Inner city Detroit was scarred and decaying and devoid of anything that looked or smelled like hope. I couldn't blame Negroes for being angry. I would have been upset, too.

Fears were realized. Across the country there was more rioting, ignited by Dr. King's murder. National Guard troops were called into several major cities, but Muskegon remained relatively calm.

And then, just after midnight on June 5, 1968, a guy named Sirhan Sirhan stalked Robert F. Kennedy at the Ambassador Hotel in Los Angeles on the night of the California presidential primary election. The assassin shot Kennedy three times in his shoulder and neck and head. He was gone twenty-six hours later.

We didn't learn about the shooting until after sunrise the next morning. It was inconceivable that another Kennedy was dead, and only a couple of months after Martin Luther King met the same fate.

It seemed everyone was either sad or angry or both. Assassinations. Middle East turmoil. The Viet Nam war. Street rioting. Protest marches. On the news, I learned about a guy with a girl's name, Abbie Hoffman, who was trying to convert hippies into yippies, threatening to screw up the whole country. As if everything wasn't screwed up enough already.

But, thank God, we had the Tigers.

I was never without my transistor radio the summer of 1968. Tiger announcers Ernie Harwell and Ray Lane were my lifeline that year. Some games were on television, but radio facilitated the essential mobility of a kid on the move.

The Tigers played well in 1967, falling just one game short of winning the American League pennant. Their line-up had been essentially the same since I could remember. Many of the players were from the Michigan area. My dad had dreams of playing for the Tigers. Maybe he could have. He showed me letters from the Tigers and Cubs. He and Bompi told me about a home run my dad hit in Tiger Stadium at a high school all-star game.

I felt like I knew each player, like they were uncles. I bet every kid in Michigan felt the same way.

Bill Freehan was the catcher. He was a rock. With a name like Freehan, he was born to receive pitches. Norm Cash played first base. His nickname was Stormin' Norman. Gates Brown was a pinch-hitter who sometimes played outfield. He was signed while he was in prison. And he didn't have a neck, but the Gator had gaudy hitting statistics. Willie Horton, Al Kaline, Jim Northrup and Mickey Stanley played outfield for the Tigers. Kaline, everyone's favorite player, was injured for much of the 1968 season. Northrup filled in. When Kaline got better, the manager, Mayo Smith, moved Mickey Stanley to shortstop and Northrup to center field. Of course, he played Kaline in right field, sending light-hitting shortstop Ray Oiler to the pine. Benching "0 for August" Oiler and playing Stanley at shortstop for the last handful of regular season games and for the entire post season was a bold and brilliant coaching move.

Dick McAuliffe and his other-worldly hitting stance played second base, and Don Wert was on third. The pitching staff was anchored by Denny McLain, who won thirty-one games in 1968. A phenomenal feat. Mickey Lolich was the star of the World Series, winning three games. John Hiller was an ace left-handed reliever that pitched in thirty-nine games during the year.

The World Series Champion Tigers were the great distraction of 1968. Yup. Thank God for the Tigers.

Sixteen

Return of the Prodigal Son
(1968-1973)

MY DAD ABANDONED Muskegon not long after our musical adventure at the Safari Club.

Just four years before, he'd led us north with the promise of a new career and a house on a lake. We'd wrapped our hopes and dreams in his potential. But cruel reality trumped forged aspirations. We were left with our hope in shreds and dreams unrealized. Alone, distressed and befuddled.

He returned home with a clean slate, Jackson's favorite son, to the place where he'd shown so much ability—quarterback of the football team, state champion basketball player and the high school all-star who boomed a home run in Tiger Stadium. Bompi and Gigi welcomed him with unconditional support. Gigi blamed my mom for the divorce, either oblivious to his drinking and the succession of lost jobs or blinded by love for her one and only boy.

There was no obvious reason for my dad's ineptness. He was bright. He was handsome. He was charming. He was loved by family and friends. He was born with the wind at his back. He flashed teasing hints of ambition. He once hung the moon.

Daddy found work after returning to Jackson and started to put his life back together. One of his new friends was a long-legged redhead named Judy Wick. Judy was in her mid-thirties, about the same age as my dad, and divorced as well.

I met Judy in August of 1969. My dad had moved into her apartment in a seedy part of southeastern Jackson. True to form, Daddy had become the pied-piper of the complex, a hit with all the kids. He took a group of them to a Tigers game earlier in the summer, without me. The kids crawled all over my dad. They loved him. He adored the attention.

The two-bedroom apartment wasn't nice, but it was okay. The doors between the rooms were textured plastic and slid open and shut like an accordion. I slept on a cot in the family room because the place came with a bonus. Judy had a daughter, Vickie, who had emerging boobs and was my age, but taller. She slept in the second bedroom.

After my dad and Judy went to bed, Vickie stayed up with me. We watched movies together. Once, she sat so close to me that our bodies touched, and that made my heart speed up and I couldn't slow it down, but I didn't want to pull away from her. It felt so good to be leaning on each other and watching television.

When I visited my dad for a week the next summer, in 1970, he and Judy, newly wed, had moved to a house south of town, near Vandercook Lake, on West Bird Street. It was a real house with wooden doors and a front porch and three bedrooms. At the east end of Bird, there was a creek that ran from Mud Lake to Sharp Lake. When my dad and Judy were at work, I'd fish the creek for carp.

Judy's temper was as hot as her looks, and she and my dad had skirmishes that were fueled by booze. Churlish chatter too easily escalated to feverish exchanges that reflected bitter and vicious ill will. Their still-new relationship featured established dysfunction that was too familiar to me, so I spent more time at the creek than at the house.

Soon, they separated and Judy filed for divorce. The nicest thing I heard one of my relatives say about her was that "she was a bitch that no one could live with." I guess my dad thought differently. Within the year, they'd married again. To each other. A second time.

When I visited at Thanksgiving in 1971, Judy and my dad were renting a cottage next to a long, skinny farm pond north of Jackson on Cunningham Road. The setting was bucolic and pleasant but for the power company's hulking, humming electric lines, running north and south along the lake.

The weather was unseasonably cold. Several inches of snow fell and a thin crust of ice had formed on the lake. The wintry scene and holiday spirit, and too much booze, possessed Judy and my dad to lead a decorating frenzy that resulted in the house inundated with tinsel and ornaments and fake snow. Daddy and I ventured into the woods behind the lake. We cut down a spruce tree, dragged it back and decorated it. The day was hectic and bizarre and fun.

Just over four months later, Brian and I caught a Greyhound bus from Muskegon with a transfer in Lansing to visit my dad for our spring break. I was fifteen and Brian was fourteen. By car, the trip took less than three hours. By bus, it took at least five. The bus station was on the north side of Jackson. My cousin Judy Steel and her husband, Fred, who was also my dad's best friend in high school, lived nearby. They picked us up at the depot and dropped us at the cottage. Daddy said he had to be at work.

The key was under the mat. We went inside. There were still remnants of tinsel and fake snow, but little else. Unbeknownst to my brother and me, sometime after Christmas and before Easter Judy and Vickie had moved out and stripped the house bare. All that remained was a mattress, card table and transistor radio. I picked it up and tuned it to the Tigers game.

My brother and I rarely got along, made even more difficult from the awkwardness of being together in the empty dwelling. It was almost unbearable. We were furious with my dad, and we snarled at each other until he finally showed up. We pleaded with him to let us stay with our cousins, or with Bompi and Gigi. Anyplace but the hollow house. He said that he and Judy were "just separated and everything will be all right." That didn't give us a place to sleep. He drove us to my grandparents' apartment. We didn't see him again that trip.

The next time I came to Jackson to stay with my dad was the summer of 1973. After summer baseball and just before high school football practice started. He was broke and unemployed and homeless, sleeping next to the water heater and sump pump in the basement of Aunt Hige's house. His appearance had changed during the prior year, from all-American and clean-cut to a cross between Sonny Bono and Super Fly. He looked like a tacky white pimp.

I hadn't been oblivious to his boozing. But I was, at long last, connecting the dots between alcohol and his serial failures. Among family and in public, his drinking was controlled and social, at times excessive but apparently benign. However, a pattern had emerged. Perhaps the signals had been there all along. But, as a kid, I was ill-equipped and myopic and too optimistic. I believed my dad could rise above adversity and bad luck and get his life together. But, after a string of lost jobs and broken marriages, he had no home of his own. A stainless steel thermos bottle had become his new best friend. And I discovered that Kessler's Whiskey, not coffee, was in the thermos at all times.

Daddy told me he had a date with a woman named Joyce. He asked me to go to dinner with them. I said, "Okay." First he took me to a bar, The Pub, where everyone knew his name. There was a chipped, faded bumper sticker stuck on the mirror, behind the bar, that said, "Denny McLain for President." After powering down some cocktails, he drove to Jackson High School, where he'd been a hero. Then to a house next door, almost underneath the bleachers of the football stadium, on Winthrop Avenue.

"Remember this house?" he said.

I told him I did. We lived in the house when I was four. At night, I recalled flipping on a light switch in the kitchen and watching mice scatter in each direction. The nearby concession stands rendered bountiful banquets to the prolific critters.

I'd lie in bed and listen to the marching band play muffled music through the walls, and I'd stare at a Jackson High Viking Football poster that hung in my bedroom and dream about playing ball.

For one home game, Aunt Hige made me a band uniform. I marched down the field with the Jackson High Viking Band. Cousin Polly played and she was my escort. Afterwards, the band members came up to me in the end zone. They rubbed my head and told me I made them proud.

"This is where Bed-wrecker lives," my dad said.

"What?"

"Joyce, my date. I call her Bed-wrecker." He was grinning. And full of himself.

"Can you believe it? She lives in our old house. What are the odds? Hang on. I'm going in to get her. Get in the back."

I jumped in the backseat and waited for my dad.

Ten minutes later he emerged with Bed-wrecker on his arm.

Joyce was an amazing Amazon whose size matched my dad's six-foot-one-inch frame. The big-haired blonde's boobs overflowed her bra and blouse. She strutted toward the car with liquored-up confidence, telegraphing that she'd already drunk herself pretty.

It felt creepy. She was visibly smitten with my dad and attractive and talkative and seemed sincere, but I was uncomfortable in the presence of a bombshell called Bed-wrecker. I hated that she slept in the house in which I used to live with my dad and mom and little brother.

I asked him to take me back to Hige's house. "I don't feel well." I wanted to go "home" and watch television with my aunt.

"That's fine," he said.

I didn't hear him come in. But I woke up at four o'clock a.m. He was next to me, breathing fire rich with booze and tobacco. His breath was rancid and he smelled of his own gas and sweat and maybe a little bit of Joyce, too. I rolled over and tried to go back to sleep. And I did, until thunderous snoring woke me again. I shook him, but he slept on. I shook him again. Then I said, "Daddy, wake up."

Frustrated, I shook him vigorously and raised my voice. Finally he was conscious, but babbling. I couldn't understand what he was saying. I thought he was talking in his sleep. But then his eyes rolled up into his head. He began to sweat and gag. He vomited on the sheets. Then he puked again. He didn't know where he was.

I went to the laundry room and I gathered soiled towels from the floor. I mopped the vomit from the sheets. I stuffed the towels and a cup of detergent in the washer and started the machine. I rolled my dad on his side so that, if he blew again, hopefully he wouldn't choke to death. I found a folding chair and unwound it next to the bed. I watched my dad for two hours. I felt sorry for him. I felt sorry for myself.

He'd fallen far. He was drunk and helpless and sick and lonely and smelled of puke and whiskey and shit. He was just a few feet from me, yet a million miles away. Vulnerable and sad and washed up and washed out. Christ, what a disappointment. What could I do?

When I heard my aunt moving around upstairs, I joined her for toast and coffee. I told her Daddy wasn't feeling well. I asked her for a ride to Bompi and Gigi's apartment, at the funeral home.

I returned to the basement, down the stairs, by the dogs playing cards and the clock that told time backwards, and under the red-nosed deer with a dozen tines and into the bedroom in the dank basement corner. I checked on my dad. He was in an unconscious state, on a continuum somewhere between asleep and comatose. He'd stopped vomiting. He was at peace. For a while.

I gathered my stuff and left.

Seventeen

Fingered

LIFE WAS GETTING better for us, so it seemed.

For the first time, I had spent two complete, consecutive years in the same school: fifth and six grades at McLaughlin Elementary. We lived in the same crummy apartment on Terrace Street, but not moving or changing schools provided a rare sense of stability and continuity. And I was making friends in the neighborhood, too.

The months and years immediately after my dad left, my mom dated occasionally, but nursing studies were her primary concern. She would shut her bedroom door and ask not to be disturbed. Brian and I would comply. He got involved with a children's theater group and, between pick-up games and roaming the streets with buddies, I was content and occupied.

The summer of 1969 was terrific. We spent a bunch of Sundays at my mom's new boyfriend's family cottage, near Hart, where I fished and learned to water ski. And, best of all, I was delightfully teased by a teenage girl.

Blessed with an abundance of water and forest, Michigan's hard-working working-class folks could afford modest second homes and cottages. In much of the state, there was a weekend migration to the country, "up north," where regular people would embrace the unprocessed outdoors.

The boyfriend's parents had a wooden canoe that we used for fishing and a small powerboat. I learned to slalom ski from my mom, but without the Salem cigarette hanging from my lips or the can of Stroh's beer in my hand.

The boyfriend's dad would fry perch and bluegill in the early evening. We ate the little buggers on a dimly lit screened porch. On Sunday, July 20, we stayed later than usual because of the moon landing. My mom didn't want us to miss it. The black-and-white television sat high, over the bar. The lights were off and all attention was on the tube. I remember my mom's face, alive with light beamed from above. Everyone was hushed to silence. It was late, around eleven at night, but we were all wide awake with excitement. I could barely make out the fuzzy images, but when Neil Armstrong, dressed in a marshmallow suit, stepped off the ladder of the Eagle and said, "That's one small step for man, one giant leap for mankind," we were captivated and mesmerized.

My mom wiped a tear from her cheek.

The boyfriend had a daughter who was sixteen years old. She had ridiculously long, bronzed legs and hair that reached past the middle of her back. One night I was sitting by myself in the cottage's family room, near the fireplace. After a shower, the daughter came into the room wrapped only in a towel. The late summer night was cool. There was a wood fire raging in the hearth, and she bent over at the waist and began combing out her hair in front of the flames. The glow of the fire surrounded her and she turned to a golden brown and looked delicious wrapped in white. After combing her hair for a minute, she flipped her tawny mane up and over her head and it slapped on her back. Then she swung her hair back over to her front so she could comb it out again. I wasn't sure what I was watching, but I stared as long as I could. I didn't realize at the time, but I was holding my breath. When I finally started to breathe again, I did so with a burst of exhaust. She looked at me and smiled sideways, with her mane dangling down, stopping just above her pretty, painted toes.

Sullying the summer was news that Ted Kennedy drove his '67 Oldsmobile off a bridge on Chappaquiddick, an island near a place with an equally peculiar name, Martha's Vineyard. Ted didn't seem to be cut from the same cloth as his dead and revered brothers, John and Bobby. It was reported that a young woman was in Ted's car, Mary Jo Kopechne. Ted met her at a party. He was giving her a ride somewhere unknown. Kennedy's pregnant wife was not at the party, and Mary Jo was lacking her panties when authorities retrieved her dead body from Poucha Pond.

In a television press conference after the incident, Kennedy avoided inconvenient truths.

During summer days in 1969, my brother and I were under periodic supervision while my mom was in school. To pass time, we pitched pennies and played marbles and poker with some of the older kids in the neighborhood. There were more pick-up games: baseball, football and kickball. And we shot hoops behind St. Jean's Church. Some days, my buddies and I would dig worms and grubs and ride bikes to the public marina on Muskegon Lake. We'd fish watery holes in the tangled, broken concrete dumped along the lake to preserve the shore. If we caught fish, we'd sell them to black people who would fish the same spots. The shoreline was bordered by a crumbling industrial complex of foundries. Toxic pollutants leached into the once-pristine lake. My mom wouldn't let me eat the fish.

At night, we played chase. A game could last for hours. Teams were chosen, four to ten to a side, and we'd agree which city blocks were in play. Hiding inside someone's house was not allowed. Trees and garages and sheds and rooftops were acceptable. Both boys and girls played. That was fun because sometimes you got to hide with a girl you liked. Big kids and small kids played, too. We would designate a safe zone. A porch usually, where captured kids would be jailed but could be freed if a teammate tagged them. The game was over when all of one team was captured. We ran and climbed and tumbled and screamed and laughed and played until the streetlights came on, and sometimes longer. The entire neighborhood was our playground. We owned every yard and fence and garden and ran and chased and hid with reckless abandon. And we were fast and free. We didn't feel poor or underprivileged. We were just kids, allowed to act like kids. And it was great.

For one week, we met a bus at school and we were taken to the State Park, a half-hour ride north of town. The AFL-CIO union paid for the day camp, so all the kids in the neighborhood went for free. We'd show up at McLaughlin Elementary at nine in the morning, wearing sneakers and shorts and t-shirts and toting paper bags with a clean t-shirts and shorts, in case we got wet. The AFL-CIO provided lunch and beverages and snacks. The first day we were nervous. But the older kids in the neighborhood assured us that day camp was great. And it was. The counselors taught us chants and cheers and amazing songs like "99 Bottles of Beer on the Wall" and a ditty about a flea that lived on a log in the bottom of the sea. The girl counselors were like the sisters I always wanted. But I didn't want to be their brother. The guys were cool, too.

After we disembarked the bus, we'd hike through the woods, down a sandy trail under a canopy of ancient pine and oak. The smell of the woods was keen. We were city kids outside the city and we loved it. We put our bags under the protection of a lean-to. We hiked through the trees and behind the dunes to a hidden lake. We played kickball and volleyball and tag and Simon Says. Twice we marched to Lake Michigan and swam in the surf. The week in the woods flew by. We were melancholy singing our final chorus of "99 Bottles of Beer." I felt like crying when the bus pulled into the parking lot of school on our final Friday.

<hr />

MY SIXTH GRADE teacher was Mrs. Barding. She was attractive, but with features that favored masculine. She wore her hair in a beehive bun, like Grandma Gigi but not as high on her head. The one thing that made me feel uncomfortable about Mrs. Barding was her large, bulbous nose that seemed to sprout black hairs, right before my eyes. She wore thick, powdery make-up and big, chunky jewelry.

I was captain of the safety patrol, an honor bestowed on me for reasons I didn't know for certain. I became a substitute crossing guard late in fourth grade, and an everyday guard in fifth grade. Then I was promoted to captain.

There were a dozen student guards at key intersections around the school. Guards wore orange belts that strapped around their waists and over one shoulder and buckled in the front. They would stand on the sidewalk at an intersection with their arms extended, effectively holding back the students until traffic allowed for safe passage.

Crossing guards were treated with respect by parents and teachers and students. As captain, I was responsible for assigning guards to intersections and patrolling the school grounds. I had two lieutenants who assisted me. The school principal gave us badges that corresponded with our rank to pin over our hearts on our belts. When we weren't wearing the belts, they were to be neatly rolled up and secured.

An additional responsibility for the safety patrol officers was to raise and lower the Stars and Stripes, as well as the proper folding and storage of the flag. Though just kids, we approached these tasks with diligence.

If, during the school day, rain began to fall, my lieutenants and I would abandon our schoolwork and spring forth to rescue the flag. We took pride in our work.

Mrs. Barding's class was great fun. She'd encourage us to be creative. We had talent shows where we'd pantomime and dance to popular music. Show-and-tell was always entertaining, and Mrs. Barding put few restrictions on us.

One of my favorite classmates was Tex O'Neill. I liked Tex because he had an Irish last name and a cowboy's first name and, if that wasn't unique enough, he was as black as tar. One day, Tex brought in his four-year-old cousin for show-and-tell. He led the little kid up to the front of the room. The two of them stood in front of us for a couple minutes, just smiling. They smiled like they'd done something terrible and knew they were going to get away with it.

Mrs. Barding was not in on the apparent hoax. She asked Tex if there was "anything else?" He said, "Yes." He told his cousin to hold his hands out. The youngster held out both of his hands in front of him, like he was trying to stop someone from running into him.

The little boy and Tex smiled broadly.

"See?" Tex said.

"See what?" Mrs. Barding said. "See what?"

Kids in the class said, "See what, Tex?"

"Count his fingers."

Tex stood next to his cousin and counted the fingers on his left hand. "One, two, three, four, five." Then he counted the fingers on his right hand, as the little guy kept his arms extended in front of him.

"One, two, three, four, five, six!"

Sweet Jesus. The kid had six fingers.

"Count them again!" someone shouted.

"One, two, three, four, five, six!"

He had six fingers on his right hand. But his hand looked completely normal. Every finger was properly proportioned. His hand looked perfect. Just as God had intended. But the little freak had six fingers. The only possible way to tell was to count them. One by one. We counted them again and again.

His imperfection was perfectly disguised.

The cousin and Tex were very pleased with themselves.

We got up from our chairs and surrounded the boy. He started slapping our hands in celebration, like my dad used to when he'd say to me "give me five, man." He'd hold out his hand and I'd slap it, and then he'd do the same for me.

Someone said to Tex's cousin, "Give me six." We roared with laughter. A kid fell down, laughing. "Yeah, give me six! Give me six!"

Eighteen

Seeing Red

I ALMOST GAGGED the first time I saw my mom take food stamps out of her purse.

It was 1968. We were at Herring's Grocery. Three blocks from our apartment. We were there to buy two boxes of macaroni and cheese for my brother and me and a carton of Salem cigarettes for her. She was calm and matter of fact and counted out the near-money like it was real. I felt sick and embarrassed and breathed a sigh of relief when I saw that no one was in line behind us. I was positive that the clerk would make some kind of demeaning comment. Instead, she rang us up and bagged our goodies. And, without a hint of anything out of the ordinary, she handed me the sack and we left.

In time, I grew accustomed to the food stamps. When my mom was deep in her studies, she'd send me to the store with a note from her that said it was okay to sell the cigarettes to me. Depending on the clerk, I was able to use the food stamps to pay for the Salems, even though "it was against the law." I used the change to buy candy bars and baseball cards. And, one time, a Fantastic Four comic book.

We also received welfare assistance from ADC, which my mom said stood for "Aid to Dependent Children." Since my dad wasn't any help and my mom didn't have a job, we needed all the aid we could get. At least until she finished nursing school.

Our apartment was smaller than the houses we'd rented. But without Daddy and Night Train, there was enough room for the three of us and a mob of hamsters we kept in a cage in the bathtub. Otherwise they kept escaping. Before we moved them to the confines of the tub, my mom accidentally broiled a runaway hamster that sealed his own fate by nesting in the insulation of our stove.

The apartment house at 1164 Terrace was big, formerly a lavish home for just one family. It reflected hints of grandeur from days long past. The space that was our kitchen had been a sunroom. A stove and refrigerator were jammed into the room when we lived there, but near the ceiling was a small stained glass window with beveled edges and divided by lead. When the sun shone through the glass, filtered by branches and leaves from a tree outside, the colors would dance across the walls and it felt like a happy place.

We had two tiny bedrooms and a bath with a tub, but no shower. And a family room, if you could call it that. There was a bay window in the room, large and out of scale. Decades before, the bay was one of several that were part of a salon of grand proportion and opulence. But the crumbling inner city chased away the affluent and prominent, and the stately homes fell out of demand. So they were chopped up into apartments. For folks who couldn't afford to live in the preferred parts of town. Folks like us.

In sixth grade, I drank my first Pabst Blue Ribbon beer and smoked a Camel cigarette. I found neither to be particularly appealing. I scored the contraband from an older kid I met shooting hoops at the playground. None of the kids in the neighborhood played on any organized teams other than those we had at our elementary school. I did hear about a kid who lived on the edge of the neighborhood who played on a Little League baseball team, but none of us had seen his uniform. And there were no Little League parks near us. We didn't care so much. Whatever the sport, we'd pick sides and play for hours on the field behind McLaughlin or on the basketball courts or in the parking lot behind St. Jean's Church. We'd play until someone broke his nose or finger or got into a fight. Or until the street lights came on.

Easter weekend in the spring of 1970, my mom took Brian and me to a party on the other side of town. We pulled up to a handsome bungalow in a modest, neat neighborhood of single-family homes with yards and dogs and kids and moms and dads. Music was playing on a phonograph.

Children my age were running in and out of the house, boys chasing girls and girls chasing boys. The screen door slammed and slammed but no one seemed to notice. The adults were invested in conversation and swimming in their cocktails and oblivious to the ruckus.

My mother and brother disappeared into the house. I found myself kicking an invisible can around the perimeter of the yard when a tall, red-headed guy popped out from behind the screen door and yelled, "Hey, Rocky, wanna play catch?"

"Guess so."

He introduced himself as Red Miller. He asked me to follow him over to his car. In the trunk, he had dusty canvas bags of wooden bats and catcher's gear and some balls and several mitts and gloves.

"Your mom says your dad was quite a ball player. Had a chance to play for the Tigers, huh?"

"Yup. And the Cubs. But I don't see him much anymore."

Red and I tossed the ball back and forth and talked about nothing that mattered. That felt better than chatting about my dad.

"How about you show me what you got?"

For several minutes he threw hard, and I threw hard back at him. Red was a pretty good athlete. He threw better than some of the big kids in our neighborhood.

He bounced me grounders and tossed fly balls and I shagged the balls and fired them back into Red. His glove popped with each throw.

"That's enough. Let's pack this stuff up."

We ambled over to his car and he opened the trunk again. I handed him the glove he lent me. He tossed it onto the bat bag and put the balls back in their place. Then he reached down and pulled out a garment bag that had been folded in half. Without saying a word, he unzipped the front of the bag and revealed a pin-striped baseball uniform. It was the real McCoy. Authentic. It had a long name across the front that I couldn't make out. Sewn onto the shoulder was an official Little League patch.

"I want you to try this on."

"What?"

I had no idea where he was headed.

"I want you on my team. You're twelve, right? And you don't turn thirteen until next fall, right?"

"Right. But Mr. Miller, I don't even live near a Little League field and my mom is in nursing school, so I don't know how I'd get there, wherever 'there' is."

"I know where you live. I'll pick you up at four o'clock tomorrow, after school. Bring your glove and cleats."

"I don't have any cleats."

"Just bring your glove, we'll figure out the cleats later. Okay? See ya, kid."

<hr />

RED GAVE ME the uniform to take home after my first practice. I put it on and stood in front of a mirror for ten minutes. I pantomimed throwing a ball and tagging someone out. Then I walked for blocks about the neighborhood, hoping that someone would ask me why I was dressed like a real baseball player. But no one was around.

We practiced and played on a groomed field with canvas bases and chalked lines. There were umpires and an announcer who called our names before we batted and said "nice catch" if we made a good play. I wanted to play well and make my mom proud.

From the day I first put on a Warner-Schuitema Moving & Storage uniform, I felt like I was part of something. I was on a team and more. We backed each other up. We cheered for one another. We played together with purpose and enthusiasm. And we shook hands with our opponents, whether we won or lost. It felt good and right to be part of something bigger than me. And, for the first time, I felt relevant and challenged and responsible and fulfilled. I wanted to be a great teammate and to win games. And, some day, to play for the Muskegon Big Reds in high school.

The big friendly guy with the red pompadour stepped through a screen door and into my life and asked me to play catch. Because of him, a light turned on inside of me.

He took a chance on kid he didn't know. And it changed my life.

Nineteen

Minding Your Meat

THINGS STARTED OUT OKAY.

I was twelve years old in September of 1970 when I entered seventh grade at Nelson Junior High. More than a mile from where I lived in the apartment on Terrace Street, the kids and the school were not unfamiliar to me. I attended adjacent Nelson Elementary for parts of third and fourth grade. And McLaughlin, my neighborhood elementary, was a feeder into the junior high. Nelson also drew from more affluent neighborhoods, west of Seaway Drive. And from some of the roughest, grittiest parts of town.

I liked not having to sit in one classroom all day. And I was excited that we were scheduled to have gym class every day of the week, with Tuesdays and Thursdays designated as pool days.

My gym class was a mix of seventh and eighth grade boys. You didn't need a swim suit for pool because everyone swam naked. More accurately, we were required to swim naked. The practice was not entirely queer to me because I'd taken swimming lessons at the YMCA when I was six years old. Skinny dipping was the rule, whether you were a guppy or a shark. For some reason, the girls didn't have to bare all. So they swam in suits issued by the school. No one knew why the boys did it one way and the girls another. That's just the way it was.

There were about forty of us in the class. We were instructed to strip and soap up and rinse in the communal shower and then form a line. Our gym teacher was a skinny, light-skinned black guy with freckles named Mr. Burt. He was a cocky little bastard who was his own and only best friend. Mr. Burt walked with huge strides and rolled from the back of his heels to the tips of his toes with each step. No doubt to compensate for his slight stature. He chirped at us incessantly and was never without his clipboard and whistle. Most of the kids agreed he was insecure and a prick, but he was also in charge.

On the first day of pool, we dutifully showered. Seventh graders started to form a line in front of the pool door, as instructed. Mr. Burt screamed, "Tighten up that line!" We had our elbows tucked against our sides and our hands clasped under our chins, in mock prayer, as we inched our peckers closer to the butts in front of us. Being careful not to touch. Mr. Burt, with his Napoleon complex, adored the fact he was torturing twenty insecure seventh graders, as he and twenty arrogant eighth graders looked on with satisfaction and delight.

Mr. Burt disappeared but the squeaky clean seventh graders maintained formation. I turned my head to the right and noticed a big, muscular black kid marching stridently toward the showers. While he might have been in eighth grade, he was several years older than us. And his pecker was the size of a zucchini. His magnificent penis swung to and fro, slapping his right thigh and then left. Keeping time like a meaty pendulum as he made his way to the line. When he reached the front, he grabbed skinny, diabetic Timmy Hummel—a preacher's kid—by the shoulder, turning him. Then the big-cocked kid slammed his open palm into Timmy's chest.

Timmy fell backwards, into the kid behind him. Like dominos, seventh graders fell to the tiled shower floor. Timmy started sobbing and hyper-ventilating. A red welt, in the shape of an open hand, began to rise up on Timmy's white chest.

Mr. Burt's whistle blasted and was amplified in the tiled shower room.

"What the hell is going on?"

The assaulter muttered something to Mr. Burt, unintelligible to us, but the words must have been insightful to Mr. Burt.

"You dumb-ass seventh graders should know that you line up behind the eighth graders. Behind them!" he screamed.

"All seventh graders on the deck."

No one moved.

The whistle blasted again.

"On the fucking deck!"

Any eighth graders in the shower scrambled out. The seventh graders spread across the floor with little open space between us. The tiles were cold and wet and soapy and slimy and gritty. I could hear Timmy whimpering.

"I want twenty-five push-ups. And I want your little baby seventh grade peckers to touch the floor on each one. If you don't (he paused for emphasis), you'll owe me twenty-five more!"

Mr. Burt counted out loud while we did our push-ups. Some kids couldn't do twenty-five so they planted their hips and dicks into the repulsive shower floor. They lifted their torsos up and down. To the best of their ability. We completed our penance and then stood in line behind the eighth graders and shuffled through the pool door, pecker-to-butt and butt-to-pecker. Pretending as though nothing had happened.

Timmy recovered from the hand-plant to the chest. I learned that the kid with the big pecker was named Benni. Before the end of the school year, he'd fathered a child.

We grew to like Mr. Burt, but just a little. And all the seventh graders agreed that if Mr. Burt had a pecker, he was hung like a baby parrot.

Twenty

What Are We Fighting For?

I WAS TEN when my mom and dad broke up. After he left, the first thing I asked my mom was "Am I gonna be stupid?"

The question was sincere. When she said, "What do you mean?" I told her the kids at school from broken families were the worst students. They acted up in class. And fought on the playground. My mom asked, "How about Mik DeBoef?"

Mik wasn't in my grade. He was a year older. But my mom was right. Mik was a good kid. His older sister Sherri was a terrific student. And from what I could tell, they were dirt poor like we were. Their dad left them, too. He escaped to California. Mik showed me pictures of his dad, who looked tan and happy. He told me that his dad used to drink a lot. And not only did he leave Mik and Sherri, but he also left Mik's two older sisters, Terri and Cris, and his mom, Mary, too. The five of them lived in a peeling, rundown dump on 8th Street off of Southern Avenue in the Nelson neighborhood.

Their little brown hovel sat next to a noisy machine shop that had gray corrugated walls and a metal roof. Inside the shop, men in hard hats and face shields would grind and weld and cut, making a racket all day and night. To the west was an industrial complex and a factory that made Brunswick bowling pins. It leaked sickening fumes from resins and glues so toxic it was uncomfortable to walk by. When the fumes got too intense, my eyes would water and my nose would burn, as though smeared with Mentholatum.

Inside Mik's house, the carpet was threadbare and stained with food and mottled with hardened gum and soiled by cats and burned black in spots by fumbled cigarettes. Trash littered the place. There were plates of partially eaten food on the floor and on tables and chairs and the couch. In the kitchen, days' worth of dishes were stacked in the sink and on the counters. And, while I never saw mice or rats, I could imagine them scavenging at night like they did when we lived on Winthrop Avenue next to the stadium where my dad played high school football.

Mik's mom was pitiful and sad. She worked as a meat cutter in a grocery store. The toll of divorce and poverty, and raising four teenagers, weighed heavily. When visiting, I'd often find her sitting in a trance and sucking on a cigarette with an ashtray on her lap in the middle of their broken-down couch. Her shoulders would be slumped as she sat in a nightgown, her short, burnt-brown hair sticking up haphazardly, gummy and brittle. She wore her hard life on her face and in her slouched and shrunken body. I always felt sorry for her, but I never blamed her for the squalid conditions. Frankly, I wondered how she summoned the energy to get out of bed each day.

When I was thirteen, Mik's youngest sister, Sherri, was fifteen. Cris and Terri were in their late teens. All four kids, in stark contrast to their house, appeared neat and uncommonly handsome. Terri, the oldest, had reddish-brown chestnut hair and full lips and dark, almond-shaped eyes and perky breasts that she showed off in tight V-neck sweaters. Cris was also pretty, but with thinner lips and lighter hair and a fair complexion. She had longer legs than Terri, but they looked yummy and ripened in their skintight Levi's. They both smoked, and when they sucked on their cigarettes their breasts would inflate right in front of my face. Sometimes they'd squint their eyes and tilt their chins and look at me. I'd have to leave the room, because I couldn't see inside their heads. And I wanted to.

Sherri was brilliant. And she could throw a baseball as far as any boy. Without fear, she climbed trees. And I watched her beat the poop-snot out of kid who killed a pigeon with a rock. But when she talked she sounded, ironically, like Minnie Mouse. However, there was nothing mini about Sherri. She had breasts the size of traffic cones. They were glorious and defied gravity. And she wore baby-size t-shirts and short shorts all summer long. When we played football, I wanted Sherri on my team, because she was good. But if she played for other team, that was okay, because then I had a chance to wrestle her to the ground.

During the summer of 1971, Mik's sister Cris spun the *Woodstock* album for us. The DeBoefs had a record player we put in the middle of a card table. We sat and stood and listened in appreciation and amazement. The music helped me put pieces together that had been just fragments of information with no linkage or association.

I watched the news on television. I read newspapers. And we talked about current events at school. I discussed things with my mom. But when I started to pay attention to the music, I found a connectivity that had eluded me.

On May 4, 1970, four college kids who were protesting the Viet Nam War were gunned down by the Ohio National Guard at Kent State University. Two years earlier, Dr. Martin Luther King and Bobby Kennedy were murdered. Race riots in Detroit in 1967 were followed by upheaval in other major cities in 1968, a reaction to Dr. King's death and what some people said were deficient and ill-conceived government programs. Race relations in Muskegon were tense during the period, but played out in mere skirmishes between whites and blacks in school yards. There were no mass street demonstrations in our town.

In 1969, Aunt Hige took me to a museum at Ella Sharp Park in Jackson. There, prints from the '68 Riots in Chicago by my cousin Michael O'Sullivan were on display. He, better than anyone, captured the anger and frustration and desperation in the faces of the people.

Also in 1969, I watched news coverage of the Woodstock concert. I was only eleven years old at the time. I knew very little about the music played there. But that would change.

During 1971, the Viet Nam War labored on, with no resolution in sight. Newscasts would morbidly present a scorecard of dead and wounded each evening. The war was something that just was. I'd concluded that countries were always at war and we had to accept war as part of life, as well as the protests and marches and sit-ins and riots.

And then Cris spun the album.

Two years after the concert, I listened to a sarcastic song by a guy called Country Joe McDonald. Something finally clicked.

Hearing his "I-Feel-Like-I'm Fixin'-To-Die Rag" was a breakthrough for me.

And it's one, two, three, what are we fighting for?
Don't ask me I don't give a damn
Next stop is Viet Nam

The music was an awakening. There was purpose to the riots. There was purpose to the marches and sit-ins. Not all hippies were bums, and not all rioting black people were bad, crazy or lazy.

"Don't ask me, I don't give a damn."

Of course they did give a damn. That was the point.

I finally got it.

Twenty-one

First Kiss

I WAS PRETTY sure that the first girl I'd ever kiss would be my dad's second and third wife's daughter, Vickie.

Vickie liked my dad's and her mom's boozing and battling as much as I did. So after that first weekend that I met her and we watched movies together and leaned on each other, I hardly ever saw her again. I'd always hoped that things would turn out okay for her. But when my dad and her mom broke up, the second time, and she and Vickie hijacked all my dad's possessions, I figured I'd never see or hear from her again.

In sixth grade, I'd ride my bike around the block where Joni Monroe lived on the outside chance that she might come outside and I'd get to talk to her. I thought she liked me, but I didn't know for sure. And there was a girl named Laura who was skinny and had big brown eyes that had their own gravitational pull. She was always animated and she had a teasing little mole on the left side of her upper lip and a big space between her teeth. She could spit water thirteen feet. I thought she was pretty and cool. But Joni and Laura were best friends, so that smelled like trouble to me.

And there was a girl named Liz that I did kiss, underneath the dining room table, after a birthday party at a friend's house. I never really counted it as a kiss because she was Greek and she had a mustache. The entire time that we were canoodling all I could think about was how scratchy her face was. I loathed the fact that she needed a shave and I didn't.

Then there was Marva Blais. I met Marva on my first day of classes at Nelson Junior High in seventh grade. She was different from any girl I'd ever met. A confident, swaggering blonde from the other side of the tracks—the good side. She was tall, or at least taller than me, athletic and tanned, and she had thick, light-brown shoulder-length hair colored by the sun and shuffled by the randomness of the wind. A yacht club kid.

The one time Marva and I tried to kiss, she came at me with her huge, lovely mouth wide open. Our teeth clanged together and the moment was ruined. Two weeks later, she beat me in a school election for treasurer of our class. Then she broke up with me, and I thought that maybe she wasn't so cute after all. And I had no idea what a treasurer did anyway.

Early in the winter of 1971, Mik and I crashed a dance at Bunker Junior High. We were glad we did because the girls were from a better part of town. I played baseball with some of the guys, so they were okay with us on their turf. Near the end of the party, I finally summoned enough courage to ask a girl to dance when the disc jockey played "Let It Be."

The girl had long, perfectly straight brown hair down to the middle of her back. She wore a soft, yellow sweater and tight-fitting, bell-bottomed Levi's and a wide belt with a big buckle. I thought she was cute, but it was dark in the gym so I couldn't see her clearly—not just due to the lack of light, but also because she was nervously looking at her shoes when she said, "Sure, I'll dance."

Mik's sister Terri taught me how to slow dance. She showed me how to put my arms around the girl's waist and hold her against me. But not too tightly. And to shuffle my feet to the left, as though moving in a small circle around the girl. She would follow me. If she didn't, I was to ask her if was okay for me to lead.

We started to dance. It seemed like everyone was dancing. All very slowly. The Beatles were singing, and I thought I heard the girl whisper "let it be" in my ear. I was drinking in the smell of her hair, which was fresh from an evening shampoo, and her perfumed neck made my mouth water. I lost myself in her bouquet. After the song ended, I intended to ask for her phone number. But when we attempted to separate from our embrace, we snapped back together. Our belt buckles had entangled. By the time we got them untangled, she was embarrassed and her friends were giggling. And she scurried away.

In February of 1971, I met a girl named Margie Briggs. She had an older brother I knew from baseball. I'd seen her at night at the outdoor ice skating rink, at the corner of Park and Southern. We skated together and threw snow at each other. Finally one night I asked her to go for a walk. We went behind the shed where we put on our skates and kept warm. She backed me up to a pile of snow so that I could be taller than her. Otherwise I wasn't.

Margie was tiny and delicate and pretty and pure. She had brown hair and brown eyes and soft freckles and a perfect little nose. When she let me kiss her she tasted like cherry lip balm. I squeezed her. It was like hugging a pillow. She had on a puffy down coat that was so thick I couldn't know she was in it, except that I was kissing a pretty little cherry head and it had to be attached to something.

And I was sure that something was equally wonderful and delicious.

Twenty-two

Large Root Beer

I LAMENTED THAT my mom stopped dating the boyfriend whose parents had the cottage near Hart, where we'd enjoyed a handful of idyllic summer Sundays.

I missed waterskiing on one ski across the glass lake and fishing from the green, wooden canoe. Most of all, I longed for the bronze-legged girl, wrapped in her white towel and bent at the waist, combing her hair in front of a hot fire and me.

But I'd graduated from Little League and I was drafted to play Pony League. And, when I wasn't playing ball, I was hitchhiking to the beach at Lake Michigan with Mik and our mutual friend Woody or chasing pretty girls across the city. I was free, a teenager at last, so I stayed out later, long after the street lights came on.

There were other guys for my mom. She was prettier than ever. She'd completed nursing school, so she was no longer a divorcee on welfare, just a single mom with two young boys. But at least we weren't crippled or anything awful like that. She even snapped up a new car for $1,995, a mustard-yellow Ford Pinto. It was the ugliest auto I'd ever seen, but our Chevy broke down. And the Pinto came with a free purse. It looked like a feedbag.

Her boyfriends tried to win my friendship by doling me cash. I figured that out early on. So when my mom had a friend over, I'd ask her for money. Whether she gave me any or not didn't matter. Because as soon as one of the boyfriends got the chance to slip me a dollar or two, they'd do it.

When she started dating a guy named Lawrence Ryan Backofen, I liked him less than any other. I didn't like him or his name. My mom told me that if I didn't fancy the name Lawrence, I should call him Larry. But he didn't like Larry. Some people called him LRB. I just didn't call him anything. He didn't talk to me, so why should it matter? He only came around a few times, that I knew of, in the summer of 1971. When he did, he was tentative and nervous. And his body was soft and doughy. I thought of him as a prissy-boy. The kind picked on at school and picked last for teams, or not picked at all.

He had a cleft in his chin and his lips were perpetually pursed. He had wavy hair and pasty skin. He wasn't at ease around me, or me around him, but my mom seemed to be attracted to the guy. He wasn't anything like my dad. Maybe she didn't want anybody like my dad. You couldn't blame her for that.

After summer baseball in early August, I took a Greyhound bus from Muskegon to Lansing and then on to Jackson to see my dad. But when I got there five hours later, Bompi picked me up at the station. He said, "Your dad is having issues."

The next day, I talked to my dad on the phone. He said he'd pick me up, but he never showed. On my third day in Jackson, he called me again, this time from a bar, The Pub. He promised to pick me up "in an hour." He never made it.

Bompi said that he probably had to go see Judy. "They're trying to patch things up," he said. I knew he wanted to stay at the bar. So he did.

That night, Bompi and Gigi took me to a place called "the Cascades." The man-made waterfall had fountains and colored lights. On some nights there were fireworks. As a little kid I might have liked the Cascades. But I didn't any longer. Then we went to The Dome. I ate a cheeseburger and froze my head with ice cream, just like I did when I was little. And that was good.

The next night we drove to the A & W Root Beer stand. I ate a rye melt sandwich and hot French fries. When I asked the carhop for a "large root beer," she said, "One LRB, coming up." I thought about Lawrence Ryan Backofen and my mom—and thought that Large Root Beer was a better name for him than Lawrence or Larry or LRB.

I visited Great-grandma Bessie. She was eighty-nine and going strong. We chatted on her back porch and listened to a Tigers game. I saw Uncle Charlie and Aunt Louise, but for just a few hours because they were leaving for a vacation "up north." I looked in on my cousins, too. But it was my dad I needed to see.

Bompi and Gigi wouldn't discuss his drinking. They said he was just in a "rough patch" and everything would be okay. I considered that maybe they were right. The week finally wound to an end and Bompi and Gigi took me to the Greyhound depot. I hugged them goodbye and boarded the smelly bus. I found a seat across from a woman who had a lazy eye and sniffled all the way to Lansing. When I switched buses, I was happy that she didn't go on to Muskegon. On the next bus, I sat across from a fat man who had four paper bags full of wet newspapers. He limped and he had the sniffles, too. But he wiped his nose on his sleeve and snorted and spit into his bags. I thought about how lucky I was to get to ride a bus.

My mom picked me up at the depot in Muskegon. As she pulled away, she told me we weren't going to our apartment on Terrace. Because, while I was out of town for the week, she said, "Lawrence and I got married. We're going to move in with him for a couple of weeks, and then to our own place, the four of us, north of town on Bear Lake."

It was like getting smashed in the face with a two-by-four I didn't see coming. I didn't even know him. I was losing my dad to booze. Now I was getting a new one, whom I didn't want. I suddenly felt like I was losing my mom, too. The one person I trusted and who stood by me and protected me and loved me and bought me chips and French onion dip and, holy shit, I couldn't believe what was happening. Nor the speed at which it was happening. I was stunned. I was bewildered. I was devastated. I was hurt. I was jealous. I felt betrayed, alienated and hated.

My dad was gregarious and athletic and entertaining. Large Root Beer had girly skin and queer lips. He talked too fast and in a condescending, pompous patois that made me ill and confused. My mom didn't try to defend her actions, but she did try to console me. I shook off her attempts to hold and comfort me. I found the stairs to the basement in Large Root Beer's house. I slammed the door behind me, and at the bottom of the stairs I was surrounded by remnants of my life. Packed away in corrugate. To be moved again. The tenth time in thirteen years.

They left me alone. I cried. It seemed like I cried for two days, but it was for hours, not days. I finally calmed myself.

My mom was a bright and pretty and gutsy woman. Sitting in that basement, I was thinking about me. And that was easy to do. I needed to consider her and Brian—us. But I didn't want to be taken away from my school and my friends and my streets. Back in Jackson, the unraveling of my dad's life was accelerating. I'd smelled and mopped up the lurid stench of his failures. But I was frustrated as to what to do.

Life was becoming harder to synthesize. I felt alone and empty.

But, just maybe, getting out of our wretched little apartment would be okay. I could make new friends. And keep my old friends. And my brother and I would grow closer. My dad would stop drinking. And land a job. Everything would be all right.

And we'd live happily, ever after.

Twenty-three

Nice Shoes

I WASN'T KEEN to move again. But resisting would have been futile.

I did feel ignored and denounced. But I wasn't about to live with my dad and watch him play Russian roulette with a whiskey bottle. So I hitched up my pants and I made amends with my mom and I embraced living with Large Root Beer the best that I could.

We moved twenty minutes north of Muskegon to Bear Lake Road, on the shore of a lake with the same name. It was a simple, single-level ranch-style house with an eat-in kitchen and a view of the lake. There was a bath and a family room and two small bedrooms and a larger one that my mom and Large Root Beer shared. The house was dog-eared and lacked character, but the proximity to the lake made up for any shortcomings. Compared to where we'd been living, the place was paradise. I didn't complain a lick.

I had no idea how my brother felt about the move or our new step-father. Brian and I continued to drift apart. His interests didn't parallel mine. His friends were peculiar and each day we seemed more disparate than alike. The transition to the new school shined a spotlight on our differences. I didn't like having to explain to other kids that we were, in fact, brothers. Over time, I saw less and less of him. He barricaded himself in his bedroom and did things, I was certain, that were dark and sneaky and dangerous.

Already an authority on moving and changing schools, I was only modestly anxious about eighth grade and meeting the kids and teachers at Laketon Junior High. The school was the only feeder into Reeths-Puffer High School. I knew of the Rockets from reading about their football program in the sports pages of *The Muskegon Chronicle*.

Growing up in the city, the only high school I thought I'd attend was Muskegon High. They had a storied history of fielding championship teams. Hackley Stadium, on Sanford Street, where the Big Reds played their home football games, was five blocks from our apartment on Terrace. The football team practiced on Wilson Field between the stadium and St. Jean's, the neighborhood Catholic Church.

I used to watch through the cyclone fence at Wilson Field as coaches ran the Big Reds through their drills. The players shouted encouragement to one another, "go Red, go Big Red!" For years, I watched the team call the man in charge "Coach Chev." His real name was Roger Chiaverini. Coach enjoyed god-like status in Muskegon because of his serial success. He left Muskegon High in 1970 to resurrect a Muskegon Catholic Central program that had gone sour. And he soon found success again. Larry Harp took over for Chev at Muskegon High. I watched him through the same fence.

Unintentionally, I created a stir when I showed up for my first day of classes at Laketon, wearing a pair of bright red Chuck Taylor Converse basketball shoes. I bought the shoes with money I made picking blueberries at a farm near Fruitport. At the time, in early August, I thought I'd be going to school again at Nelson Junior High and one day to Muskegon High School. So the choice of red made sense.

I stuck out with the gaudy shoes. A cocky kid named Greg Mann introduced himself to me. He asked if I was going out for the football team. I told him I hadn't given it much thought, but I knew I needed to belong to something fast.

"Come on out. You'll have fun. We're gonna be good."

"Okay. Probably will."

"Nice shoes, by the way. See ya."

I went out for the team as Goldilocks — Greg — suggested, and I was impressed with the speed and athleticism of the players, especially a black kid named Gordon Evans, a man among boys. Gordon pushed six feet and he was fleet and he had defined muscles and grit. He was designated to carry the ball and the eighth grade Wildcat team to many victories. Goldilocks was the quarterback, and a guy named Paul Jacobsen was another good ball carrier. And there were others. The coach asked me what position I wanted to play. I told him "center," a lineman position, which was preposterous since I'd led my Pony League baseball team in steals. But that's what I said and where the coaches played me.

Ironically, Goldilocks and I won "best combination" at an awards ceremony after the season.

In my eighth grade yearbook he wrote:

To a real cool kid and good friend. Remember all the good times goofing around...have fun over the summer. Hope we can get together and raise some he__. Be sure to be careful—accidents cause people. A.F.A.
— Greg

TWO MONTHS INTO eighth grade, I alerted my mom that I needed a ride into town on the upcoming Friday night because the Traverse City Trojans were to play the Muskegon Big Reds for the "mythical" state championship. And I couldn't miss it. They were ranked one and two, respectively, and the game was a re-match of the 1969 game where Coach Chev lost to the Trojans 7–0 when a Muskegon pass was intercepted by a giant white guy who rumbled fifty yards to score the only touchdown.

The contest was sold out even though they'd trucked in additional bleachers. Dozens of buses from Traverse City lined the streets near Hackley Stadium. There was uncommon electricity in the air. The energy and excitement was enhanced by the distant sound of the bands warming up on the adjacent campus.

I had five dollars and no firm plan. My mom told me to hold one finger in the air, above my head and near the will-call window of the ticket booth. There was a chance that someone with an extra ticket would sell one to me, or I could sneak in with the band or hop the fence.

Just a few moments after raising my hand and shouting "I need one!" a man in his forties asked me what I was doing. I said, "Trying to buy a ticket."

"How old are you?"

"Fourteen, almost."

"By yourself?"

"Yup. I used to come here by myself all the time."

I told him that I attended Nelson Junior High when I lived on Terrace Street, but that now I lived in the Reeths-Puffer school district, and that I used stick my nose through the fence of Wilson field. He stopped me by saying, "I get it." He was grinning.

"My wife fell ill today. Would you like to sit with me?"

"Shoot, yes. Thanks."

First we entered the concrete tunnel under the old stadium, and I knew why we were there. We nodded at each other and smiled as we heard the Big Red marching band approach. Once inside, the percussion section punched out a raucous beat. The noise was deafening and perfect. The band's high-stepping became more animated and the musicians exaggerated the swinging of their instruments and the articulation of their drums. The drum line consisted of snares and tenors and bass drums. They were trailed by a dozen cymbal players that spun and flashed their instruments before crashing them together with delight. Hairs stood on the back of my neck. I had shivers and goose bumps. You couldn't have beaten the smile from my face.

We climbed to our seats on the forty-five yard line. I was the sole kid among adults in our section. I didn't care. Across the field, thousands of Traverse City faithful were locked side by side in random groups of six to ten. They swayed left to right to left to the rhythms of their own marching band and they sang their fight song and cheered wildly as the Trojans ran onto the gridiron.

A teenager—a light-skinned black kid dressed to look like an Indian warrior—took the field in front of the Big Red student section. He stomped out a spirited Native American dance within a circle formed by drummers. The atmosphere of the spectacle surpassed my inflated expectations. After the dance, the players and coaches were introduced and the ball was kicked off and the battle ensued.

I soaked in the sounds and the smells of coffee and popcorn and hot dogs and pipe tobacco. We were packed shoulder to shoulder. No one complained. The evening was cool, but not cold. We were witness to one of the greatest Michigan high school football games of the decade, if not ever. The Big Reds won 20–18. The final outcome was in doubt until the end. It was over too quickly. The man talked with me in the stands until they cleared. He was kind and patient and, no doubt, a great dad to some lucky kid.

That night, he was mine.

＊―――――＊●＊―――――＊

IN NINTH GRADE, I reported to football practice and suggested to the coaches that I was no longer a lineman. They hesitated, but I proved my mettle.

Fran Pike was the assistant and Dennis Pallett was the head coach. Coach Pallett was more short than tall. He had tightly-cropped, kinky dark hair and his eyes were a little too far apart. He barked and spit at us incessantly. Coach tried to be gruff and tough, but he never quite pulled it off. We could tell he was, if truth be told, a gentle man. And, in an ironic cruelty, Coach Pallet was born with a cleft palate. It was because of the cleft palate that Coach Pallet spit when he barked. His condition also made him the rarest of breeds—a coaching homophone.

Eighth grade star Gordon Evans damaged his knee the prior basketball season and opted out of ninth grade football to focus on hoops. The coaches featured me at halfback. I scored on a seventy-yard run my first carry of the year and drew a penalty for spiking the ball. For the season I led the team in touchdowns and yards gained. We had big farm boys like Jerry and Steve Wirt opening gaping holes. I often ran untouched thanks to them.

We went 6–0 in league games and we were Seaway Conference champions, outscoring our opponents 112 to 28. Our lone loss was to Coach Chev's Muskegon Catholic Central frosh, in our last game of the year.

I played basketball at Laketon and rarely started, but I enjoyed my teammates. Just being on a team was important to me. We won all sixteen of our games.

I ran track, too. And chased girls.

＊―――――＊●＊―――――＊

ONE GIRL I chased, and caught, was Gail Babcock. I'd gone out with longer, blonder and prettier girls, but Gail was the first for whom I felt something more than the Neanderthal urges that weigh heavily in the loins of all teenage boys. And she was cute. She was delightfully adorable with her big brown eyes and mole on her upper lip, and she was attractively coy and reticent. But it was her maturity that set her apart. And her parents.

Her dad and mom were ordinary, honest folks who raised five children in a tiny house that was filled with love. I fell in love with Mitch and Judy because their unspectacular lives were plain and bland and boring and constructed on a foundation of trust, and because everything about them was solid and good.

And they treated me like a son, with dignity and care. I never told them how I felt about them. I hope they got something back from me.

I sure got something from them.

Twenty-four

Growing Up Fast

FROM THE INSIDE back cover of my high school yearbook my sophomore year, written unmistakably by the careful and patient hand of a female, in blue, with a ballpoint pen:

Where to start...we've been through so much together, a lot of happiness and a little bit of sadness. I can't begin to say all I feel for you, but I can say I never expected to feel or share so much with one person like I have with you. You've taught me a lot about myself and brought out feelings I never knew I had. I've come to know and understand you, though I must say there are things about you I may never understand. Maybe that's good, I don't know. You're the first person in my life, the first person I've ever shared myself with, and I've never needed or wanted anyone else. Maybe I shouldn't be writing this in here because quite a few people will probably be reading it...I know some of your feelings toward me and I hope you'll always keep them. I think I grew up fast after meeting you though maybe sometimes it doesn't seem that way at all. I trust that you'll always remember me. I'll never forget you, after all who ever forgets their first love? You be good to yourself...there's so much more I can say, maybe some day I'll tell you all my inner secrets...I love you, Gail.

There were things about me that Gail would never understand. Because I didn't let her. I didn't let anyone. I kept my dad's unraveling locked up tight, inside. A secret that I shared with no one. Not my mom or friends or coaches or teachers or Gail. I tried to talk to Bompi and Gigi, but they dismissed me. They saw what was happening to my dad. Maybe they tried to talk to him. To get him help. To reason with him. But how do you reason with a drunk? Though one hundred and fifty miles away in Jackson, he was ripping my heart apart every day with his inexorable spiral down. I felt frustrated and helpless and impotent.

I was outgoing and gregarious most of the time. But I could be aloof as well. And when I was, it was because I wasn't there. I was standing in a window, pulling back the drapes, looking outside at snowy streets, knowing that he could be in the next car coming around the corner. Or I was waiting on the steps. Or in a parked car, when he went in "for just one." Or I was in my bedroom, late at night, praying that he would come home, before I cried myself to sleep. I wasn't there because I was still waiting, hopelessly, for my dad.

He hadn't seen me play a single Little League or Pony League baseball game. He missed every football and basketball game and track meet. And then he finally appeared at a football match my sophomore year. An away game. I didn't know he was going to be there. We lost. I started and played halfback on offense and then played part of the game at cornerback, on defense. My dad intercepted me on the way to the team bus.

"Too many arm tackles," he said.

"What? Hey, Daddy!"

"Too many fuckin' arm tackles. Lead with your shoulders and hit 'em with your body."

"I didn't know you were coming. Yeah, I wasn't happy with my defense, either."

While I was speaking, he wobbled. Then he started tilting forward, toward me. I noticed his eyes were bloodshot and out of kilter. He stepped forward to catch himself. His boot landed on top of my foot and he fell into me. I caught him. Then I smelled the cigar smoke and booze on his breath and jacket. He was embarrassed about the stumble. He angrily pushed off, turned and staggered away. Then he gave me a dismissive, behind-the-back wave. He mumbled something. I didn't know what. He disappeared into the parking lot.

I went to my team bus and someone said, "Who was that?"

I said, "No one."

So much had been expected of my dad. He had amazing physical gifts. He had size and speed and agility and brains that rivaled none. He had grit and guts and gumption when he came out of Jackson High School in 1955, prepared to vanquish all comers. But instead, high expectations were neutralized by the frailty of his humanity. A broken leg led to broken dreams and three broken marriages. And he was breaking me.

———————————

MY BROTHER AND I went to see my dad and our family in Jackson for Christmas of 1974. I was a junior in high school and Brian was a sophomore. I had my driver's license and my mom and Large Root Beer let me borrow one of their cars. I drove and my brother rode along. We traveled a windy, snowy three hours downstate. I didn't miss the bus rides or the bus stations or the plentitude of unsavory characters who frequented both. I certainly embraced controlling my own schedule, and shaving time off the trip was nice, too. During the drive we didn't talk much, but we didn't argue either. So that was good. I wondered what my dad would be like. I wasn't always certain because sometimes he seemed okay, but increasingly he wasn't. And while there wasn't a reason to expect things to stop getting worse, I held out hope there was a chance that things would get better on their own.

We spent Christmas Eve and Christmas Day with my dad and Bompi and Gigi and other relatives. My dad was witty and entertaining and a little bit smug, because he'd recently had a handful of feature stories published in the *Jackson Citizen Patriot*. His drinking around the rest of the family at our holiday celebrations seemed contained and restrained. If there were any issues, they were invisible to me. We had a good start to the holiday. I was hopeful that his writing signaled a new beginning and that things were getting better, that his "rough spot" was over.

Daddy had escaped the dank, dark bedroom tucked in the lonely corner of the basement of Aunt Hige's house. He was renting a scruffy little trailer near Somerset Center, in the rolling hills south of town.

He was dating a woman named Opal. She seemed friendly, but I didn't like her fusty name. And she was noticeably older than my dad. She was a tired and hard-looking woman with deep facial creases and hillbilly hair stacked high on her head. She wasn't nearly as pretty as my mom or Judy or Bed-wrecker, and she was frumpy and plump in a bad way. Opal lived in an overgrown, ramshackle farmhouse near the trailer park and adjacent to a farm that wasn't hers. I'd been to the house once before. My dad stayed there for a while. When I stopped by to visit him, I found him washing his hair in the sink in the kitchen, using a tea kettle for hot water. I asked him why and he said, "Because the fuckin' water heater hasn't worked for a month."

Christmas night, after we left our family celebration, Daddy asked Brian and me to join him at Opal's to play Euchre, a card game in which he excelled. I didn't want to go to the old farmhouse, but I didn't want to say no. Neither did Brian. We didn't want to disappoint my dad. And after all, the holiday had started off great.

Perhaps he'd been drinking all day and I just hadn't noticed. He'd often carry a stainless steel thermos that he kept loaded with liquor. But he must have had other methods of disguising his boozing. And when he was sneaking, he must have drunk moderately so as not to be discovered but still drinking enough to get him to that place where his mind and body told him he needed be. And on this night he must have been drinking for hours, because after we got to Opal's he got smashed fast.

We were sitting at a green laminated kitchen table, six of us on chairs and barstools, and my brother and I watched and listened while Opal and two of her friends and my dad played Euchre. Daddy would shuffle and deal and share his strategic and tactical insight, during and after each hand. They sailed through games in rapid succession, with one hand taking no more than a few minutes. After an hour, I noticed my dad's shuffling and dealing had grown clumsy. Then his speech became unwound and he lost his ability to shuffle the cards. He struggled to speak coherently. It wasn't that he was slurring his words. It was worse than that. He was unable to form words. He was fighting with himself. Just to speak.

The other card players were bombed as well. And, while not in the same condition as my dad, they were distracted and unconcerned, or perhaps oblivious. I could see my dad's frustration building, as though he realized he'd gone too far. Or was it just that he couldn't shuffle or deal? I wasn't certain why he became so damned frustrated. But, while sitting in his chair, he reached his hands up above his head and then brought them down with all of his drunken might. He slammed his palms into the kitchen table, upsetting tumblers of booze and ashtrays stuffed with butts. In an apparent attempt to stand and make some kind of declarative statement, he fell backward, turning over his chair, crashing to the floor. Opal and the other two drunks burst out laughing. My dad lay on his back with his arms and legs flailing like an overturned, drunken turtle. Helpless and forsaken.

Brian and I sat and watched it happen. We were there, but disassociated. The scene was real and surreal. At first we were having fun. Daddy was playing quickly and brilliantly and engaging us with stories and jokes and card-playing tips and then, in what seemed like only a few moments, he fell off an inebriated precipice. It was stunning and frightening. He had taken himself to the edge. And he didn't stop.

I'd seen the end result before. His eyes rolling about his head. The loss of balance. The slurred speech. But I'd assumed he'd gotten there gradually. Instead, on this night, it was as though he went from zero to sixty in seconds and then he launched himself off a cliff.

Brian and I were atypically united in cause. Without talking, we slipped off our perches and went to my dad's aid amidst the raucous drunks still bellowing in laughter. We hoisted my dad to his feet and guided him to the car. The driveway was a lumpy, icy, wintry mess. It exacerbated the challenge to keep the three of us upright. My dad spoke Babylonian all the way to the car, and when we loaded him into the backseat he was semi-conscious. His mustache was wet and white with snot.

Back at the trailer, we dragged and danced him up the steps and dumped him onto his bed.

I searched every closet and cupboard and nook and cranny. I scoured each and every inch of the trailer for beer and whiskey. I found what I could and I loaded a grocery bag. Then I searched his car. I drove the booze a few miles east and deposited the bottles and cans into a dumpster. Behind the Artesian Wells bar.

He wasn't getting better after all. His work—the writing—was a red herring. I didn't know what do to.

We left the next morning before he woke.

I HAD MY favorite teachers growing up. In elementary school, it was my second grade teacher, Mrs. Vada E. Ferguson. She'd let us march around the classroom and sing "She's A Grand Old Flag" while we high-stepped and slapped erasers together. She smiled broadly and led the singing, swaying back and forth while she played the piano. We'd forget about everything, except how proud and patriotic we were.

In junior high, Mrs. Witt, who we sometimes called Jan, was my favorite teacher. She'd let an epithet or two slip out once in a while. One Halloween, we covered the trees and bushes at her house with toilet paper. When we came back the next day to admire our handiwork and clean up the mess, she made us cookies and hot cider and she opened the windows to her house and played loud music. Jan allowed us to get closer to her in ways that other teachers didn't. She was one of the first to treat us like adults, though we didn't deserve to be treated that way yet.

Donald Helmus was my favorite teacher in high school. He was wired differently. That made him fresh and unexpected and unorthodox. I think he made some kids uncomfortable. I know he made the school adminis-tration uncomfortable. But you had to take Mr. Helmus with a grain of salt, because he was completely full of shit, and that's what made him special. He entertained himself while he entertained us. And in the process he taught us French Literature and French History and French Geography and, of course, the language as well. And I learned from Mr. Helmus that zigging instead of zagging made life more interesting, so why not?

Ms. Moore wasn't one of my favorite teachers. Maybe because she was boring and brutish. But she was also smart and progressive and bold. My junior year I took a college prep literature class with Ms. Moore. *The Feminine Mystique,* by Betty Friedan, was required reading. As a post-pu-bescent male, my take on the women's liberation movement was that it was about a bunch of nasty-looking, fat women trying to create laws and regulations that would give females an unfair advantage over men in the workforce and any place else that they needed a big, fat leg up.

The premise of the book was that housewives were pissed off because their lives were unfulfilled since motherhood and marriage were not adequate for a woman to become self-actualized. Things were further screwed up because men controlled the media, and the media reinforced the idea that, when done properly, the homemaking role was fulfilling and meaningful. And if a woman wasn't happy, then she was obviously neurotic.

My great-grandma Bessie, who was ninety-two years old in 1974, worked decades in a spring manufacturing plant as a laborer. My mom was a social worker and then a nurse. My dad's mother, Gigi, worked as a retail clerk. With few exceptions, O'Sullivan women were not June Cleavers. And, while I didn't know if they were fulfilled in their jobs,

I wasn't sure any O'Sullivan men were either. First and foremost, if they had work they were glad for it. The whole self-actualization thing was, if not irrelevant, secondary to survival.

But then we started to talk about penis envy. I learned that penis envy was a concept of Freud's. The gist of his idea was that when a little girl discovered that she'd been cheated out of having a penis, all hell broke loose. There was a sequence of events that began with the little girl developing sexual impulses toward her mother. But with no penis, Mom was a dead end. So then, the little girl would desire her father. But of course, the father-daughter thing would get in the way. Ultimately the little girl wanted a penis of her own. And all the manly power that came with it.

I didn't know if any of that stuff made sense. But the concept of girls wanting penises was something worth exploring.

The book got us talking. We agreed with big Betty. Freud's ideas seemed a stretch, if not bizarre, and perhaps he didn't give women enough credit. What was most instructive was that we were talking about topics that were rich and relevant and deserving dialogue. We were sixteen and seventeen years old, debating women's rights and civil rights and what was right and wrong. The discussions helped us decipher our sexuality and roles. And we were challenging each other and learning how to build arguments. And how to disagree, but still get along.

We were growing up, fast.

⚬————⚬●⚬————⚬

I WAS AN occasional starter on our junior varsity hoops team, but basketball wasn't my best sport. When I heard early my junior year that we were establishing a girl's gymnastics team in my senior year, I couldn't erase from my mind visions of limber and lean, lovely lassies with ribboned hair tumbling and prancing about in black tights.

Title XV of the Education Amendments of 1972 was the law that revised Title IX of the Civil Rights Act of 1964. The primary outcome of the law's change was more athletics opportunities in high schools and colleges for women. But the statute also cracked opened a door for guys to compete in women's sports when a comparable sport wasn't available to men. If that meant zigging instead of zagging, then I wanted a piece of that.

With a copy of Betty Freidan's book in my back pocket, I sat down with Dan Wright, the athletics director and head varsity basketball coach at Reeths-Puffer.

"Coach, you're up to speed on Title IX and all that business, right?"

"Yup."

"Well, I wanna be on the gymnastics team."

"I didn't know you were gymnast."

"I'm not, yet. But if you say you'll support me, by this time next year I'll be ready to try out."

"Is this some kind of prank?"

"Nope."

Coach stood up and walked around in a tight circle, slightly hunched over with a pigeon-toed gate. It made him look like he had a broom stick broken off in his butt. After a minute he said, "Sure."

When football season ended, I started taking gymnastics lessons with nine-year-old girls. Some of their parents thought I was some kind of sicko or pervert. But when they learned I was captain of the football team, their concerns were alleviated—though not entirely.

And who could blame them?

Twenty-five

Somebody's Hero
(1975-1976)

I USED TO think the scariest times of my life were when I was just a kid. I'd wake soaked in sweat in the middle of the night, feeling like a human gyroscope, with the world whipping around me, speeding out of control and I was spinning, too, but not at the same speed, and I'd scream for my mom. She would hold me and I'd beg her to "make it slow down." She'd tell me that everything would be all right. She'd sing to me. But that didn't help. She'd turn on the lights. But that didn't help, either. Then I'd hold onto her even tighter because I knew, if I let go, I'd be thrown through the wall and into space where I'd burst into flames, then come crashing back to earth, dead and burned to black, shattered into a thousand tiny pieces.

By high school, those adolescent nightmares had, thank God, diminished to isolated events. But the imaginary had been replaced by the crueler reality of growing up at the speed of life. Tortured in helplessness, I watched my dad stumble ever-closer to the edge of a drunken abyss. And no kid was exempt from navigating high school's confounding stratification of freaks and geeks and jocks and nerds. The experience, naturally and painfully, propagated my own insecurity and self-doubt. My brother and I had stopped talking entirely. Ironically and unfortunately, our sole common denominator was my dad. Brian was fighting his own demons. Struggling to find himself. His own aberrant behavior had alienated my mom and Large Root Beer and me. Brian was peculiar and unapproachable and had grown increasingly obese. His odd behavior, and odder friends, made him an embarrassment. When my mom told me he was transferring to another high school for his junior year, I was selfishly relieved.

My mom and I got along fine, but her man was Large Root Beer. And he was good for her. He provided us with what we didn't have when we were in the city on Terrace, living on meaner streets and meager means with an uncertain future. With him there was the prospect of better times and comfort in our apparent financial stability. And that was good.

My final football season started with little hope for improving on the prior year's sole victory. But I played for my teammates and the band and the smell of popcorn and hot dogs and pipe smoke and the chance to smash heads and dance around tacklers and do it at night—a dream come true, win or lose, from the times I watched the Big Reds practice through the fence at Wilson Field, and then play next door under Friday night lights. We lacked depth and had no great players. Too many of the big farm boys who used to plow holes in our opponents' lines had quit football to earn money for beer and cars. But we sucked it up. And played hard. And, most often, we still came out on the losing end.

We beat Ludington 17–0 at our homecoming game. Terry Jensen, Greg Mann, Paul Jacobson, Chip David and I got to miss Coach Cook's half-time homily because we were riding in Corvette convertibles (furnished by the Western Michigan Royal Corvette Club, of course) and sitting next to pretty girls wearing tiaras and God-awful tacky dresses. I escorted Jennifer Tuttle, who was one of the smartest girls in our senior class. To the delight of all the boys, she was skinny and had a tiny butt and boobs so big they had their own ZIP code. Nancy Olsen, Kay Somerville, Cindy Cleveland and Becki Sodini were also on Homecoming Court. Jake and Becki were crowned King and Queen, which was perfect because they'd been dating since they were in their mothers' wombs. They were charming and funny and cute, and in a month it would all be forgotten. So who really cared, anyway?

A week later, the local newspaper said we lost a "heartbreaker" to Spring Lake. It was a freakishly summery night in October. It was an away game. We were hitting harder and breaking more tackles than was our typical pattern. I was playing tailback and filling in on defense, as well as kicking and receiving punts.

I missed a field goal early in the game. And after our third touchdown, I pushed an extra point kick to the right. I thought it was within the upright, and so did my teammates, but the referee signaled "no good" and the score remained 20–7.

My dad kicked and played quarterback in the single wing formation for the Jackson Vikings. He used to tell me about a kick he missed and lost a game, and that he swore it was good. But the ref said "no good," and he felt oh-so-miserable for letting his team down. That's how I felt whenever I missed a kick. And I felt like shit this time, too. I didn't want to run back to the sideline, but I did. I told Coach Cook that I was sorry. He slapped me on the butt and I ran back out onto the field with the kick-off team and I booted the ball to our opponents.

After holding Spring Lake on downs, they brought in their punt team. I went back to receive the kick. I misjudged the ball's trajectory but I caught it, awkwardly, over my left shoulder, which spun me around and when I regained my balance and planted my right foot behind me to push off the turf and begin advancing the ball, it was as though I had been shot in the leg. My hamstring convulsed into one massive knot. I went down and the whistle blew. I tried to straighten my leg. In seconds, a coach and the training staff were on the field. After a few minutes, with stretching and massage, the cramp subsided, so I hustled over to the sideline. Again I went down with more muscle spasms, but a crew was kneading the knots and they were feeding me water and a trainer was pushing the bottoms of my cleats at my toes toward my knees in order to stretch my calf and hamstring. I was flat on my back with my helmet off when my dad appeared, inches from my face.

As far as I knew, after playing football for the previous five years it was only the second time he'd seen me play. And, like the first time, he was stupid drunk. He was on his hands and knees, smelling of bad whisky and cigars. He was yammering about my missed extra point. He was spitting as he tried to talk. Finally, someone grabbed him by the shoulder, to pull him away. He resisted.

I screamed, "Get out of my fuckin' face and leave me alone!"

And he did. He found his feet and stumbled away and over the rope that was supposed to keep parents and fans off the sidelines. He disappeared from my sight.

Someone asked, "Who the hell was that?" I kept my mouth shut.

We relinquished our 20–7 lead. Spring Lake scored two more touchdowns and two extra points and we lost 20–21, because of my missed field goal and extra point. Gail was sweet and tried to console me after the game, but I went home and cried in my room. I cried about the missed kicks and I cried about my dad and I cried myself to sleep. When I woke up the next day, I was stiff and bruised from tackling and being tackled, and from the cramps in my legs. I remembered my dad, on the sidelines, and I prayed that no one would figure out that the drunk guy in my face was my dad.

OUR FINAL FOOTBALL game of the year, and of my career, was against Muskegon Catholic Central—the same bunch of Jesuits that ruined our undefeated freshman season. They were ranked high in the state and had only a single loss and featured Lou Bass, a quick-as-shit black kid with a smile so big his head could hardly contain it. Lou and I played football and baseball against each other for years. He was one of the best to ever play at Catholic, and an all-around great kid. I loved him to death. Coach Chev led their team, so not only were we out-manned, we were also out-coached. We were used to that. But we played the gutsiest game of our lives that night, losing 22–10. We had a chance until late in the game, when a bad break turned the tide the wrong way. But every man played to his potential. And I was able to find some pride in the flotsam of another losing season. When the Catholic kids shook our hands and slapped our butts after the game, you could tell from the purposefulness in their grip and the expressions on their faces that we had given them a scare. We had earned their respect. Even Coach Chev shook our hands with resolve. That felt good. It made losing, again, just a little bit easier.

I CALLED MY dad a dozen times on Thanksgiving Day, and he didn't pick up. Bompi told me he hadn't talked to him for weeks. I hadn't seen or spoken to him since the humiliating Spring Lake game.

After Thanksgiving dinner with Bompi and Gigi and a handful of other relatives, I decided I'd try to find my dad. No one offered to join me.

I drove out South Jackson Road, until dead ending at two-lane US 12. I took a right onto the highway and, after traveling two hundred feet, I made a left into the trailer park. I followed Southhampton Road until I reached the eighth trailer on the right.

I was worried and angry. Probably more angry than worried, since he'd appeared plastered and unannounced at my football game and he hadn't bothered to take our calls.

His car was parked beside the trailer. I pulled in behind it.

The trailer door was unlocked, but apparently no one was home. The lights were off. There were empty cans of Bud and Miller scattered about his dinette. Dirty clothes were draped over the backs of two folding chairs. Discarded boxes of macaroni and cheese and vacant cans of baked beans and Vienna sausages littered the kitchen. His bed had not been made and his sheets were soiled and discolored. The place smelled of beer and liquor and smoke and shit.

I speculated that he was at Opal's, but her phone had been disconnected and I'd promised myself to never go back there again. Perhaps he was too embarrassed to see me after the incident at the football field. And I wasn't sure how I felt it either. I wanted to see him, but at the same time I didn't.

I left him a note.

Stopped by. Must be a problem with your phone. We've been calling. Hope to see you at Xmas. Love, Rocky

I stepped out of the trailer and down the cinder block steps and by his car on the way to mine. Out of the corner of my eye, I noticed his body lying sideways on the backseat of his car. He was clutching his ever-present stainless steel thermos. His best friend in the whole wide world. On the floor near the backseat was a partially consumed bucket of Kentucky Fried Chicken. And another victim, a "dead soldier," an empty jug of whiskey. He was seemingly alive, but not conscious. I could see his chest expanding and contracting, but so infrequently that at first I thought he wasn't breathing. He was dressed nicely, in a red button-down shirt and gray blazer with silver flecks that matched his goatee. He wore black half-boots and dark pants. He had gotten himself all wrapped-up to go somewhere, to meet someone. Maybe me. But instead, he ended up at the chicken store with his favorite duck, a fifth of Kessler's.

The car door was unlocked. I opened it and he woke, almost instantly. But when he spoke, he slurred his words. I couldn't make out what he was saying.

I said, "Come on."

I helped him out of the car and up the cinder block stairs, but he missed the second step. He scraped his shin and smashed his knee, but it didn't faze him. I was able to get him into bed, only removing his jacket and his boots. Doing the only and best thing that I knew to do, I emptied the trailer of every ounce of alcohol that I could find. And, like I'd done before, I drove the bottles and cans to the Artesian Wells bar. I heaved them into the dumpster. I drove back to the trailer. He seemed okay. Passed out and oblivious to me. But okay.

I wadded up my note and tossed the paper into the trash. I called Bompi and Gigi. I told them that Daddy was in the trailer, in his bed, and that I was driving back to Muskegon. They could figure out the rest.

Rock bottom came soon. Just a week after Thanksgiving, Bompi called. He stoically reported that my dad was gravely ill and in the hospital, complications from alcohol poisoning. And, no doubt, the abuse he had heaped on himself for most of his short, young life. Bompi had discovered him in his trailer, unconscious and stewing in his own shit and puke. He called an ambulance. They hauled him away.

I was hardly surprised. I used to have a reoccurring dream about my dad, sitting in his own feces and vomit and holding a whiskey bottle to the side of his head and pulling its trigger as though the bottle was a gun. If the whiskey bottle didn't fire, he'd toss it to the side and grab another and drink it and pull the trigger on that one. He'd repeat until he found one that worked. And finally, a bottle would fire. When it did my dad's head was blown to bloody pieces, but his body remained, and he kept pouring bottles of whiskey into the black hole between his shoulders. A headless vessel. Impossible to fill.

He was released from the hospital just days before Christmas. He appeared at our family gathering on Christmas Eve. He was sober, but greatly diminished. His face was long and drawn and he didn't walk. He shuffled, bent at the waist and hunched over. He swung his arms to help propel himself forward, but he appeared to be clawing at the air in front of him in an awkward and unnatural advance that, thankfully, ended when he reached a chair, where he collapsed to his ass. And forced a smile.

I was frightened for him. I'm sure we all were. I had no confidence that he would grow strong and stay sober. And, though he was with us, he was distant, still feeling the pains and pangs of withdrawal. The embarrassment must have weighed heavy on him. It did on us. As well as shame and disgust and frustration and humiliation. Ten years lost, maybe more. Now he was worn down and beat up and the wit and banter and good looks were gone, or dormant. No longer evident. And I wondered if he could ever recover.

Gigi used to tell me that she and Bompi had just one child because she became so miserably sick during her pregnancy. "I used to lay spread-eagle in the middle of the wood floor and pray that it would end," she'd say.

One and done. Their sole hope rode on the back of their prodigal son.

<hr />

I COULD BE aloof and loquacious, and the former became more the norm after the holidays. I was more insecure and self-critical and my confidence had been compromised. I was annoyed with myself for not stepping forward and intervening, somehow, before my dad nearly drank himself to death.

The forest across the road from our home on Bear Lake became my companion and confidante. I walked down snowy trails for hours. I contemplated my own failures and the calamity that my dad had become. I measured the hurt that he heaped on me. I muttered to myself, "Why me and not someone else?" But, then again, I knew my friends had their own burdens to bear. And, whether fair or not, that's just the way it was. I'd walk and walk and nothing changed, but for some reason trudging through the snow and listening to myself moving forward through the muffled woods, thinking and reflecting, made me feel better.

I returned to the gym and the mats and my newest teammates, the gymnastics team, all with boobs and moods that both perplexed and entertained me. I was the only guy who made the team. As a matter of fact, I was one of only two males competing in the conference. And the only straight one.

Shelly Bassett and Jill Pitts and Sue Chilcote were high-flying daredevils who marveled me with their fearlessness and flexibility and athleticism. Kim Ross caught my attention for other reasons. Her golden brown hair, parted down the middle, framed dark eyes that danced under always expressive eyebrows. She was tiny, of course, but in tasty proportions. Her skin was as flawless as her lips, which seemed frozen in a wispy, seraphic smile. When I landed on my head, Kim would slap me on the butt and tell me to "try it again." I became her project and she cajoled and teased and coached me to become a pretty good gymnast.

We had a connection that was difficult to define—part sexual, perhaps.

But not really. We never so much as held hands or kissed, but she was my secret passion. I'd give her a ride home after meets and visit her on weekends. She and her mom rented a modest cabin in the woods. Pretty and single and lonely, her mom was charming company, and I welcomed the chance to sit and talk with her and Kim. And we often did. I didn't tell Gail or any of my friends about Kim and me. They wouldn't have understood. I didn't understand. How could I be "just friends" with such a pretty girl? Maybe I didn't tell them because I wanted more than that from Kim. Maybe I saw Kim and her mom struggling and broken and poor and it was painful, and too familiar. They were like we had been a few years before. I wished I could help, but I couldn't. Or maybe I did.

Kim made my heart flutter and race. She was bright and pretty and good all the way through. Maybe too good for me. So I let her be.

We won five meets. Damn good for a first-year team. I competed in tumbling and vault and trampoline. I placed in every meet. And, miracle of miracles, I took home a fifth-place ribbon in vault at the conference championships. Those girls were great athletes and tough nuts. I appreciated being treated as their equal. It taught me a lesson or two. I figured Betty Friedan would have approved.

⚬—⚬●⚬——⚬

MY DAD AND I didn't talk until spring. He called to ask how baseball was going. I told him "okay." I asked him how he was doing. He'd traded the booze for Tab, drinking twelve cans a day. But his head was clear and he had a new job counseling troubled kids.

Our conversation was awkward and uncomfortable. There were no apologies. No expression of regret or acknowledgement of the public and private humiliation. But we were talking. And, just maybe, I'd get him back some day.

⚬—⚬●⚬——⚬

MY FINAL YEAR of high school, we lost more baseball games than we won. A shallow pitching staff doomed us. I was irked by an in-game strategy that was sterile and benign. We needed to bunt and steal and hit-and-run, to put pressure on our opponents. But our coach was complacent and inexperienced. So we were bad and dull.

I played centerfield and third base and pitched, when I had to. Pitching was never a natural position for me. I was incapable of throwing consecutive strikes. We had only twelve players, and just five seniors. I used to scratch my head as to how, out of a senior class of three hundred kids, we could field such a small team. Two of my best buddies, both superb athletes—Ray Owens and Paul Jacobson—played and we kept each other laughing and, together, we tried to manufacture wins. But there were few.

My house was the last stop for the "activity" bus. Our school district was predominately rural. We lived in the southwest corner, near the end of the district line. First the bus would swing north toward Dalton and Twin Lake, then meander through the bucolic county. After an hour of stop-and-go and stop-and-go, I'd be home.

Baseball had wound down, with only two remaining games. My high school career was almost over. The lofty expectations I had as a cocky ninth grader were largely unmet. I captained the high school football and baseball teams to losing seasons. My dad was disappointed in me. I represented his second chance to capture the dreams that had been dashed for him. It weighed on me. Insipid coaching and my own forgettable performances meant glory days wouldn't be. Instead we'd live with the reality of our fate. We were who we were. And we weren't very good.

I watched the mailboxes pass by in front of newly leafy trees and then houses and then trees again. The bus continued to regurgitate kids from high school, and some from our junior high who rode the bus as well. I began to read a book and dozed off, but woke to a tap on my shoulder.

It was a seventh-grade boy. I'd seen him on the bus before.

"Sorry to bug you. I was wondering something."

"What was you wondering?" I smiled, hoping he understood my poor grammar was intentional.

"Well, my mom and dad have been taking me to the football games for years. I've been watching you play. You're number 44."

"I was. Yup."

"We went to some baseball games, too."

"Okay."

"If it wouldn't be too much trouble, may I have your autograph?"

My mind rewound to the days that I'd stand outside the fence at Wilson Field and watch the Muskegon Big Reds practice. The players would yell, "Go Red! Go Big Red!" Once I snuck into a Muskegon basketball game. I sat behind the Big Red bench. Just before the second half, I asked Cal

Tatum for his autograph. He gave it to me, on the back of a program I'd picked up from the floor. It was a thrill for me. Cal smiled. Happy to oblige.

He was looking at me. Dead straight in the eyes. "Please."

"You know, you're not the first kid to ask today."

I smiled and winked at him. I think he knew I was kidding, but I wasn't sure. He handed me a pen. He asked that I sign the cover of his notebook, so his classmates could see it. Then he handed me a clean sheet of paper. "Sign here, too. I'll keep this in a safe place."

He stuck out his hand to shake. And I shook it. Then I held out my hand, palm up, and I said, "Give me five." He slapped my hand and smiled.

We both turned to watch the trees and mailboxes flicker by.

I felt warmed and wanted. And proud to be somebody's hero.

Twenty-six

Hope

INSTEAD OF PULLING us together, my dad's newfound sobriety became a wedge pushing us further apart.

He drank the booze to escape the reality of his serial failures. And when he drank, his debacles became more pronounced and darker, thus the need to drink more. The cycle fed on itself. Two decades of disappointment didn't disappear when the booze stopped flowing. My dad needed to deal with that.

He'd told a thousand lies to hide his drinking. He'd abused those who loved him and those who didn't. Money was squandered on sluts and booze and smokes and ponies. Two boys, now young men, had been abandoned, without a father, for a decade. Maybe we never had one. Maybe he was drunk from the beginning. We just didn't know it.

He hurt us.

He let down his hometown.

The lies and tears and hopes and dreams and shattered promises, and the people connected to them, they were all still there. Sullied in the wake of his selfish disregard. The debris of his disease soiled the lives of many. He had to wrestle with that. And I didn't think he was up to it. He looked pitiful shuffling around on Christmas Eve. And on the phone in the spring he was distant and guarded and different. Maybe different was good, but different was different. Where we would go from here? I didn't know. And I was scared.

I was really scared.

———————◦•◦———————

THE DECISION TO go to Hope College was not obvious, and perhaps odd to people who knew me. Hope's connection to religion was integral to the college's mission and history and the fabric of its being. I had turned my back on God soon after I was able to reason. It didn't help that, from the pulpit, Grandpa Sweetland scared the Jesus out of me when I was just a puppy. But I was drawn by the school's reputation for academic excellence and the success of its athletics programs. And intrigued by the prospect of cavorting with long-legged, blonde-haired Dutch girls.

I'd been through Holland before, but I'd yet to visit. In May I finally made the one-hour trip south from Muskegon to see the campus firsthand. There were few students around. The Kletz, the student union, was almost empty. "Between terms," someone explained. I walked the place, green and pristine and placid, by myself. Deciding to get an unadulterated sense of Hope with a self-guided tour.

The buildings were unlocked. I walked through dorms and the library and Lubbers, where most of the business classes were taught, and through the rolling Pine Grove in the center of campus. I liked the massive, proud, old stone-and-brick buildings, the intricate stained glass of Dimnent Chapel, and the sense that the campus was built to be there, forever, around a piney park. Everything was so neat and clean and in its place. So very Dutch.

I circled Graves Hall to College Avenue, where I found a prodigious anchor. A plaque explained that, in 1851, four years after the people who settled the Holland colony sailed from the Netherlands, the Reverend Van Raalte started a school, the Pioneer School, with the purpose of educating young men and women. The Pioneer School would become Hope College and this school, according to Van Raalte, "is my anchor of hope for this people in the future."

The symbolism of the anchor was simple, yet powerful. I was seduced by the history and tradition. And the idea of hope. The thought of me, increasingly cynical, attending Hope because of a metaphor linked to God and faith and the belief that there existed something more powerful and purposeful than chance guiding our lives. It was all too perfect to resist.

A smart-ass could use hope once in a while. And God knew I needed some.

So Hope it would be.

Twenty-seven

Woody

I MET Patric Woodard in 1970, not long after Red Miller asked me to join his Little League baseball team.

Patric's younger brothers, Terry and Michael, played on the same team. Woody came to the games at Sheldon Field with his older brother, Buzz. For some reason, all the Woodard boys befriended me. They had an older sister, Debra, who had big freckles and bigger boobs, and their mom and dad were named Billie and Harold. They lived in a small, wooden two-story home across the street from Hackley Hospital, less than a mile from our apartment on Terrace.

Harold was an accountant at Clarke Floor Machine. He was quiet and patient and wise. Harold always kept calm in a house that never was. Billie spent her time cooking and doing laundry. She'd stack the five kids' folded laundry on the stairway for the kids to take upstairs. She said, "I haven't been upstairs in years and I have no plans to go upstairs." I had been upstairs and I was absolutely certain that no adult had been up there for many, many years.

Woody didn't play organized sports. He was tall, a string bean, and uncoordinated and not the kind of athlete who would do what a coach wanted him to do. Other kids said he was crazy. He was, but he wasn't. Woody didn't quite fit in. But he did, too. I saw him eat a six-inch night crawler in front of three teenage girls one night. They said "gross" and "disgusting" and laughed and squealed. Then they gave him five dollars.

At a carnival, in downtown Muskegon at the Seaway Festival, Woody played a game where, if you threw a ping pong ball into a goldfish bowl, you won the bowl and the fish. When the carney handed Woody the bowl, he plucked out the goldfish and ate it. He played the game for free for the next thirty minutes and swallowed three more fish, belched and then walked away to the applause of a hundred people.

In 1971, when my mom, unexpectedly, married Large Root Beer, Woody and I grew closer, partly out of necessity. I wanted to spend my weekends with Woody and friends in the city, and Woody wanted to get out of town. So we took turns staying at each other's houses.

My mom and Large Root Beer liked Woody. Our dog, Minx, loved him. Woody constantly fed her under the table while we ate dinner. When other kids were drinking and using pot, Woody didn't because he said he didn't need to. But, increasingly, he got into trouble. His crazy behavior descended into risky behavior. He did things like pry a pay phone off a brick wall with a crowbar outside Muskegon High School.

Once Woody and I stayed the night at Mik's house, near our old place at Park and Southern. Mik and Woody and I sneaked out the window of Mik's bedroom. We slid down the roof to a tree limb. From the limb, we were able shimmy down the tree trunk to the ground. We'd planned to walk over to Nims Elementary School in the Pinchtown neighborhood to see if we could find girls. On the way Woody started to check the doors of parked cars. When he found one unlocked, he rifled through the glove box and lifted an 8-track cassette player. Mik and I insisted that Woody put it back. He said, "No." Mik and I told Woody we were going home. Woody said, "Fine. See ya."

Woody ran down an alley toward Nims. We turned around and started the mile-long walk back to Mik's. When we heard a man yelling and cursing a couple of blocks behind us, we surmised that Woody had continued his larcenous ways.

A few minutes later, we saw a cop car pull onto the street where we were walking. The cop began working his spotlight up and down the driveways and between the houses. Mik and I dove into a low spot between two garages. When the cops got to us, the beam passed just over our heads. Our hearts tried to beat through our chests. We were scared shitless.

Certain the car was gone, we ran two blocks to Seaway Drive, a divided highway with a cyclone fence on each side and a median and two lanes of traffic each way. We waited by the fence in bushes for traffic to clear before we sprinted across the highway and over the fence on the other side and two blocks to the safety of Mik's house.

About to climb the first fence, Mik threw an elbow into my ribs and pointed a block down Seaway. It was Woody, all arms and legs, scrambling across the highway with his arms full of other people's stuff. We laughed while we scaled the fence. We met Woody back at Mik's. We cursed him. And then we told him about the cops. He said he screwed up when he jumped into a car with the hood up and didn't bother to check to see if someone was working on the engine.

Before we could drive, we'd hitchhike to the beach at Pere Marquette Park on Lake Michigan. We'd swim in the Big Lake and then hike up the soaring, parabolic sand dunes that stood a hundred feet above the shore. Woody insisted that if we got going fast enough when we ran down the windward slope, we could fly.

I believed he thought he could.

Woody would hike up the dune time and time again. He'd sprint down the face of the sugar bowl of sand until his spindly legs couldn't keep up with his body and he'd tumble out of control, spinning and rolling down the dune until friction trumped gravity and he'd come to an abrupt stop, spitting sand and sometimes blood. Then he'd say that he felt "just a little bit of lift" from the air, before he crashed.

Woody was a year older than I. The summer he got his driver's license, in 1974, I asked him if he wanted to meet my dad. And stay with him for a couple of days. And fish. We borrowed my mom's car.

Woody and my dad got along famously. My dad was writing, occasionally, for the *Jackson Citizen Patriot,* and he was sporting a beard. Woody called him "Ernie," as in Hemingway. My dad thought the nickname was brilliant. And, because Woody could drive, my dad could drink like Hemingway while Woody was there. So he did.

After fishing late one night and then going out to dinner, Woody was driving my dad's car down an isolated part of South Jackson Road. My dad asked Woody to "watch out for raccoons on the side of the road." He said that you could see their eyes glow when the headlights shone into them. The first time we saw the glowing eyes, Woody let the car drift to the side of the road and he executed a pair of blameless raccoons. My dad asked Woody why he hit the raccoons.

Woody said, "I thought that's what you wanted me to do." My dad responded with a drunken chuckle.

I felt sad and sickened.

Twenty-eight

Glory Days

I WASN'T CERTAIN if Cliff McMillan was gay or not.

He lived down the street from me on Bear Lake Road. He graduated from Reeths-Puffer as well. But two years before me. Cliff was attending the local community college when I graduated from high school. His dad, Ken, was a business rep for one of the unions, Local 100. Ken was friendly and jolly. And he had a gargantuan gut. It earned him the nickname Big Mac.

Big Mac would come home from work and lower himself into a huge, brown recliner. Cliff's attendant mother, Drue, would meekly deliver dinners on a tray that Big Mac would balance on his gut as he reclined in his chair and off of which he'd eat steaks slathered in butter and sour cream and enormous cheeseburgers and pies the size of Frisbees. Then he'd drink whiskey, straight up, and fall asleep in the chair. Once I tried to wake him, but he snored me away.

Cliff claimed to date a girl for a while, but no one ever saw them kiss or hold hands. When we went to bars and clubs, he'd talk to girls. But he didn't seem to take interest in them. They loved him because he was smart and funny and chubby and safe. I didn't care if he was gay, as long as he kept his thing away from me. So when he told me he'd enrolled at Hope, I said, "Let's be roommates."

Cliff had an old ugly brown Ford Mustang with just enough room for our stuff. In late August of 1976, I hugged my mom goodbye and waved at Large Root Beer and patted Minx on the head. Cliff and I rolled away from Bear Lake and Muskegon and drove an hour south, down US 31, to Holland and Hope.

We arrived on campus to learn that there was an issue with our housing. We'd been reassigned to the "International House." A building the college called a "cottage." It was adjacent to campus and home to ten brown guys wearing flowing white robes.

Ms. Vandersomething, the Director of Housing, explained that because Cliff was an upperclassman and a transfer, he received the lowest priority for a dormitory assignment.

"Plus, you chose each other as roommates. And dorm demand exceeds supply. So, unfortunately, the International House is the only place to put you together."

We said bullshit without actually saying bullshit because, after all, we were at Hope College. Cliff got frustrated. He quit school. Right then and there.

Ms. Vandersomething watched through the window of her office, in Dutch-disbelief, as Cliff stomped out to his car, unloaded my bags and boxes and dropped them at my feet.

"Cliff, we'll figure this out."

"No, we won't. It's just not supposed to be."

"Huh?"

"I'm not supposed to be here."

I was stranded on the lawn, in front of the housing office, with no roommate and no transportation and no place to live. On my first day of college.

I went back into the building and told Vandersomething that Cliff was gone and not coming back. She took her index finger and tapped her temple twice and said that there was a sophomore history major in Durfee Hall who needed a roommate. "Follow me."

There was no answer to her knock. She opened the door with her master key. The room was already furnished and decorated. In addition to a bunk bed and desks and chairs, there were hundreds of miniature solders in numerous battle formations, apparently representing various nations and conflicts throughout time.

You could barely move in the room without disrupting an engagement.

I looked at Vandersomething and she shrugged her shoulders. Without saying anything, she led me out.

All I yearned for was a place to lay my head—and a wall with a poster of Farrah Fawcett.

We walked back to the housing office and my pile of belongings on the side of the street. Vandersomething told me she'd put me on a waiting list. I said, "Okay." She asked what I was going to do.

"I'll figure something out."

I tracked down Dave Stevens in Kollen Dorm, a friend and teammate from Reeths-Puffer. Dave used to block for me, the best he could, on the football field. He was witty and bright, in the top ten of our graduating class. But he came across as dull because his head was shaped like Charlie Brown's and he spoke in an inflectionless monotone that could induce sleep in an insomniac. Dave had been randomly paired with a pimple-skinned, purple-faced freshman named Doug. They said I could sleep on the floor of their dorm room until I found a place to stay. I crashed in a bag for two nights. Then I hitchhiked, with my baseball glove and cleats and uniform in a duffle bag, thirty miles to Grand Rapids and a Big Boy restaurant, where I caught a ride to the eastern part of the state to play in the American Legion baseball state championship.

I played center field for the best ball team I'd ever been on. We were sponsored by the Fraternal Order of Police in Muskegon. We were coached by a half-crazy Cuban, Albert Fernandez. Coach wore his sheriff's deputy uniform to practices and games. He recruited some of the best players from the counties in and around Muskegon to play on his traveling American Legion team. He coached an exciting fast, furious, unselfish game built on speed and teamwork. We stole and dove and ran and batted and bunted ourselves through the months of July and August. We beat the best teams in the western part of the state. We earned our way to the state finals. And when we got there, we won the whole enchilada.

After three glorious days of baseball, one of my teammates dropped me off at Kollen late Sunday night. With a state championship trophy under my arm, I walked up the stairs to my temporary dorm room to discover that Dave's roommate, Doug, had grown weary of me sleeping on the floor, so he moved in "with some wacko."

Doug told Dave, of his new room, "There were a thousand toy soldiers in battle formation, but no one sleeping on the floor."

Twenty-nine

The Pull

DAVE ASKED IF I was going to the Pull Rally. I told him he was the fourth person to ask.

He droned, "I heard it was a great way to meet girls," and he wondered if I'd seen the "sweet-ass blonde" picking up mail, just after lunch, in the dorm lobby.

If he'd asked me about a redhead or a brunette, maybe that would have registered. We were on a campus littered with genetically-bleached Dutch girls. Noticing a blonde was akin to detecting a singular blade of grass in the verdant lawn that fronted our dorm.

It was our second week on campus and the initial nervous apprehension had begun to wane, but the college experience was still embryonic, and I was in full absorption mode as each day brought new things that were dizzyingly different from what I'd known growing up in dreary and humble and crumbling Muskegon and Jackson. And, for the first time, I was around kids with purses and wallets chubby with cash. They drove sparkling cars that their moms and dads bought for them, and their moms and dads owned companies or were senior executives or architects or doctors or politicians. And while there were kids of modest means, preacher's kids and kids like me, I was being introduced to an unfamiliar world of privilege and preference and prestige.

That evening Dave and I walked across the street to a small auditorium a few hundred feet from our dorm. We took seats in the sixth row next to each other. Other freshman cautiously entered. There were several familiar faces, but for the most part they were kids that Dave and I had yet to meet. He stuck me in the ribs with the tip of his elbow when his blonde came in. I could see why she caught his fancy. Her mane was a curious milky blonde and uncommonly straight and fell to the top of a pleasantly defined buttocks that must have had a spring wound tight inside because her bottom seemed to lift her to her toes with each step.

There were a handful of serious-faced upperclassmen on the auditorium stage. They wore red t-shirts with white numbers "78" stacked above the blue letters "PULL." Dave leaned over to me and said, "I guess that means we're 80 Pull." He must have been right. We were the class of 1980, and what little we knew about The Pull, we did know that juniors coached freshman and seniors coached sophomores. These guys would be our coaches, for the next two years, if we tried out and made the team.

The leader of the 78 Pull shirts was a short chap with pronounced cheekbones and bushy sideburns that disappeared into a head of curly hair. Another Goldilocks, but more brown than golden. He was wearing gym shorts and running shoes and white athletic socks that ascended into the shape of a "v," stopping a foot above the floor in the middle of a calf muscle that was freakishly large for a guy so vertically challenged. He had Popeye forearms and piercing eyes that hovered above a harmless smirk that said he was honest and good. Like most kids at Hope.

The muscle introduced himself as Brian Hipwell, "Or just call me Hip." His voice was restrained but scratchy and high-pitched. He said he knew we had a lot of questions but he asked us to "just sit back and relax and watch a slide show."

As images flashed by and music played in the background, the coaches added commentary to clarify what we were seeing. We learned The Pull was a tug-of-war, but not really. It was unlike any tug-of-war from anywhere or from any time, and the pictures proved so. As did its history.

Each man pulled from a pit. The coaches told us there were eighteen pits to a side. The pits, ironically, looked like graves and were about five feet long and three feet wide and two feet deep. They were dug end to end, so that from the first pit to the last was more than a hundred and twenty feet in distance. The other team also had their eighteen men and eighteen pits, but they were on the opposite side of a river, the Black River, which was a hundred and fifty feet wide. The Pull rope was formed by three woven strands of Manila hemp, five hundred feet long and as taut as steel conduit when each eighteen-man team was leveraged against the other.

They showed us pictures of towering fabric barriers suspended from poles that prevented the team on one side of the river from seeing the other. Each Puller had a girl kneeling next to him, relaying signals from a coach who was standing in front of the first pit with his back to the fabric screen and the river.

The Pull Coach calling signals was like a coxswain for a rowing crew. But instead of rowers he had Pullers. And in lieu of just instructing and imparting cadence, the Pull Coach also used hand signals. Each signal had a prescribed purpose. The coordination and sequencing of moves that preceded the efforts to take rope from the opponents required precise and specific actions.

The girls — Morale Girls, they called them — were essential cogs in the process of taking and protecting rope. When Pullers were in their locked in positions, their heads were back so they couldn't see the signal-calling coach. The girls relayed the commands.

Pullers were positioned on top of and around an inch-and-a-half thick rope. Legs were thrown over the top of the rope and Pullers had their hands positioned down between their legs, as though prepared to pull a wooden stake out of the ground. But instead of standing, they were horizontal. And in lieu of a wooden stake, they were pulling the colossal rope.

Some pictures showed the Pullers, all of them, in a position off and under the rope, but in an athletic stance apparently ready to throw their hips up and their heads back. In fact, they showed more pictures of Pullers doing just that.

Expressions on the Pullers' faces reflected exceptional intensity, uncommon concentration and excruciating pain. The girls were equally focused and involved in their vital roles as they relayed signals, mopped perspiration, repositioned padding, served water and fruit, taped bloody hands and provided encouragement and support and energy.

The presentation ended and the room buzzed with excitement. My face felt flushed. I wanted to Pull more than I ever wanted to run track or play baseball or football or any other sport. The Pull was unique and extraordinary and demanding, and I was anxious to get involved. Dave, next to me, grunted in affirmation and pleasure.

Hip and the other coaches, Stauffer and Big Bob and Howie, pulled chairs to the front of the stage and sat and shared bits of Pull history. They said The Pull started in 1898 but since 1910, on a Friday in early October, Pullers from the freshmen class had competed at the Black River against Pullers from the sophomore class. Whoever made the team, they said, would be forever a part of Hope College history. Our lives would be changed in ways that we couldn't imagine. I whispered to Dave, "This is why we went to college."

We learned that *Sports Illustrated* featured The Pull in 1966. National media coverage was not common, but not unusual. It didn't matter after we saw the pictures and measured the intensity in the eyes and voices of the coaches.

They closed the meeting by telling us when tryouts would commence and that it would be more difficult than football and wrestling and other sports, but the rewards would be tremendous and the memories indelible. Then Hip said, "Be careful tonight."

We began to exit the auditorium and, after most of us were outside, we were annihilated with buckets of cold water from the roof and a barrage of water balloons from every other direction. The provocateurs wore shirts that said "79 Pull," the sophomore class, our adversaries.

We were forced back into the building, stunned and soaked and cold and annoyed. Big Bob asked, "What are you guys gonna do now?"

I said, "I've got an accounting quiz tomorrow. And I'm going study. But not until I've drowned a couple of those 79 Pull bastards."

Hip and the other coaches tossed us bags of balloons and said they'd see us at practice. We proceeded with an hour-long, campus-wide water balloon fight that was staged honorably and in good fun. When the 79 Pullers finally disappeared into their dorms, we did the same and then showered and changed. Dave and I talked late into the night about the hope and prospect of Pulling.

<hr/>

WE RETRIEVED OUR practice rope from the basement of Kollen dorm, hoisting the beast onto our shoulders and running and chanting, as a group, to a meadow and field a few blocks from campus. Thus commenced three weeks of six-days-a-week training that would culminate with The Pull, on Friday, October 1, 1976.

The initial days emphasized conditioning. We didn't get on the rope, but we did weed out weaker and less determined freshmen. Later the first week, we dug practice pits and the rope was tied to a series of small trees, four to six inches in diameter, in an overgrown part of the park. There was enough flex in the trees that we acquired a sense for gaining rope, but we also learned that coiled trees were worthy adversaries and would take rope back if we were not properly locked in.

When in the locked in position, the top leg was wrapped around the rope and the feet were at the top of the board, just under the rope. The outside of the calf muscle was pressed painfully against the rope, creating tension and friction. In the ideal position, you were on the balls of your feet against the board in the front of your pit wall. Your hands were in a constant pulling position, between the legs and gripped onto the rope. The rope exited your body under the arm opposite the leg wrapped around the top of the rope. And, importantly, the top shoulder was not rolled forward, but was square and balanced over the rope. If the Pull Coach gave the signal to "strain," then the top shoulder was thrown back, torqueing the body and putting additional pressure on the calf muscle against the rope.

There were two primary rope-taking tactics. One was an on-the-rope heave, where we shimmied down the rope into a crouched position and then exploded together toward the back of our pits, but never actually dismounting the rope. This was effective at taking small amounts of rope, but didn't offer the leverage of airborne off-the-rope heaves.

Off-the-rope heaves involved the Puller throwing his top leg off and over the rope and then placing the foot of that leg at the top of the front wall of the pit. The lower foot was positioned near the bottom of the pit wall. The hands didn't change position, and the Puller's hips were pressed tightly against the underside of the rope. The Puller was, in effect, in a squatting position, but almost horizontal, as though having to pull some-thing out of the pit wall in front of him. Only half of the Pullers would take this position at one time and, for the second it took them to take that stance, the other Pullers would strain in their locked in positions so the rope didn't slip back toward the other team.

Once all eighteen Pullers were in the ready-to-heave stance, they'd be able to see the coach in front of pit one. When that coach gave the signal to heave, all eighteen men would detonate. Thrusting their hips up and throwing their heads back. The veins on their necks would look like they would burst. Their Morale Girls would shout "heave-heave-heave-heave!" Then the coach would give the signal for half the men to lock in. A second or two later, the other half would be directed to do the same. It was critical that while half the team was locking in, after a heave, the other half continued to heave so as to maintain any gains. When the Pullers locked in, they needed to do so quickly and crisply. To protect stolen rope.

We spent hours practicing the timing and sequencing. When we heaved in perfect unison, the force produced was extraordinary and eventually even the trees in the woods would succumb to our efforts.

Morale Girls were an essential component to the tradition of The Pull. While their job could have been done by a guy, and vice versa, the nature of pairing guys and girls provided sexual tension that added to the texture of the experience and completed the promise of building teams of men and women, working together, to complete a titanic task. Morale Girls were not only cheerleaders. They were partners and participants and indispensable, in every respect.

My Morale Girl was Luanne Ramaccia. She lived on the girl's side of Kollen dorm and was from a well-to-do family in Franklin Lakes, New Jersey. I didn't know if she chose me, or I her, but we became partners and dear friends. She wrote me poems and washed my clothes and made me cookies and brownies and decorated my room and offered encouragement from the moment I met her. She was witty and bright and had olive skin and straight brown hair and a tiny nose that flared when she was irked with me. She was an appropriate complement to a kid who was more wise guy than gentleman. Her sisterly guidance was welcomed and embraced. We made a great team within a team.

Luanne and I were assigned to pit one. I told Hip that Gerry Decker was the best Puller on the team, and that he deserved to be in the first pit. Hip said, "Gerry pulls on the left and I was a right-side Puller, like you."

I said, "So what?"

Hip said, "Dammit, O'Sullivan, get in pit one and shut up."

Hip taught Luanne and me why the first pit was distinct and strategic. When the other team inched up, to prepare to heave, he said, "If you're at harmony with the rope, you should be able to feel the slightest change in tension. You need to become the rope."

He told me that when I felt the tension change, I should yell, "They're coming!" We would defend by straining in our locked in positions, staying on the rope but throwing our shoulders back and pushing off the balls of our feet. If we were quick enough and strong enough we might even take rope as the other team inched up to throw a heave.

The downside of being in the first few pits, Hip explained, was that we would feel every heave from our opponents. But the better we strained and held our lock-ins, the more insulated the back pits would be. It was important that we absorbed as much of our opponents' efforts as we could. Hip said that if I let rope slip through my hands, it would likely slip through Gerry's hands and down the line. We were the front line of the assault, defensively and offensively.

Gerry was amazing. Once, during practice, I was able to break and watch his technique. When he came off the rope to throw a heave, not once did he touch the bottom of his pit. In a gravity-defying move, he would swing his right leg out from under the rope and plant it at the top of his front pit wall. In an instant, he would shift his left foot to the bottom of his board and rotate his hips under the rope without losing contact with the rope or his front wall. He was then crouched and coiled and ready to spring up and backward into a violent heave that no other Puller could equal. He was a champion wrestler and compact and hard as stone and, without a doubt, the best Puller on our team. Maybe any team, ever.

They didn't take us to the river until the day before The Pull.

College administrators orchestrated the clearing of brush that had grown since the prior year's event. Strings had been set on stakes, so that we knew where to dig our pits. Precisely aligned with the pits across the river.

Silent grave diggers we were. The freshmen rarely won The Pull—only a handful of victories in eight decades. The sophomores usually won. They were more experienced and usually bigger, and no sophomore wanted to endure the indignity of being beaten by freshmen. And no sane person wanted to have hundreds feet of hemp ripped through their hands, inches at a time, two years in a row. The sophomores had the advantage.

Once our pits were dug, the coaches double checked our alignment and made certain our boards were properly positioned in the front walls of our pits. Then we left to have dinner together.

The next day we gathered in front of Kollen dorm at 3 o'clock p.m., an hour before The Pull. Students scurried from Friday afternoon classes. They wished us luck as they passed. The campus emptied before our eyes, as freshmen and sophomores and juniors and seniors and faculty and staff made their way to the Pull site, just north of campus.

Morale Girls taped padding over our ribs and we pulled on our crisp new "80 Pull" shirts over our pads. We collected our water bottles and other supplies, and we boarded our bus for the short ride down to the river to make final preparations and, ultimately, battle ourselves and the 79 Pull Team.

On the ride, the coaches read letters of inspiration and motivation from former Pullers. Hip spoke of the bonds that we'd built over the previous three weeks and about how, win or lose, we would grow from the experience. We were about to participate in one of the most unique spectacles in all of athletics. They reminded us of the story *Sports Illustrated* once did about The Pull, and that we were about to become a part of Hope College history and lore.

The scene had changed overnight. A reddish-brown wooden snow fence encircled the pits, a barrier that kept parents and students and other onlookers back from our graves. A fifteen foot-high wall of fabric had been draped from poles between pit one and the Black River. The same had been assembled on the other side. I could read through the fabric, backwards, the words "79 Pull" and, facing us on our shield, "80 Pull." I felt a chill of pride.

There were hundreds of onlookers lining the fence. Some wearing t-shirts that said "66 Pull" and "70 Pull." And others. At least a dozen classes were represented. Alumni proudly commemorating their time on the rope. And in the pits.

I searched for my mom and Large Root Beer in the swelling, murmuring crowd. I knew they were there somewhere. But not my dad. He was still sober, as far as I knew, but he hadn't taken interest in me at Hope. When I described The Pull to him over the phone, I wasn't able to convey the epic essence of the event. Or perhaps he just didn't care.

My gut began to churn and my mouth filled with saliva. I was ready to fill the bottom of my pit with puke when Gerry embraced me and said, "You ready?"

I said, "Sure."

Luanne gave me a smile and a nod. I felt like we were prepared, but I feared the unknown. It was not a homecoming football game or a double-header in baseball or a track meet. It was The Pull. The freshmen had put their faith in us to win. All the even-year classes that preceded us were counting on us as well. For nearly a century, freshmen and sophomores had been Pulling against each across a river the color of night. The stage was ours.

The rope had been extended from the back of our anchor pit, through my pit, and then disappearing under the suspended wall between the river and me. I stepped around the barrier to see the rope, slack and drifting with the current of the water. It passed over a rowboat that sat in the middle of the river with two men, one with a walkie-talkie to his ear. Then the rope went back into the river until reappearing on the distant bank and under their barrier and, no doubt, extending across pits one through eighteen of the 79 Pull Team.

We were told to take our positions in the pits. When the horn blew I'd been coached to seize the rope in the front of my pit and throw it back to Gerry. He would do the same, as would the Pullers behind him. We were to reel in the rope as fast as we could, because the more rope we earned at the start the more we had to lose. The horn sounded and in a mad flurry we reeled and reeled, and when I could reel no more I yelled at Hip. He signaled the Morale Girls to lock us in. And we locked in. Almost immediately, Hip ordered on-the-rope heaves to tighten and stretch the rope so that when we got down to business we would, hopefully, take rope through the hands of our opponents and not just stretch it.

For thirty minutes, we threw on-the-rope and off-the-rope heaves — mostly the former. We gained small increments of rope. We felt occasional heaves from our opponents, but it seemed the rope was continuing to stretch. Neither squad was gaining ground at the expense of the other.

The coaches walked along our pits and shouted encouragement. They pleaded with the crowd to cheer louder. Hip shouted, "It's time to step it up!"

From in front of my pit, Hip implored the team to "make 'em feel this one." He proceeded to give the signals for an airborne, off-the-rope heave. When I was in the position to heave, I could see in Hip's face a change of intensity. I felt a surge of power, and so did seventeen other men and eighteen women and the throng hanging over the fence.

The heave was powerful and magnificent. Based on the movement of a piece of blue tape that Hip had placed on the rope, we advanced the rope two inches in our direction. Then we lost an inch back, across on the river, when we locked in.

Hip went nuts.

He was furious. He berated us while he bounced, like a mad ball, up and down and around the pits nearest the river. I could hear Big Bob and Stauffer and Howie chiding Pullers in the back pits.

"You cannot give back what you take. You must preserve your gains. You must lock in quickly and crisply. You must."

Hip returned to his signaling position. He asked me what they were doing on the other side of the river.

I said, "How the hell should I know?"

He reminded me that I was in the first pit for a reason. It was my job to know.

In the excitement, I'd forgotten my role. My duty was to sense change in the rope's tension. With a hundred and fifty feet of rope stretched taut across the river, if there was slack created when our opponents inched up I should have been able to feel it. The tighter our team was locked in, the more likely I'd feel the rope relax or even move while the other team prepared to heave.

I heard the crowd, but I didn't want to. I closed my eyes and I slipped away. I focused on the rope and, not long after, I thought I noticed slack, but I hesitated. And then I shouted, "They're coming!" And they did. But I'd waited too long. An inch of rope burned through my hands. Hip said, "Great job, Patrick."

I didn't feel like I'd done a great job. We'd just lost an inch of rope, but Hip meant it. He knew we could feel the other team. If we could feel the other team, then we could defend better against their heaves. I shouted over my shoulder and apologized to Gerry. He said, "That's okay. You'll be ready next time."

I felt slack in the rope before the next dozen heaves. I shouted, "They're coming!" to Hip. We were quicker and more aggressive in straining. Not only were we neutralizing their heaves, but we were taking rope, too. The team on the other side of the river was either fatigued or technically flawed or undermanned. It didn't matter. We had an edge.

Seventy minutes into The Pull, we got more aggressive. We threw a series of off-the-rope heaves. In total, we gained a foot. We threw more heaves and the piece of blue tape passed under my arm and into Gerry's pit behind me. We knew that with each heave the huge hemp rope was burning through the hands of the sophomores.

We smelled blood.

The coaches conferred and agreed that we'd pause for five minutes, before we made a big push. The crowd was in a frenzy and students who had been on the north side of the river and crossed the bridge back to our side reported that the sophomores were close to not having enough rope to keep their anchor Puller in pit eighteen. No team had ever won a Pull after one of their pits had been popped. Once Pullers had to double up in the pits, the outcome was inevitable. But no team worth a damn would surrender. Tradition dictated that once the rope no longer reached pit eighteen—then seventeen, then sixteen—the homeless Pullers would join their mates in the remaining pits with rope and do their best to delay the inevitable. But face defeat courageously and with glory.

We'd seen the gruesome images from previous Pulls, with two Pullers in a single pit. More than one Puller in a pit was less effective because two Pullers couldn't properly position themselves on the rope in a single pit. To see the excruciating pain on their sweaty, filthy, doomed faces must have been unbearable for parents and professors and classmates who were helpless on the sidelines, knowing what was ordained but hopefully taking pride in watching their team lose with honor.

I felt slack in the rope and yelled, "They're coming!" We gained an inch on their heave, and we hardly felt a tug from the other side. That was when Hip gave the signal for consecutive, multiple heaves. We'd thrown two or three heaves in a row, but always locking in between them. To minimize rope loss. But Hip sensed the other side had lost their will. And that we should attack. So we did.

He held up three fingers and the girls screamed, "Three-three-three!" There was a murmur in the crowd and, though I was fatigued, the hair stood on the back of my neck. I whispered to Luanne, "This is it." Hip gave the signal for off-the-rope heaves and half the girls shouted for us to "inch up" into the ready position, our legs out from around the rope, hips underneath and eyes trained on Hip. And then came the command for the other nine Pullers to inch up, as the nine already in position strained to maintain rope. Then Hip leapt into the air, throwing his hands to the heavens, and the crowd roared as the girls shouted, "Heave-heave-heave!" But we didn't lock in. The next command was to inch up. We did. And we heaved again. And then we inched up a third time. And we heaved again. And when we did, Gerry and I, and the rest of the team, crashed into the backs of our pits. Someone in the crowded shouted, "You popped a pit!"

The romp was on.

Luanne was crying and smiling. I was exhausted and I yelled back to Gerry and asked him how he was. He said, "Great" and that he wanted more rope. I barked, "We want more rope!" Hip said, "So do I."

We threw several sets of multiple heaves and we took four to six inches with each thrust. The atmosphere was jubilant, but the coaches implored us to maintain our intensity. Hip tore down the fabric barrier and we kept throwing heaves. We didn't care if the other side knew what we were doing. There was no stopping us.

After one hour and forty-two minutes, the rope went slack. We reeled it across the river. The wet rope piled up in my pit and around me. Parents and students came over the fence. We rejoiced in disbelief. I could only imagine the hideous scene on the other side of the cold, dark river, but we were swimming in tears of joy and triumph.

What a team.

The celebration continued on the bus ride back to campus. The chanting and cheering was incessant—until we crossed paths with the bus carrying the 79 Pull Team. In front of Durfee Hall, and without prompting, we hushed and sat in our seats and gazed at them, and them at us. There was no taunting or jeering or boasting or finger-waving or fist-pumping. We sat, passive, in solemn respect, because the bastards fought a tough and honorable fight. They hung onto the rope in the face of defeat, doubled-up in their pits with hemp shredding their hands. They hung on until they couldn't hang on any longer. They hung on when they knew they would lose. They hung on when their parents and coaches pleaded with them to let go of the rope. They just kept hanging on. It was easier to win a Pull than to lose one, but even when you lost, you really didn't. The 79 Pull Team was great.

THE ONLY PLACE more popular than the library, but no less important an institution at Hope College, was Skiles Tavern. The appeal of Skiles was simple. It was close to campus and it was cheap. They served small plastic pitchers of Papst Blue Ribbon and unimaginative, greasy pizza. No one complained. The joint stunk of Marlboros and Camels and stale beer and burnt grease. Hope kids, loudly and merrily, sang "drink jug-a-lug" songs and drained their pitchers of ale and gobbled up pizza.

Spoiled, horny frat boys mingled with spoiled, chaste sorority girls, and lowly independents mingled with both because, at Skiles, prejudice and pedigree were checked at the door, and Hope kids were all-for-one and one-for-all.

One chilly, damp, drizzling weekday evening, I finished my studies and my feet took me to Skiles. I wound up sitting and drinking beer with a lubricated gaggle of giggling girls from another dorm. A couple of them were Morale Girls, but the others were new to me. One girl in particular, Mary Beth Van Dis, I found to be cute and chatty and animated.

Mary Beth was an atypical Dutch girl, with dark hair, but she was adorable and had cornered the market on perkiness. She entertained me with stories about growing up in Kalamazoo, where her dad had a shoe business. And, like a lot of Hope kids, I learned she was a legacy. Her dad had preceded her at Hope and he was a sports legend at the college and, "doggonit," Marybeth said, she wanted her kids to go to Hope, too.

Mary Beth asked me why I came to Hope. I told her that my dad was a sports legend, too. And a fall-down drunk.

She punched me hard in the arm and said, "Stop being silly." Then I told her I came to Hope because of the anchor in front of Graves Hall. She said, "That's even sillier." She laughed so hard she had to excuse herself.

When she came back, I noticed her face was flushed. We talked until everyone else had peeled away. Then she asked me if I'd walk her to her dorm. I said, "Sure." We pulled on our jackets and left.

We walked two blocks up Columbia Avenue and talked about nothing important.

"Let's walk around campus, okay?"

"Okay," I said.

We turned right on Tenth Street and passed Durfee Hall. We wound our way through the conifers in the Pine Grove and by the President's house. Finally, we looped around Graves Hall and by the giant anchor. She hugged my right arm with both of hers and put her head on my shoulder. She laughed into my jacket, then said, "No one really comes to Hope just because of a silly anchor."

"I did."

Mary Beth said, "Come this way, Patrick O'Sullivan. I want to show you something." She led me back toward the Pine Grove. I took her hand as she reached back to me. She pulled me around Graves Hall to an entrance to the building opposite the side with the anchor. In ever-trusting Dutch fashion, the door was unlocked. She led me inside and I obediently followed her down the stairs and through a pair of blonde, wooden doors. I found myself in a place that I didn't know existed.

"Where are we?" I asked.

"Schoon. Isn't it pretty?" she said.

"Schoon?"

"It's a chapel. For meditation. No one knows it's here."

"It's nice," I said.

She put her arms around my neck and wrapped a leg behind my knees and flawlessly executed a wrestling take-down move. I fell to my back on the indigo carpet of the underground chapel with one of Hope's finest. I wondered what the preacher, my grandpa Sweetland, would think.

We held each other. She kissed me with urgency. We laughed. I told Mary Beth that I should walk her to her dorm. She looked into my eyes, perhaps measuring for sarcasm. But there was none. Then she said, "Okay."

I waited on the sidewalk while she let herself in. She smiled and waved, with just the top of her hand. Then she turned and disappeared inside.

———————◦◦◦———————

AFTER PULLING AND the adulation and attention we received for our stunning victory, college baseball was a major league bore. The biggest issue was that we were meteorologically challenged. We had no indoor practice facility, unless you counted hitting plastic whiffle balls in the basement of Kollen. The official season was only six weeks long, ending in early May. In Michigan that meant we were still on the fringes of sledding season. We were as likely to play in snow flurries as sunshine and, because the season was condensed, we played all double-headers, which meant at least four—often bone-chilling—hours for each pair of games, and interminable bus rides to and from our opponents' fields, where there were always more players on the field than fans in the stands.

Our blue and orange vintage school bus was driven by a cranky old bloke called Bunko, who doubled as our team manager. Bunko acted like he detested us, but that was because he loved us. In spite of his tired, angry eyes you could see in his actions the kind of deep-seated commitment that was common in Hope's coaches and faculty and staff.

Ray Smith was the assistant baseball coach and the head football coach. Smith played at UCLA and in the Canadian Football League, and he had smile lines permanently etched in his face. He was a legend at Hope already. He had a commanding presence. Coach Smith was a man of honor and integrity, as was the head baseball coach, Jim Bultman. Bultman assisted Smith on the football team, but he had the lead job in baseball. They seemed bonded, like brothers.

They coached and we played a brand of baseball that was as conservative as the religion and politics at Hope College. I missed the aggressive, damn-the-torpedoes, go-for-broke, hit-and-run, base-stealing game that I learned from Albert Fernandez. But I played for Hope because I respected the coaches and I liked my teammates.

I was proud to wear the uniform.

Thirty

Sophomoric

THE SUMMER OF 1977 was pleasingly punctuated with the news that my dad had married, for a fourth time, to a woman who worked in the hospital ward where he attended AA meetings. Much to my surprise, she was not like Judy Wick or Bed-wrecker or Opal. She was pretty and delicate and quiet and patient. My dad was better for it.

They lived in the same mobile home park in Somerset Center and on the same street, but in a new, nicer trailer. They purchased a lot on a nearby lake and planned to build a small house of their own. Daddy seemed to find purpose in life again.

His new wife's name was Mickey. She told me to call her mom and dad Lady B and Uncle Don. They were charming and kind and generous and seemed to welcome my dad, the recovering abuser and gambler and drunkard.

Daddy was still in his job at the Adrian Training School. His life had a tempo and rhythm that was real and sustainable. Everything seemed good.

❖————◦●◦————❖

THERE WAS EVERY expectation that we would win our sophomore year. Not since 1941 had victorious freshmen been upended, as sophomores, by the latest freshmen class.

*The most important tradition concerning The Pull is that the sopho-
mores should win it—because they are bigger, stronger, older and, like
sophomores all over, superior to the callow freshmen in every way. For this
reason the sophomores at Hope annually tremble at the thought that they
might be the ones to disgrace age and dignity by losing to the frosh. And
every freshman class clings to hopes that it might prove to be the David
chosen to upset the Philistines.*

—*Sports Illustrated*, October 17, 1966
Lynn Simross

The best of the 79 Pull Team that we beat the prior year became the
coaches for the next freshman team, representing the class of 1981. Now
juniors, the coaches lost as freshmen and sophomores, but they were
worthy and determined and dedicated to breaking the string of defeats for
the odd-year teams.

After three weeks of draconian practice, we returned to the banks of the
Black River to validate our prior year's victory, in the battle fought almost
every year since 1898.

At four o'clock, the horn blew and the rope was reeled in. A historic
confrontation ensued.

I knew in fifteen minutes that this Pull would not be like the prior year's
engagement. I could feel little or no slack in the rope before our opponents'
heaves. Several caught me by surprise and I wasn't able to warn Hip. An
inch of rope burned through my hands and Gerry's, too. But he and I were
resolved to be the front line of defense and buffer the attack. With time
and focus I got better at detecting slack in the rope and anticipating their
heaves, and we were able to strain and diminish their impact.

Our heaves were met with determined defense. We found it difficult
to maintain our gains as our lock ins, following our off-the-rope heaves,
were not as crisp as needed. Then, in a most unfortunate coincidence, the
freshmen threw a heave while we were inching up and preparing to throw
one of our own. They shredded our hands for three inches of rope.

We were collectively staggered. Our coaches decided to order more
conservative on-the-rope heaves and we began to win back rope, but in
small increments. After two hours we had gained several feet, but scouts
reported we were still feet away from popping a pit on our opponents'
side. We kept grinding on and increased the frequency of our heaves. Our
progress was painful, slow and exhausting.

Most Pulls were over in less than two hours. I heard Hip say that it was almost 7 o'clock p.m. and that it was "time to get to work." We'd been engaged for three hours and were beyond fatigued. My fingers were cramping. I looked at Gerry behind me. He was still maintaining perfect form, but I heard mumblings from coaches that there were Pullers suffering in the back pits from bruised ribs, torn skin and dehydration. The coaches went from pit to pit to fire us up for a final push.

Darkness was creeping in. There was a new sense of urgency to finish the battle and we began to throw, exclusively, more aggressive airborne off-the-rope heaves. We started to take rope in bigger chunks. After ten minutes, and a series of heaves, my right hand cramped into a claw-like clench. I fell to the bottom of my pit. Hip called for medical help. But I got back on the rope. Gerry shouted encouragement. We threw another series of heaves, and we took more rope. By 7:30 p.m., three hours and thirty minutes into The Pull, we knew we would win again.

Television cameras had abandoned the north bank of the river for our side as the outcome became apparent. The camera lights provided additional visibility as daylight waned. The coaches told us we were taking a brief respite before the final onslaught. They used the time to prepare the crowd and the Pull Team, waiting for the moment when they felt we were ready, mentally and physically.

Luanne wiped my face with a damp cloth and put a straw in my mouth so I could take water. Pullers were shouting up and down the line of pits, "This is it!" and "End it now!" Excitement was building in the pits and in the crowd. It was time to pop pits and reel home victory.

Three hours and thirty-five minutes into The Pull, we began throwing multiple off-the-rope heaves and the rope came to us three to six inches at a time. Then, in one beautiful heave, Gerry and I and sixteen others hit the backs of our pit walls. We knew we had popped a pit on the other side. For the next ten minutes we threw heave after heave with just momentary breaks between them.

One of the television cameramen threw down his equipment and stood between my pit and Gerry's. He pumped his fist and he screamed at us to "heave-heave-heave!" We continued to take rope. We knew, on the other side of the river, they were doubled up in their pits. The end was near. Finally. After three hours and fifty-one minutes, the rope went slack. We reeled it in and fell on each other in tears.

Then someone said, in morbid disbelief, "They called it a draw."

We later learned that parents of the freshmen Pullers had become terrified and enraged and pleaded with school officials to end the engagement out of concern for the safety of their children. But there was no provision to end a Pull without a winner taking all the rope. During the final thirty minutes, it had gone from dusk to nearly dark in the woods on the north bank of the river. Rope was burning through the hands of the freshmen, the newest children of Hope. Near the end, as our heaves became more effective, the last Puller in line, their anchorman, was violently yanked forward with the rope knotted around his waist. His teammates' hands were being ripped to ribbons and the darkening woods echoed with screams of agony. Amidst blood and gore.

We had the advantage of the camera lights, which was not any plan of our own. And, while the outcome had been decided before the lights were a factor, school officials had to make a decision.

So they called it a draw.

We felt betrayed. Our freshmen opponents were phenomenal Pullers. They sowed seeds of doubt in our minds, but we overcame their Davidian efforts. We won. But we lost. We were angry and sad. We felt hollow and used.

There was a void in our guts and in our hearts. But, with dignity, we garnered the bitter taste and acrid smell of a most important lesson.

Life wasn't fair.

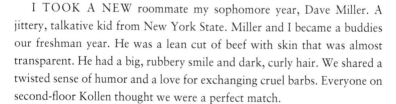

I TOOK A NEW roommate my sophomore year, Dave Miller. A jittery, talkative kid from New York State. Miller and I became a buddies our freshman year. He was a lean cut of beef with skin that was almost transparent. He had a big, rubbery smile and dark, curly hair. We shared a twisted sense of humor and a love for exchanging cruel barbs. Everyone on second-floor Kollen thought we were a perfect match.

Early in the semester, Miller said he needed pocket money, so he picked up a job at a local tavern not on the college drinking circuit. He tended bar six nights a week, drank on the job and stumbled home obliterated each night. On his night off, he went to the same bar and returned to our room stumbling drunk again. His behavior became increasingly disruptive and disturbing and disconcerting. I attempted an intervention.

Learning from what I didn't do with my dad, I confronted Miller. I told him he needed help and that I would do whatever I could to be supportive. He assured me that he had everything under control. After a short reprieve, the pattern resumed. My sleep was interrupted by a drunk every night. Miller continued to dismiss my efforts to help him.

So I moved out. And at the end of the semester, Miller moved on. No longer welcome at Hope and expelled from school.

THE CANCER HAD likely been lurking, dormant, for years. By the time Uncle Charlie's doctors detected misfortune, his fate had been sealed.

He was sixty-six when he passed away on Christmas Eve of 1977. A popular man, hundreds attended his funeral.

His larger than life presence and gruff ways intimidated some of my cousins. But he'd been my fishing buddy since I was a four year old. I'd fish from the end of his dock on Clarklake for hours. Sometimes he'd take me out on his pontoon boat and we'd float above the sunken island. We'd fish until we ran out of worms. Back at the cottage, he'd show me pictures of trophy smallmouth bass that he and his friend Dr. Ludwig caught in the waters around Beaver Island. He promised me that he'd take me there some day. But he died before he could.

After we buried Charlie, there was a raucous, drunken wake at the cottage. There were no fights this time. But when several of my cousins marched stridently through the family room with shotguns cradled across their chests, there was a moment of awkward and tense uncertainty. They continued their parade out the patio door to the listing dock which sat frozen in the lake.

After a minute of silence, the guns erupted. We reflexively jerked. All of us. We'd expected the explosions, but their proximity rocked the cottage.

Twenty-one times, they fired.

The cadence was irregular. But the salute was visceral and sincere and applauded and toasted, a hundred times, inside the house.

Sad and alone, Aunt Louise shook her head and smiled and said, "Damn kids." Then she sipped from her bottomless glass of booze.

MY MOM WAS bemused when I called her late in the second semester of my sophomore year. I told her I was one of five students in the class of 1980 to be named a George F. Baker Scholar. She asked what that meant. I responded that before long I'd be preparing sweet potato falafel, buckwheat cheese straws, buttermilk biscuits and yummy macaroons, and that maybe someday I'd open a bakery—because that's what Baker Scholars did—and that she'd be proud of me.

She said, "You're full of shit," and begged for the truth. I told her it was a big deal for business students at Hope. The scholarship would fund trips to New York and San Francisco and would help open doors so often closed to kids like me.

"I'm proud of you," she said.

"Thanks. Me, too."

I called my dad as well. He'd been sober for two years. We struggled to find our own connection. His relationship with Mickey was encouraging. The stability and normalcy she brought to his life was positive and refreshing. But he was still detached and unengaged with me and my life at Hope. I yearned for there to be something more, but a mountain of embarrassment and humiliation and shame was piled high between us. And would not soon erode.

"Congratulations on the award. And ummmm, I'd like you to come live with Mickey and me this summer," he said.

"Live with you?"

"And she's pregnant."

"What?"

"Mickey's pregnant. Just a few months. You're gonna get a baby sister. Next October."

"I can't wait," I said. "I can't wait."

BASEBALL AT HOPE, my sophomore year, started with the ever-cranky Bunko driving us in our 1950s school bus five hundred miles south to the Volunteer State, where we kicked off a seven-day southern-swing with a double header against Middle Tennessee State. After we pulled into campus and parked, students gathered around our Flying Dutchman bus and marveled that the vehicle made the trip "all the way from Michigan." Bunko muttered, "It'll make it back, too."

Against the University of Georgia, I started in right field, the same position played by Al Kaline, my favorite Detroit Tiger. To get to the ballpark, our orange and blue bus wound through the center of Georgia's campus, down Sanford Drive and by venerable Sanford Stadium. Television sports announcers would say that Sanford was where Bulldog football teams met their opponents "between the hedges."

In the sixth inning of our first game, Georgia had a man on first with one out. The batter ripped a line drive over our first baseman's head and to my left, my glove side. I fielded the ball on the second hop and, in my field of vision, I could see the runner from first hell-bent on third base with the Bulldog coach waving him into the bag. When I reached into my glove, I plucked the ball cleanly, with my middle and index fingers across the seams. I had a chance to throw the guy out. I made the best throw I could and one-hopped the ball to our third baseman. He tagged the runner and then he fired the ball to second. We almost doubled-up the guy who hammered the hit. I got a few whoops from my teammates and a "nice toss, Yankee" from the Georgia dugout. After the final out, I ran off the field. Coach Bultman intercepted me, outside the dugout.

"You had no business over-throwing the cut-off man." He went on to remind me of the ramifications of an errant throw. I said, "Yes, sir," and jogged over to the bench, where I got a wink and a smile from Coach Smith.

I was benched for the second game of the double header. It was a clear day. A couple of us told Coach we were going out to the bullpen "to keep loose." We did play catch. But also, we rolled up our sleeves and rubbed cocoa butter on our pale arms and marinated in the southern sun.

Between innings, Georgia's head coach loped out to our bullpen. He had a lump in his cheek the size of a hard-boiled egg. He spit streams of tobacco juice as he offered muffled congratulations on my throw.

He said that the kid I threw out was "an onion eater from Valdosta, Georgia" whose daddy owned the biggest Vidalia farm in the state. "That boy had been hotter than a two-dick billy goat. He needed a taste of humble pie. Damn good throw, boy." He offered us some of his chewing tobacco. We explained that we couldn't accept because we didn't use tobacco at Hope College. He laughed because he knew we were joking — but of course we weren't — so he tossed us a bag of Red Man.

We'd been led into temptation and in minutes we had hard-boiled eggs of Red Man in our cheeks and we were spitting brown, viscid tobacco juice and soaking up the Georgia sun. I was no longer pissed at Coach Bultman and apparently he had forgiven me. He waved me in from the dugout to pinch-run for our bow-legged catcher. I clawed the wad of chaw from my mouth and tossed it aside and hustled in from the bullpen and pulled up just short of Coach for my instructions. He asked if I'd been chewing tobacco. I stood mute. He pointed to the brown slime dripping off the letters "H-O-P-E" on the chest of my jersey.

Things were never quite the same again between me and Coach.

Thirty-one

Europe
(Summer 1978)

WHEN I MET Wally, we were both freshmen. He was a business student, like me, but a local kid. Raised in a life of privilege.

Wally drove a late model, burnt-orange Chevy Camaro. He had a credit card and a wicked, guttural laugh produced in the back of his throat. You could see the influence of his Dutch ancestors in his blue eyes and light brown hair and big bones. Wally's dad was an executive and swung a lot of weight at Herman Miller, an office furniture company based in nearby Zeeland and an entity praised worldwide and worshipped, second only to God, at Hope. The College nurtured its relationship with Herman Miller's management, many of whom were Hope graduates. The company and its employees were a wellspring of capital for the school. Many Hope students sought jobs with Herman Miller, thus continuing the self-sustaining, symbiotic relationship.

Over burned bagels and cream cheese and coffee in the Kletz, Wally rocked in his chair and rubbed his hands together and announced he was planning to attend the London May Term in England and that I should join him. I was intrigued, but the program was pricey. A call home to my mom and Large Root Beer bore no fruit, and neither did a chat with my dad. So I opted to double the balance on my student loans.

We lodged in London at a hostel across the street from the British Museum, near Bloomsbury Gardens and Russell Square. We were just blocks from Fleet Street, Covent Garden and Piccadilly Circus, which—to my surprise—was a round, open space at the junction of two roads, with nary an animal or clown in sight.

We visited Buckingham Palace, Trafalgar Square, Westminster Abbey, Saint Paul's Cathedral and The Tower of London. And by train we took a day trip to Bath in Wales. Our professor, Dr. Barry Richardson, had arranged tours of factories in Wales and across London and visits to the Bank of England and to the courts, where we watched debating barristers in dark robes and powdered wigs.

To get from here to there we either walked or rode the Tube, London's worthy subway system. We ended each night at a neighborhood pub called The Swan, where we tipped pints until midnight with merry Londoners.

Always dog-ass tired and with bellies full of beer, our crude housing was only a minor inconvenience. We shared a second floor room with four other guys from Hope. We had three bunk beds—each with a skinny mattress, sheets, a pillow the size of a notebook and a blanket made of wool from malnourished sheep. The building had one large community loo, which led to frequent, awkward coed encounters. I failed to grow accustomed to seeing nail polish on pedicured toes in the stall next to me.

Wally and I never intended on spending the entire term in London. After two weeks, we advised Dr. Richardson of our impending departure. He offered his support as long we promised to keep a journal and returned the day before our scheduled flight out of Heathrow. The next morning we caught the first train to Dover.

WE WERE ARMED with a copy of *Europe on $10 a Day* and Eurail passes for transport, via train, anywhere in Europe, and we were unencumbered for two weeks.

Our train arrived in Dover, where we transferred to the docks and boarded a hovercraft for passage across the straights at a narrows of the English Channel. The winds were brisk and the water was choppy, and Wally tried to drink a bottle of Heineken but nearly chipped a tooth as we bumped across the seas. The white cliffs that surrounded the port of Dover shrunk in the distance as we approached France and the village of Calais.

Once in Calais, Wally lost his cultural safety cushion of the English language. He told me that the twenty-one miles across the channel felt like a million miles, and that France was nothing like England. He became nervous and chatty as we walked the streets of the village in search of beer and bread and cheese.

We had two hours before our evening train departed for Paris. Wally was in want of a tranquilizer, and we were both in need of sustenance. We happened upon a tidy épicerie and bought food and beer. Wally relaxed after I proved that my French was proficient enough to buy groceries. We sat in a placid little park on a green, wooden bench and cut chunks of creamy Camembert from a white wheel of cheese. We chased it with bites of a crispy baguette and beer that was warm. We didn't care. We were in the north of France. And on top of the world.

We hiked to the station and I reviewed the timetables. Everything was just as we'd researched in London.

The station platform was empty but for two trim, brightly-attired young women who appeared disoriented and perplexed. The girl most animated and seemingly in charge looked like a young Elizabeth Montgomery from the television showed *Bewitched,* with auburn hair that the actress some-times wore, but not always. She didn't twitch her nose, but she did wave at me, signaling that she wanted me to approach. I told Wally, "I'll be back in a minute."

Neither girl read or spoke French. While they believed they were on the correct platform, they didn't know for certain and wondered if I would assist them. I assured them they were in the correct spot if they intended to go to Paris and the Gare du Nord. The not-so-witchy one, who looked like the television witch, introduced herself as Catherine Christmas. She was a rookie stewardess. She and her sister were traveling to Europe for the first time. They'd been intimidated since arriving in France, where "no one seems to speak English, like they did in London." I advised them, in my best French, that they were safe and in good hands. If they wished to travel with my friend and me on the train to Paris, we'd be glad to make their company.

I left them and joined Wally. He asked me what the girls wanted. I told him they offered to spend a couple days in Paris with us. He laughed and punched me in the shoulder and called me an "ass." Then, over the same shoulder, he saw the girls walking our way. He dropped his chin and raised his eyebrows and a smile spread across his face.

The four of us went back to the épicerie and we bought more cheese,

Beaufort and Tomme de Savioe, and bottles of Bordeaux and more warm beer and baguettes. We wrapped our booty in paper sacks and strolled to the park and sat on the bench for an hour. Then we walked along the streets of Calais, returning to the station to catch the train to Paris.

CATHERINE AND JULIE were from St. Louis. She flew for TWA. Her sister was considering the same occupation. They'd spent three days in London, but were looking forward to Paris. Then they planned to return home. Wally and I listened, with uncommon attention, and smiled and laughed. We were hypnotized by the two delicious young women, both nicely wrapped in sundresses on the express train to Paris with a couple of college boys from Michigan.

We broke bread and shared cheese and bottles of French wine and barely noticed the countryside fluttering by the almost-empty train. It was Sunday evening and we had the car to ourselves but for a lone gentleman in a tailored gray suit. Our conversations divided, Julie with Wally and Catherine with me, my attention was focused on the eyes and nose and lips of the first-year stewardess who looked too fresh and young and delicate to be free to roam the world.

The man in the suit had been eavesdropping and was probably humored by Wally and me trying to be interesting and entertaining and with more wine, no doubt, we grew louder and more obnoxious. But regardless, he appeared next to Catherine and he handed me a piece of paper that said, "Hotel Bervic, four rue Bervic." He explained in English, superior to my French, that the hotel was near a Métro station less than a kilometer from Gare du Nord, in the Montmartre area and beneath the Basilica of Sacré Coeur. The accommodations would be tired, but clean and safe and cheap, and not likely to be listed in our guidebook.

"*Merci, monsieur,*" I said.

"*De rien,*" he responded.

Gare du Nord was as vacant as our train. It was supposed to be the busiest station in Europe, but not on this late Sunday evening in May. There was a magnificent arch of stone and glass and so much iron to admire, but my brain was jelly after all the travel and beer and wine. We needed to find our hotel, so we stepped out into the unexpectedly tranquil streets and flagged a cabbie. We shoe-horned our bags into his trunk and the four of us squeezed into the back of a Citroen with Catherine on my lap. We sputtered just a few blocks and were deposited in front of the hotel.

There was a sign on the door with instructions to mash the button if arriving after hours. An exuberant gentleman answered the buzzer and welcomed us and introduced himself as Claude. He explained, in understandable English, that he had rooms available, but lacking private baths. I told him we were delighted to be there and about the businessman on the train. He nodded and smiled.

Claude assisted us with our bags. There was an awkward moment when he tried to put Catherine's in the same room as mine. I explained that it was a coincidence we were traveling together. The sisters would share one room, and Wally and I the other.

I said, *"Bonsoir, mes amis"* to Catherine and Julie, and we agreed to meet at eight o'clock in the morning. Wally and I went to our room where we talked about our good fortune. We hoped the girls were doing the same.

I slept hard and woke early and was on the street before seven. Wally was still down and out cold. The neighborhood was awake as well. And, to my surprise, in Montmartre there were more men and women of African and Asian decent than I'd expected. Rue Verbic was only a block long. I wandered through several narrow streets and avenues and boulevards and by clubs and studios and then above me on a hill I saw the unmistakable white domes of the Sacré Coeur. I smiled and thought about my high school French teacher, Donald Helmus, and his relentless, entertaining and educational slide shows.

We met in front of the six-level hotel, as planned. I explained that I'd mapped our day based on landmarks and the location of Métro stations. Catherine looked edible in another sundress and strappy sandals, a picture of sartorial perfection, and we were off to explore the world's most romantic city on a brilliant spring day.

As we walked to the nearest Métro stop, I described that Paris was divided by the river Seine and that north of the river was called the right bank, or La Rive Droite, and south was the left bank, or La Rive Gauche, and the city was further sectioned into arrondissements and that they should think of them as neighborhoods. Wally and Catherine and Julie were absorbed by the vigor in the streets. And oblivious to me.

The Métro station was a jumble of winding stairs. We navigated through whispering, hustling Parisians and when the doors of the subway car closed, the princesses from Missouri were soft-hued coral in a sea of drab, their cheery dresses beaming sunshine on the ebony uniforms of the city's people.

We exited near the Arc de Triomphe and marched east on the Avenue des Champs-Élysées. The girls shopped windows and Wally and I marveled at the dark, lean women of Paris, confidently strutting in dark heels and pencil skirts and sucking cigarette smoke in through their Gallic noses. A man abruptly stepped in front of me and grabbed Catherine by the arm and started jabbering at her, a finger pointing in her face. I stepped between them and asked him, in French, to please slow his speech. And he did. He said he was an undercover police officer. We were in an area ripe with pickpockets. The girls were instructed to carry their bags against their bellies and not their backs. Wally and I were advised to put our wallets in our front pockets. We complied. He smiled and welcomed us to Paris.

Just east of Place de la Concorde, we entered gardens that ran north of the Seine and to Musée du Louvre, the world's greatest museum of art. Short for time, I had one objective: to see Leonardo da Vinci's inscrutable Mona Lisa and the timeless smirk that Mr. Helmus called the Gioconda smile.

We continued our trek east along the Seine to Île de la Cité and the Cathédrale de Notre-Dame de Paris, ancient and unexpectedly dark and dreary inside. The great church was home to the fictional hunchback and was protected by gargoyles and adorned with flying buttresses that provided flair and integrity and glory to her blistered facade.

We crossed Paris's oldest bridge, Pont Neuf, and walked to nearby La Sainte-Chappelle. There, I had to see the ancient stained glass windows that Mr. Helmus showed us in his slide shows, where deep reds and blues glowed, enhanced by delicate framework of stone mullions and tracery.

In the Latin Quarter we caught our breath and wetted our tongues with chilly beers. Catherine pressed the side of her knee against mine as we sat in a café and people-watched.

With the day closing fast, we skipped Saint-Germain-des Prés, the oldest church in the city, and we turned our backs on the muted vitality of the Latin Quarter and took the Métro to École Militaire and the grassy park, Champ de Mars, where we made our approach to the Iron Lady of Paris.

The Eiffel Tower, a thousand feet tall in a city void of skyscrapers, commanded the sky with no peer. As we approached, Julie and Wally broke off to search for refreshments and Catherine squeezed my hand and then wrapped her arms around my head and over my shoulders and kissed me on the cheek. She held me tighter, pulling herself off the ground and into my arms. She sighed and began to cry and, for a moment, I was a prince and she was my princess. It was a day of dreams, and she was raining tears of ecstasy.

I imagined.

"My feet," she said. "My flippin' feet. They're a bloody mess."

Her feet were blistered. She couldn't walk another step. The sandals that had started the day delicate and sexy had cut her to shreds. She discarded them in a trash bin. Catherine rode me, piggyback, to the street where we intercepted Wally and Julie and hailed a cab.

I bought Band-Aids, salves, gauze and tape, while Catherine soaked in a tub. It must have been painful, given her puffy eyes and chafed nose. I patched her feet. She looked pretty and pitiful and vulnerable. I apologized for running her ragged through the streets of Paris. She professed that she and Julie could not have imagined a more perfect day.

The girls begged forgiveness as Catherine felt too sore and miserable to join us cavorting in the bars and cafés near the hotel. They were going to retire early. We said we understood. We'd see them off at eight in the morning.

I said, *"Bonsoir."*

Rejected and dejected, our buoyancy deflated, we took a cab to a pub at the top of Montmartre. With a view of the city, all dressed up in her lights, we drank beer and ate pommes frites and planned the next stage of our tour. We lamented the absence of our princesses from Missouri. We toasted them and us, clicking our glasses together, and we drank. And then we drank more. And we staggered down the winding backstreets of Montmartre until we stumbled to our home away from home, Hotel Bervic.

We woke late, blurry-eyed and thick-headed. At the reception desk, our host handed me a note from the girls. It said that after trying to call it a day they realized they were in Paris "for a reason." They looked for us, but we were nowhere to be found. They ate dinner at a nearby café and checked our room again at midnight. But we were not in. They thanked us for "the grand tour of Paris." Catherine left me her phone number and address and Claude admitted he gave Catherine my address, from the registration card. I told him that was fine.

With nothing more to say, Wally and I shuffled into the street with our heads throbbing and our hearts bruised. We bought dark coffee and croissants from a street vendor, cleaned up and packed our bags and walked, in a funk, to the station to catch the next train to the seaside town of Marseille.

MARSEILLE WAS GRAYER and grittier and more industrial than we'd expected. So, after a short day and night, we traveled east along the Mediterranean Sea to Cannes—hitchhiking, not by train. Just because we could. And for a change of pace.

We checked into a bed and breakfast, then walked two kilometers to a public beach, fronted by dozens of boxy and bland eight- to ten-story hotels and apartments. The day was sunny and bright, but cool. We were by ourselves, sitting on sheets and towels we'd borrowed from our innkeeper. We drank beer and felt sorry for ourselves because two days before we were college kids with two beautiful women in Paris, smitten and convinced we were objects of their desire.

After enjoying several breakfast beers, we were about to head back to the inn when a thirty-ish brunette appeared next to our encampment. She had on a simple, midnight-blue shift and carried, over her shoulder, a beach bag on her left side and beige, heeled sandals in her right hand. She looked like she could perhaps be a retail clerk from a fashion boutique on her lunch hour.

She pulled a white bed sheet from her bag and spread it across the sand just to the left of us. Then she stepped into the middle of the sheet and reached behind her back and, dexterously with her thumb and index finger, unzipped her dress starting from behind her neck and then down her back. The shift dropped to the ground, requiring just two shimmies of her hips to complete the transaction. She stepped out of the garment and neatly folded it and stowed it away in her beach bag. Clad only in white, lacy panties that shown brightly against her tawny skin, she sat and then lay down. Her panties disappeared against the sheet and her hair, the color of sweet molasses, fell in waves beside her head.

Wally and I agreed, in a silent pact, that it would be premature to leave. We drank more beer, until our bladders objected, and then we had no choice but to abandon our station. I said, "*Au revoir*" to our new friend. She said, "*Caio.*" On the walk back to the inn, we agreed that the princesses from Missouri weren't that cute after all.

From Cannes we went to Nice where we rented mopeds and traveled, ill advisedly, in a cold drizzle on hilly highways overlooking the Mediterranean Sea. We buzzed twenty kilometers all the way to Monte Carlo in Monaco, where we broke a hundred traffic laws but returned safe and soaked to our not-so-nice hostel in Nice.

Our last day and night along the Mediterranean coast was spent in Menton, where the Alps begrudgingly fell into the sea and where we slept, for free, on cots in a storage room behind the kitchen of a grand, old seaside resort because we couldn't afford the expensive rooms. A kindhearted manager felt sorry for us.

The following day, June 8, 1978, we traveled by train, all night, and arrived in Geneva, Switzerland for one evening and a boat cruise on the lake of the same name. We dined on French fries, washed down with beer, and lamented the rain and fog and wished we were in Paris or Cannes.

The next evening we rolled through Germany, then into Brussels for a short stop, and on to our final destination, Amsterdam, before hustling back to London and our flight home.

By the time we reached Amsterdam, our asses were dragging and our brains were pulp. We had circled much of Europe in less than two weeks and traveled at night to save time and money. Our diet consisted of cheap beer and cheap wine and cheese and bread and French fries. The train station was chaotic and frenetic, and sketchy and swarthy characters tugged at our bags. We muscled our way to a cab stand and gave a driver the address for our inn, hoping for the best.

While Mother Nature shined on us in London and Paris and Cannes, since then we'd been victim to dreary, damp days and nights. Amsterdam was no different. I needed a hot bath and a long nap and, thank God, our place was neat as a button, but three levels up. We were the sole guests of a silver-haired woman who spoke perfect English. She greeted us with welcoming hugs. But we must have smelled like a Greyhound bus.

I bathed and, when I returned to the room, Wally was gone. He'd left a note that said he had an errand to run, which was surprising since I'd been his travel guide for ten days. It was the first time he'd shown independence.

When he returned, he was fidgety and perspiring. He told me he'd met a man, near a bridge, with dark skin and knotted hair. I knew he was describing a South Moluccan. Our guidebook warned of the Moluccans and their association with drug trafficking. Previous generations of Moluccans were paid protectors of the Royal Dutch East Indies Army, once based in the Indonesian Archipelago, during the days of Dutch imperialism, and were later, effectively, trapped and isolated in the Netherlands. The result of political and geographic complexities too complicated for me to comprehend.

Wally began to sit on one of our two single beds, but pulled a wad of aluminum foil out of his pant pocket just before he hit the mattress. Then he told me he was stoned because he'd smoked pot, laced with opium, with the dark man. He unwrapped the foil and exposed a molded, cube-shaped brown mass and he smelled it. Wally laid the foil across his lap. Then he began rocking back and forth and rubbing his hands together. He giggled from the back of his throat and licked his lips and giggled some more.

He said it was hash and that he bought it cheap. The dark man promised him a good high. He mashed the foil into a ball and then flattened one side. He stuck a straight pin into the foil and, on the other end of the pin, he molded the brown paste so that it was suspended above the foil base. Wally grabbed a water glass from the sink in our room. He lit a match and tried to light the mass while holding the glass over it to capture the smoke. He tried for five minutes to ignite the dope. I asked him if I could pinch some of it off.

He said, "Sure, go ahead."

I smeared the brown paste between my thumb and index finger and I drew its scent into my nose. I congratulated Wally.

"You purchased shoe polish from the Moluccan. Not hash."

That night we pub-hopped along coffee-colored canals and made the requisite visit to Amsterdam's red light district, where hideous women sat in store fronts on chairs behind plate glass windows wearing heavy make-up and cheesy lingerie and petting cats on their laps and, apparently, waiting to be picked and then pecked by poor-forlorn-forsaken-schmucks.

When our train arrived in London, we returned to the hostel across from the British Museum, retrieved the luggage from storage and showered and made Heathrow with minutes to spare. We flew to the States after refueling in Newfoundland, the birthplace of Grandpa and Grandma Sweetland.

I was nervous, but not apprehensive, about spending two months in a trailer with my sober (hopefully, still) dad and his new and newly pregnant wife, Mickey.

And I was eager to chip away at the rampart that had risen between us.

Thirty-two

Living With Daddy, Again

THE SUMMER OF 1978 was the first that I didn't play organized ball since a serendipitous meeting with a man called Red, the Little League coach with the scarlet pompadour. He took a chance on me, and changed my life.

Baseball had been good to me. I played center field for a state champion American Legion team. My senior year of high school, I finished second in the county in hitting and made All-Conference. I had a tryout with the Dodgers and two with the Reds, and I earned my varsity letter in college. But I was a realist. I had no future in the game and my interest was waning. So, for the first time in a decade, I stepped away.

And then there was my dad. His turnaround was incomplete, but breathtaking nonetheless.

He was all-everything growing up. Big and fast and handsome and charming. With a chance to play baseball for the Cubs or the Tigers, his dad, Bompi, insisted he go to the University of Michigan to play baseball and football. But a broken leg on a Wolverine practice field put a shattered end to his field of dreams.

Then he met my mom and she got pregnant. And Mommy, with my heart beating inside her, denied to her mom and dad that I was there. But I was.

What came easy to my dad as a kid did not as an adult. The glory days of high school were washed away in a tide of whiskey. He failed his test as friend and worker and father and husband. And he used the booze to take him to a place where negligence didn't matter to him.

Growing up was difficult, so he didn't. He got drunk instead. And he was mean and critical and abusive. After a decade, my mom said, "No more."

He returned home to Jackson. His second chance became a third. He borrowed money and lied about why. He bet on the ponies. He divorced two more times and he treated me, and everyone else who loved him, like dog shit.

Then finally, in December of 1975, he drank enough to kill himself, but not quite.

Two months prior, he'd shown up obliterated at my football game. Then on Thanksgiving night I found him dressed in a blazer, unconscious in the back seat of his car. I heaved him into his trailer and, for old times' sake, I drained the rank dump of all its booze. The next week, he put a whiskey bottle to his head and pulled the trigger. On Christmas Eve he shuffled back, sober, into our lives. And he acted as though nothing had ever happened.

Of course he did. He was a narcissist. Conceit and self-absorption made his affliction even more difficult to overcome. And, in recovery, admission of his flaws was required before the healing would be complete.

It would take time. I knew it would take time. We all knew it would take time. The pestilence of his addiction and the stubbornness of his vanity meant we had to be patient with a man who didn't deserve it. But then again, he did. He was sober. He was trying. He was succeeding. And I wanted to be a part of it.

At first his sobriety seemed tenuous, but then he married Mickey and, with her, he gained his footing. When she became pregnant, he went from steady to confident. He was ebullient when he spoke of their soon-to-be baby girl, Molly.

Mickey was my dad's fourth wife. She meant the world to him. But Molly, the baby inside, was what would make that world turn. With her came the opportunity to be the father and husband he should have been. The expanding bump in Mickey's tummy represented hope, faith and redemption. Molly would be his savior.

He worked different shifts at a minimum security prison, the Adrian Training School, where he counseled juvenile delinquents, convicted felons and addicts, like him. He'd been there two years. The longest he'd held a single job.

I found work, after returning from Europe, with the help of a quiet little blonde named Julie, who was the friend of a friend from Hope. Julie was a summertime waitress at a popular dive called the Golden Nugget in the Irish Hills area, fifteen minutes east of the trailer park.

I was a host and cashier and bussed tables, when required. And I kept a list of patrons who were held hostage in a bar in the basement where they paid too much for weak drinks and waited too long for empty tables. A curtain of blue-gray smoke hung in every room, and cigarettes seemed to dangle from everyone's lips. Ashes fell like snow. The food was either over-cooked or undercooked and, mercifully, fried. No one cared. They arrived tight from booze and left even tighter. But I appreciated my job and I liked working with Julie. Sometimes, after closing, we'd go out to eat. We tried to date, but we were better at just being friends. So we stuck to that.

Twenty years of heavy drinking had diminished my dad. Still hand-some, the hard living and toxic effect of years of too much booze and tobacco had weathered his face and robbed him of the sinew and muscle that had connected and wrapped his mighty bones.

"Watch this," he said.

Daddy eased himself to the floor of the trailer and attempted to pop off ten push-ups. The first five were okay, but for six through ten I found myself clenching my fists and pushing my toes into the cheap carpet of the trailer, as though I might transfer my strength to him. "I'll be strong again," he said. My dad was only forty-one. He was still a young man.

I considered dropping to the floor beside him. Counting out loud, from one to ten, together. Then we could have stood and held each other. And maybe I would have said that I was proud of him for overcoming great odds. For beating the booze and overcoming homelessness. It was so good to have him back.

"Daddy, it's so good to have you back."

I didn't.

I wished I had.

But he was getting better. That's why I was there.

THOUGH HE WORKED different shifts, my hours were consistent.

So there were days that he and I were both off together. And we fished every chance we could.

There was only one road to little Moon Lake, deep in the woods. It began at the back of the trailer park. A hilly, serpentine half-mile of two-track that was rutted and rocky. My dad used his Gremlin like a Jeep, and we slipped and climbed and banged our way back to the lake. And each time we arrived, it was the same. When we fished Moon Lake we were always by ourselves. Together and apart.

We had a small, silver aluminum johnboat, with three benches and a flat bottom. We kept it upside down in the reeds near the launching area, next to a faded green canoe and a wooden rowboat, with a v-hull, that never moved. To prepare for our excursions, we'd buy red worms and minnows at the bait shop. We kept the minnows in a tin bucket perforated with holes that sat inside a bigger bucket with no holes that allowed us to keep the minnow water fresh and cool and full of oxygen.

The lake, shaped liked a piece of a jigsaw puzzle, was only several acres in size. An electric motor was all the propulsion required to navigate to our favorite holes. Fed by artesian springs, the water was clear but the color of iced tea, stained by nuts and seeds and leaves that fell to the lake's bottom each fall. Opposite the single access point that was carved through tall trees was a bank protected with thick bushes below a modest bluff that rose to leafy fields. Lily pads flanked the bank around the entire lake. Just beyond the pads, the water dropped off to depths beyond the length of our anchor line.

Our favorite quarry were black crappie. They thrived in clear water and fed on zooplankton and insect larvae. Moon Lake was a honey-hole for the fish. Our preferred bait for the speckled fish was the live minnows. We'd use lightweight spinning tackle and small hooks in spite of the crappies' huge mouths. In June the crappie were still on their beds, in five or six feet of water, but would eventually migrate deeper, near structure invisible to us, and could still be caught throughout the summer with trial and error.

We talked while we fished, but not about me. He seemed to avoid me. And if we talked about him, it was high school and the state championship basketball team and the single-wing offense they used in football. And we talked baseball. About the home run he hit in a high school all-star game in Tiger Stadium. Briggs Stadium when he hit it. On Trumbull Avenue in Detroit. We talked fishing. A safe subject. And during our conversations something random would prompt him to tell a story, and then for ten minutes he would weave a fictional tale that would end with a remarkable punch line that would set us off laughing until we rocked the boat, which would reawaken us to the task at hand.

One day we discussed Uncle Charlie and Beaver Island. I reminded my dad of Charlie's unfulfilled promise to take me there. He said that he'd like to go there some day, with me. I felt good about that.

We were close, but distant. Together, but apart. As we sat and fished and talked, we danced around the darkness that pushed us apart. I was too hurt and too immature to take us there. He was too proud and too embarrassed—and still too immature himself. Twenty years apart in age, but floating in a tub together in the middle of a lake, we were still too much like kids to work through our issues.

◆────────◦●◦────────◆

IN MID-AUGUST, I finished my last Saturday night working at the Golden Nugget and Daddy and I went on our final fishing trip of the summer. Our battery charger had not functioned properly, so the electric motor was useless. We grabbed a couple of oars from underneath the trailer. On a still day, gliding over the protected pond, manpower was sufficient to get the ten-foot johnboat to where she needed to be.

We fished. He told me more stories. We laughed until we rocked the boat. He drank copious quantities of God-awful Tab pops, the soft drink addiction that replaced the booze. And we fished some more.

Summer's heat had driven the fish to deeper water, so we had not been as productive as earlier trips. But we had a stringer to be proud of filled with sunfish, bluegill and four slabs of black crappie.

Daddy pulled up our anchor—a clothesline tied to a U-bolt frozen into a cement-filled coffee can. I dipped the oars into the water and I pulled us across Moon Lake, toward the boat launch carved into a copse of towering oaks.

Just a few minutes from shore, outside the lily pads and in a fathom of water, my dad shouted, but in a whisper, "Stop!"

"What?" I said.

"Jesus Christ. Jesus Christ. Look at that!" still whisper-shouting.

On the lake bottom, an enormous snapping turtle was slowly but purposefully plodding across a strip of sand. The monster's triangular head appeared to be the size of two fists. From our vantage, the turtle's carapace was as big as a manhole cover and scaled with brown pieces of armor. The tail was inches thick at the back of the shell and extended two feet.

My dad said, "Let's catch her."

"What?"

"Let's catch her."

"What we gonna do with her?"

"We'll eat it."

"We'll what?"

"Eat."

"Are you crazy? That's nuts."

He opened the tackle box that was under his seat and he pulled out a fish stringer made of chain. The stringer was attached to three feet of clothesline, intended to secure the stringer to a cleat on the boat. He tied a steel-leader, attached to a three-hook night crawler harness, to the last position on the stringer. A crude but creative set-up.

He worked nervously and feverishly. I kept the boat positioned over the snapper.

Daddy ripped a sunfish from the other stringer, exposing bloody gills. He ran the three hooks from the harness through the belly and head and tail of the sunfish and started to lower the carnage to the lake bottom.

"Put me right on top of it," he said.

I did. He leaned over the side of the boat and slowly extended his arm down until the bait was in the turtle's face. And, with a violent thrust, the beast nailed the dead fish. At least one hook engaged the turtle's mouth.

Daddy was lying on his stomach across the back of the boat and his arm, up to a foot above his elbow, was below the water's surface. He was trying to pull the turtle off the bottom, but to no avail. We were listing toward the turtle. I feared capsizing. We were an inch from taking on water. But they were in a stalemate.

"Please let go," I said.

He didn't, but thankfully the turtle released from the bottom and began to ascend, not voluntarily, but from my dad's determined efforts. In less than a minute, the turtle surfaced.

The reptile's back had accumulated decades of moss. The snapper's tail had dorsal-like scales that were an inch high at the base. Only one hook remained in the turtle's mouth, which was opened wide beneath a nose that looked like a beak. The beast was balancing by waving scaly legs that were tipped with impressive claws. I thought I heard the turtle hiss but I wasn't sure because my dad was banging around the boat in search of something. I watched in disbelief as he grabbed one of the oars and was preparing, apparently, to render the beast unconscious.

He'd tied off the stringer-hook devise to the oarlock on the turtle side of the boat and he'd taken the oar from the opposite side and raised it over his head, when I yelled at him.

"What the hell are you doing?"

"Soup!" he shouted. "We're gonna make soup."

He took two controlled swings at the turtle and connected, without effect, to the head, once. Then he took a third madly wild swing that almost capsized the boat.

"Stop! Are you crazy? Let it go, Daddy. It might be a hundred years old. Let's let it go. Please. Please, let it go."

He sat back on his seat in the stern of the boat. The wildness in his eyes tamed, but not entirely. The turtle was a sad, angry island floating next to us. Her head was extended uncomfortably. The bloodied sunfish had vanished, but one large hook was still lodged in the turtle's mouth.

He slid the tackle box toward me, across the deck. I opened the box and dug around until I found a rusty pair of wire clippers. I leaned over the water and reached as close to the turtle's gaping mouth as I dared. Her neck was still extended, but she seemed to understand that I meant no harm. I clipped the wire harness and the turtle's head pulled back into her shell. Free from the stringer.

And, seemingly in no hurry, the giant submerged steadily, returning to the floor of Moon Lake, no worse for wear, a predator with just one enemy—my dad.

"God, that was fun," he said. "God, that was fun."

Thirty-three

Molly and Woody
(Late 1978)

I FELT LIKE more a man in full, than not, when I returned to Holland and Hope for my junior year.

I had a surge in confidence after a month of rich and novel experiences in Great Britain and Europe. Musing of Catherine, my Parisian princess from Missouri, never failed to add bounce to my step and illuminate my day. Work at the Golden Nugget was banal but satisfying, and I watched Mickey's belly expand with Sister Molly inside. I felt a new, but alien, sense of responsibility for the baby to be born in October. And as Molly grew, so did faith in my dad's recovery. He had purpose and was committed. And over the summer he and I laid the groundwork for reconciliation.

I moved into a five-bedroom college-owned cottage called Dosker on Central Avenue, across from Centennial Park. My roommate was a hairy beast of a kid, more yeti then man. He featured a five o'clock shadow by noon and was covered, but for the palms of his hands, with the coat an Airedale rolled in the dust of coal. For reasons too peculiar or sinister to understand, no matter the weather or season, Duncan typically went shirtless in our house, exposing a pillowy upper torso with nests of black hair that surrounded a pair of inverted nipples. Female visitors found his semi-nude appearance to be strange and unnerving. And it was to no one's surprise that he rarely dated. We'd have to plead with him to cover himself in the event that parents or friends visited. He would sulk, for show, but begrudgingly comply.

When fully dressed, his wardrobe was simple: dark t-shirt, jeans and square-toed, scuffed, caramel-colored boots that announced his arrival. Duncan was genetically incapable of walking. As though perpetually pissed or late or eradicating an infestation of cockroaches, he stomped everywhere he went. An effective early-warning system for those who preferred to avoid him.

And he didn't speak in the conventional sense. Duncan machine-gunned his words. Remarks shot from his mouth in rapid-fire succession. His lips were thin and hardly moved, and the speed and lack of precision in his word formation made him almost impossible to understand. Over time, we learned his dialect. He was bright and witty and pitied no fools. They were doomed to wither in his oral barrage of caustic condescension, and we cheered him on because he deserved it.

Duncan was pre-med, and becoming a doctor was an imperative over which he obsessed. He studied more than any other kid I knew at Hope. His preferred venue was a bathtub on our second floor, for which he'd built a shelf that spanned its width. There he would review his anatomy and chemistry and biology work and drink copious quantities of hot tea that he made with an electric water pot that rested on the shelf, over the tub. I'd remind Duncan that if the pot fell into the tub his death would be certain, and he'd feel acute pain when each follicle on his hairy body exploded from its roots.

He'd fire back at me, "So-be-it-who-cares-about-the-pain-I'll-be-dead-anyway."

Although Duncan had an awkward outward appearance and countless neurotic idiosyncrasies, he was a fine person. He treated me with kindness, and I believed he loved me like a brother. I counted on him to be a pal when I needed one and to disappear when I needed that. His friendship was real and enduring. But for the fact that he lived like a feral pig and was known to drink from a bong when he thought it was a bottle of beer, he was the best roommate I'd ever had.

❖────────❖❀❖────────❖

POSTERS WERE TACKED and taped around campus announcing The Pull meeting for the incoming freshman. The class of 1982.

They wandered into the auditorium like we had two years before, apprehensive and curious and perhaps more fearful than we were. The prior year's three hour and fifty-one minute Pull was epic. It was the longest documented tug-of-war to have occurred anywhere, at any time, ever. And it ended in a contentious draw. They knew they'd be pulling against a special group of athletes, experienced and determined and yearning for validation.

Bob Lamb and Gerry Decker and I sat in chairs across the stage and faced the frosh. We told them that, in retrospect, we'd been too complacent and not confident enough. We feared losing more than we wanted victory. Everyone on the south bank of the Black River thought we'd won. Rope was coming to us with every heave, near the end, and when it went slack we reeled it in and embraced and kissed and cried.

Then we were told, "It's a draw." We were devastated and felt cheated and betrayed, but then we learned The Pull had been called a draw due to ambiguities in the rules. And out of concern for the safety of our opponents. We explained, as understandable and defensible as it was, we knew what really happened that day. We'd won the rope, but didn't win The Pull. And that was a bitter pill to swallow.

We stopped talking and let them sit in silence. We let it sink in. There was no nervous shuffling of feet or staring at the floor. They just looked back at us. Then we flashed slides set to music and we let them sit some more. We told them that they were our redemption. We came up short. They wouldn't. We failed. They wouldn't. We couldn't pull again. They could.

During our speeches, I heard muffled footsteps on the roof of the auditorium. The sophomores were about to do us a customary favor.

Our team stepped outside and was ambushed with buckets of icy water and water-filled balloons. They scrambled back inside and a guy named Freddie said, "I'm gonna kill those bastards." We gave them balloons and instructions and told them to detest the sophomores, but the night was about fun and tradition and that retribution would come on the first Friday in October at the river. And they'd never be the same again.

They were a better team than we were. We pushed them harder than our coaches pushed us. Freddie and Ron and Lou and Pete and so many others—they were freaky good. But they were pulling against guys who knew what it felt like to have rope burn through their hands and to double-up in their pits. And the sophomores were bigger and more experienced and smarter. It was expected that they would win. When sophomores lost, as they occasionally did, they had to live with the embarrassment and humiliation for years. Forever.

The horn sounded at 4 o'clock p.m. and the reel-in commenced. But as agreed to after the prior year's longest Pull, there was a stretching period during which each team was required to throw on-the-rope heaves. After the rope was stretched, college officials marked the rope with tape. If there was not an outright winner after three hours, then the teams would lock in and the distance from the first pit's front wall to the tape would be measured on each side of the river. The team that had gained the most rope would be declared the winner.

Gerry and Bob and I had committed to each other that we would not win or lose by measurement. If our team failed to win, they would do so by spilling their guts in their pits. They would win by ripping the rope through the hands of their foes, or they would lose by having it ripped through theirs.

After the stretching period, officials marked the rope. There was another signal. Then we methodically executed on-the-rope heave after on-the-rope heave. If there was any additional stretch left in the rope, we wanted it on our side of the river. So we went after it hard. We gained feet, not inches. And then we paused.

The rope was taut. Freddie was in pit one because he was fierce and gritty and stubborn and streetwise. And if any man on our team could feel the other team coming, it would be Freddie. But that's something you only find out on the day of The Pull. It required tight lock-ins on our side and just a little bit of sloppiness or fatigue in our opponents to create enough slack in the rope, across a hundred and fifty feet of river, to be felt in the first pit.

They threw a heave and Freddie didn't feel them coming. They burned us for an inch of rope.

We threw three on-the-rope heaves, and we got the rope back.

Then I heard it. "They're coming!" Freddie screamed. I gave the signal to strain and eighteen Morale Girls bellowed "strain-strain-strain!" Eighteen Pullers threw back their shoulders and pinched their calf muscles against the rope and pushed against their boards from the balls of their feet, and the sophomores didn't budge the rope.

"They're coming!" he shouted. I gave the signal to strain and we strained. And again, they didn't take any rope. We were almost an hour into The Pull and, while we hadn't won a significant amount of rope, Gerry and Bob and I sensed that it was our Pull to win.

I conferred with the other coaches and we agreed to throw our first airborne off-the-rope heave.

The airborne heave captured two inches, but we lost almost an inch on our lock ins. I went ballistic and so did Gerry and Bob. We berated the Pullers. We called them "sissies" and "punks" and told them we were disappointed and exasperated. After three weeks of busting our butts and theirs, they'd lost all their gains because of sloppy lock-ins. It wasn't entirely true, but it was vintage Brian Hipwell, our former coach. He did the same thing to us and it seemed to work then, so we'd planned to do the same thing to our guys.

Gerry marched up and down the middle pits, Bob worked the back and I screamed at the guys in the front. Freddie, in pit one, was irked. He called me a "bastard."

We urged them to strain harder while their teammates inched up. We pleaded with them to heave in unison. Their lock-ins had to be crisp and precise. We reminded them we were there to win The Pull by taking all the rope. There would be no measurement.

Freddie's concentration waned and he missed a sophomore inch-up and heave. We squandered an inch. They threw two more heaves, but Freddie felt them coming. We held our ground. We were two hours into the Pull when we ratcheted up the intensity.

The next off-the-rope heave netted two inches, and we kept it all. We threw four more heaves with comparable results. Then we worked the pits, shouting encouraging words. We could see whetted hunger swelling in their eyes. They could taste sweet victory. We encouraged the crowd to support each heave. Their energy began to build as well.

Two and a half hours into The Pull, the rope was coming in four-inch chunks. After one amazing thrust, Freddie and seventeen other guys hit their backs on the rear walls of their pits. We'd popped a sophomore pit.

The sheets that sheltered our signal-calling were torn from their masts. Redemption and retribution were at hand, but the brave bastards on the other side would not capitulate. They had guts. They refused to get off the rope, like the prior year's team, even as they doubled up in their pits. And then finally, after two hours and fifty-six minutes — just four minutes shy of a measured end—the rope went slack and Freddie reeled it across the black water. Bodies soaked in blood, sweat and tears piled onto one another. Gerry and Lamb and I embraced. Parents and classmates poured over the fence, joining the celebration.

Against great odds, eighteen men and eighteen women had pulled together, a team united, to beat a squad of nut-tough sophomores that had survived the previous year's longest-ever, historic Pull.

God, it was good.

———————◦•◦———————

I FELT A WARM and mysterious involuntary pull toward one of the frosh Morale Girls, Leanne Fiet. From Cleveland and a preacher's kid, she wasn't cut from prom queen cloth, but I was partial to her prominent cheekbones and big white choppers and pouty lips. Her hair was brown, kissed with streaks of sun, almost to her shoulders and often tucked behind an ear. She was petite and lean and athletic and her eyes were dark and kind and had a depth and dimension that gave them their own voice. They seemed to speak to me in ways that were different and complicated, but natural and honest.

We took it slow. There was no hurry. We met two or three times in the Ketz for bagels and coffee. I think we were both trying to understand, without discussing so, whether our connection was real and the vibrations sincere and the energy sustainable. And over time, we mutually agreed, without saying so, that it was.

She was grown up. There was a deepness to her that defied my expectations. She was, beyond question, her own person, confident and with purpose. She was strong and determined and uncommonly real. She was grounded and practical, but in love with life and a world in motion.

Methodically we got closer, enjoying more of each other's time, and she was within reach on October 16 when I received a message from the dean of students. It was urgent that I call my dad.

———————◦•◦———————

HE PICKED UP on the second ring.
"Hello, Rock?"
"Yup. It's me. What's going on?"
Daddy told me that his new baby, my sister-to-be, had been full-term

and stillborn. Mickey was okay. They didn't know what went wrong. He kept his shit together and remained stoic. But he was devastated. He should have been.

With Molly, so died my dad's best chance to prove he could be a proper father.

"I'm so sorry. I'm so very sorry," I said. "Will you and Mickey try again?"

It was an untimely, insensitive question. I regretted it before I finished the sentence. Before the pause became unbearable, I told him I'd see him in a month, at Thanksgiving.

"That's good," he said, and hung up.

I cried for my dad.

In Leanne's arms.

———————

NOT LONG AFTER I reached the trailer park south of Jackson for the Thanksgiving holiday, television news was covering the Jonestown Massacre—a mass suicide of a religious cult in Guyana. Hundreds died. It was incomprehensible. They'd followed their so-called spiritual leader, James Jones, to Africa from San Francisco.

The horrible headlines deepened our collective misery and made mourning Molly's death even more onerous. We turned off the television and the morose images faded to black.

Then the phone rang. For me.

It was Patric Woodard's mom, Billie. She apologized for tracking me down. She said she'd called my mom in Muskegon, looking for me, and I said, "What's the matter, Billie?"

"I'm sorry to bother you when you're with your family, and on Thanksgiving weekend, but...uh...Patric was killed in a car accident and we...I know he...would like you to be a pallbearer."

Woody had been working as a youth counselor in a half-way house, not unlike my dad's new vocation. He and another buddy of mine, Rex, had been drinking beer and watching football at the Red Rooster, a popular tavern on Scenic Drive between Muskegon and Whitehall.

The road's name reflected its nature. The two-lane wound along Lake Michigan's eastern shore, sometimes through dunes and majestic trees. At too high a speed the road was as dangerous as it was beautiful and, when covered in snow and ice, treacherous, too.

Woody's penchant for risk-taking had grown over the years. Though he'd discovered alcohol and pot later than most, when he did use it was as though compensating for lost time.

As kids, we'd sprint down Lake Michigan's dunes, chests forward and arms out, extended beside us. Woody swore he could feel the lift of flight before he crashed into the sand. He loved speed and danger. Born without a governor for fear, he feared not. He didn't fear life and he didn't fear death and, while his life was short, death came quickly.

Woody's Blazer went straight when Scenic Drive didn't. The car sailed off a dune and into a grand, old oak. Woody and Rex were catapulted from the vehicle, objects in a hailstorm of glass. The Blazer landed on Rex, in the woods, but he escaped with merely broken bones and attended Woody's funeral in a wheelchair.

Woody lived life near its edge. And he'd gotten too close.

Thirty-four

Landslide

SECOND SEMESTER CLASSES at Hope started on Monday, January 8, 1979. That night my mom called, distraught and with more horrific news.

My first cousin Mark had been killed in a motorcycle accident. My Aunt Gracie's only child. She called him Marko, and so did I. We'd been friends since we were little kids. Mark lived in Royal Oak. He never knew my buddy Woody, but they were similar — young, untamed and now dead.

Leanne was a devoted source of needed love and comfort, and together I thought we'd get through the interminable, snowbound Michigan winter. I had spring and baseball to look forward to. She'd not seen me play. With Leanne in my life, I felt a renewed interest in the game. I knew the unforgiving season of gloom would yield to brighter, warmer days, and the drumbeat of ruinous news would fade.

On Friday, March 9, Leanne and I met for coffee and bagels in the Kletz and made plans for the evening. That afternoon, my cousin Polly's husband, Joe, a doctor, called my cottage. I was taking a nap after classes. I picked up the phone, still in a haze.

"Rock, that you? It's Joe Seeger."

"Hi, Joe. Yup. It's me. You woke me. Catnap."

"Sorry."

"No, that's okay."

"It's your dad, Rock. I have bad news."

"How bad?

"Bad bad."

Joe told me that my dad had been complaining of a headache for several days, but didn't think anything of it. "But today," he said, "the headache became intense and unbearable," and according to Mickey, he recounted, my dad slumped to the floor and began to vomit. He lost consciousness and Mickey called an ambulance. He'd likely suffered a cerebral hemorrhage. His condition was grave. The outlook, dismal.

I felt nauseous. My head was spinning. I called Leanne and she helped me find transportation to Muskegon. Once there, I borrowed my mom's car and drove three hours to Ann Arbor, where my dad was hospitalized. Bompi and Gigi were waiting, of course, and Cousin Polly and Joe and Aunt Hige and her second husband, John. And poor, anguished Mickey and her mom and dad. One at a time, I hugged them all. I told Mickey I was sorry and she said, "Oh, Rocky, I'm sorry, too."

I needed to see my dad. Bompi showed me the way.

His head was twisted and cocked to the side. His chin was jutting up with a mask over his face and hoses running into his mouth and down his throat and up his nose.

There were dozens of tubes and wires and clamps and machines that were beeping and blurting. A respirator clacked and wheezed. The frenetic scene was in stark contrast to my dad, who was as still as stone but for his chest being forced up and down by the wind whistling in and out of the ventilator.

Nurses scurried about checking machines, flipping switches and punching buttons and needlessly moving things around. Bompi went to my dad's side, patting his arm and calling him "Bub" and telling him "you're going to be all right."

A doctor entered the room and introduced himself. He explained that, most likely, a blood vessel in my dad's cranium had been leaking for several days which explained, he said, why he'd been having headaches. Because the bleeding continued unabated there was no place for the fluid to go, which lead to further trauma and exceptional swelling of the brainstem. There was evidence of minimal brain activity. Virtually none.

I said, "What does that mean?"

The doctor said my dad's prospects were grim. He looked at me and shook his head from side to side. Then he dropped his eyes to the floor and turned his back to me and walked away.

Bompi said, "A lot could change."

I told him that I'd just heard the doctor say my dad was, effectively, brain dead. My grandfather just shook his head, disappointed in me and my lack of faith. I looked at my dad and at my grandfather and I whispered to myself, "He's his only son."

I stayed the afternoon in the waiting room with my family. There was talk about how important "the first forty-eight hours" were and that "the swelling could go down" and that "miracles can happen." My feelings oscillated between anger and hope and helplessness and sadness. I ached for Mickey. First her baby and then this. And my dad was worse than dead. Alive, but not. Unconscious with no practical chance of a normal life. For her sake and for mine—for all of us—I hoped he wouldn't survive the night.

I went back into his room, but not for long. Even if somehow he ever woke from his coma, he would never be the same. I didn't want him back. If I couldn't have all of him, I didn't want any of him.

God forbid if my family had to take care of him—a vegetable—after he'd put us through hell. He'd wallowed in guilt since the day he took his last drink. He was embarrassed and humiliated for what he did to me, and us. He was yet unable to express his transgressions and ask for forgiveness. And now, he never would. He'd been sentenced to death, or dumb and dumber.

I told Mickey I loved her and that I was sorry. And I was. I was sorry for what happened to Molly and my dad and I was sorry for what would come next. Whatever that was.

Home was where I needed to go. To be with my mom and then back to Hope. I arrived in Muskegon at midnight and crawled onto my bed with my clothes on. I cried myself to sleep. I wanted to hate God. What God would shovel so much shit on one kid? What God would raise a man from the dead just to crush his head? What God killed friends and uncles and cousins and little babies?

My mom was stoic as I told her the news. In my presence she never spoke an ill word of my dad. Not ever. Not while they were together or after he left us or when he spiraled down. Maybe there was some of him in me. And she saw it. It was the good stuff. Maybe she still loved him, too. The good part. She took the highest of roads. I loved her for that.

I got a ride back to Holland Sunday night and I lay beside Leanne. She let me tell her my sad story and she held me and listened and I cried some more. And so did she.

I called Coach Bultman on Monday and I quit the baseball team. He said, "I understand." I doubted that he did. I didn't tell him about my dad.

For the next few weeks, to sleep each night, I popped Valium and smoked pot and drank too many beers. Unconscious, I dreamt of Molly and Woody and Mark and my dad, all of us, in a johnboat fishing with minnows and poking giant snapping turtles. Uncle Charlie shouted, from shore, "Let's go to Beaver Island." We'd toss Charlie cans of beer and Tab. He'd wade into the Moon Lake with a fishing net and scoop up the cans, wearing his silly captain's hat slightly askew.

We'd laugh at Charlie until the boat rocked me awake.

I HIT THE books, a worthy distraction from my dad's condition that, according to my grandfather, had improved considerably. "Your dad is breathing on his own," he told me over the phone. "The ventilator has been rolled away."

A month after the incident, I sought counsel from one of Hope's chaplains, Pete Semeyn. He and I were connected — by Muskegon, not chapel. We shared a curious bond from the first day I met him my freshman year. A former football player, he was a big guy with prodigious shoulders and a thick head of dark hair flecked with silver. He was handsome and sported a toothy Hope College grin, requisite for anybody that was somebody on Hope's staff.

Pete's smile was sincere. He was real, with no façade, and he let me talk to him. He didn't tell me that God would take care of me or that things would get better or that all things happened for a purpose. He listened and nodded his head and looked through my eyes into my heart. Pete asked if I was doing all right, and I could tell that he meant it. I told him that I was okay and that Leanne was there for me and my friend Dave Stevens and my roommate Duncan and my other buddies. I was going to be fine. I just needed to talk.

We chatted in the basement of Dimnent Chapel and, for a while at least, I felt sheltered from the landslide of ruinous woe that weighed on my soul and confused my mind and weakened my heart and shredded my faith. From one day to the next I wasn't sure what was up or down and sometimes getting sideways was the only way to feel right. We talked until it stopped feeling natural. Then I knew it was time to leave. I held out my hand and we shook and he put his left hand on my shoulder. He didn't say anything—he just gave it a squeeze. How great it would have been to have had a dad like Pete.

As I was wrapping up my final exams, Bompi called. He said my dad had been transferred to a hospital in Jackson. He was doing much better. I asked what that meant.

He said, "There are a thousand things. You just need to see."

I told Leanne that I didn't want to go. She said she did. She'd not met my dad and only knew part of his story. She didn't know about his drunk days. That remained a secret I kept wrapped up tight. Tucked away.

She knew I was pessimistic about his recovery. Smothered in guilt and reproach. She thought it would be best if we went, together. I knew I couldn't go by myself.

I borrowed a car. Jackson was two hours away and we talked the duration. We never had trouble talking, Leanne and I. We were friends and lovers and the words came easily. We talked about Hope and her sorority and her brothers and growing up in Cleveland. About her mom and preacher dad and her childhood that wasn't idyllic, but was good. She loved her family and embraced their imperfections. Maybe that was why she could be fond of me.

We arrived at the hospital about noon. We walked up to my dad's floor and to the nurse's station. I told a nurse who I was and why I was there and she said, "Follow me." She led us to my dad's room. The door was open, but Bompi wasn't there. She said my grandfather had gone to get a bite to eat.

"He's here every day, your grandfather. He comes in the morning and at lunch and after dinner. He sits with your dad and talks to him and prays. Every day."

"I know. Bompi's a special man," I said.

"And then he drives across town to see his mom, your great-grand-mother," she added.

I said, "Yup. Great-grandma Bessie broke her hip. She's ninety-seven, you know?"

Of course she knew. Bompi made certain the entire staff knew about his mother, of whom he was exceedingly proud. We all were.

The nurse nodded in affirmation. "I'll leave you with your dad."

He was on his side and facing the door. I was surprised to see his eyes open. For a moment I felt faint hope. But it was short lived. When I approached him I saw that his eyes were empty and milky. He was unresponsive to my touch and voice. It was just as I'd expected. He was still more vegetable than man. Nothing had changed.

I took Leanne by the hand and led her to the hallway.

"That's all I can do."

"You sure?"

"I'm sure."

We stood and I held her hands in mine. And she read my eyes. She didn't say anything. She just read my eyes. I told her that the man "in there" wasn't the man I wanted to remember.

"I'll go in," she said. "I don't mind. I want to. I want to spend time with your dad. And I think it's fine if you don't want to. I don't blame you. It's okay. It'll be fine."

We stood in the hallway. I looked at my feet. I felt like a coward. A chicken-shit bastard too self-absorbed to sit and hold the hand of my own dad. But I couldn't do it.

She squeezed my hands, then turned and went into his room. She closed the door. I found a chair in the hallway. I sat and waited. I felt grateful for her. I was in awe of Leanne's patience and faith and courage. In all of which I was woefully deficient.

When she returned, she smiled and tilted her head just so. That meant everything was all right between us. It looked as though she'd been crying, but maybe not. I decided it was best not to ask. I offered her my arm, which she accepted, and we walked away.

We didn't talk as much on the drive back. Not at first anyway. We stopped at a diner to get a bite but neither one of us was hungry, so we just nibbled. And then we went on our way. I wondered what Leanne thought of my fear and apprehension. She had remarkable intuition, developed and acute. She seemed to accept and perhaps understand my numerous flaws, but I wasn't sure how. I didn't understand them myself. If she was confused and conflicted, I couldn't tell.

She held my right hand as I drove down the road. Her touch kept me upright when all I wanted to do was find a corner and curl up and cry. But she led me back home. Where we stood tall and held each other. And I was eternally grateful to have her at my side.

Thirty-five

The Cottage

DURING THE SUMMER of '79, work became a welcome and necessary distraction. My duties helped keep my mind off the black barrels of woe, overflowing with steaming shit, that seemed to roll without relent over my soul and into my recent life.

Leanne was waiting tables in smoldering and dreary Cleveland. In Muskegon, I lamented that it would be September before I saw her again in our safe haven of Holland and Hope.

Great-grandma Bessie passed away in June. She was a ninety-seven-year-old marvel. My dad had been moved to Medical Care, the same facility in which she resided—her final days an ironic convenience for the family.

When we buried Bessie, so went generations of secrets. I attempted to navigate the torrent of information that came rushing out of Bessie's box of mystery. I called Bompi to tell him what I'd uncovered: obituaries and funeral home receipts; a newspaper article about Great-grandpa Patrick's awkward, drunken death in a ditch; details about the suicides of Uncle Emmett and Cousin Hortense; the existence of the half-brother, Robert, from Toledo. Did he know him? I asked for his help and perspective.

He said, "Not now. I can't talk about that stuff right now."

He continued to hold vigil over my father, his love unabated and unconditional. His faith never wavering. Bompi was an amazing man.

My grandmother had given up, I learned. She refused to visit him. I couldn't blame her. But of course, how could I?

I also worked as a program counselor at a playground weekday mornings and as a lifeguard and swim instructor at a beach on Bear Lake in the afternoons. I played "Simon Says" with little kids when it was too cold to swim. They were cute and innocent and I treated them well, except for the spoiled ones who were belligerent. I was extra nice to them. Because that wasn't what they wanted from me.

As often as I could, I also worked for a subcontractor, third shift, cleaning air handlers at Muskegon Piston Ring. We'd crawl into oversized dust collectors wearing goggles, respirators and hard hats with lights. We'd unfasten and then replace long, tube-shaped fabric filters connected at the floor and ceiling. There were hundreds in each enclosed metal box. The dust was gray, like cigarette ash, but as light as baby powder. We worked shifts of twenty minutes on and twenty minutes off. I'd make more money in one night than in a week on the playground and at the lake.

After work, black and muddy from head to toe, I'd drive home sitting on a towel. I'd strip to my briefs outside where I'd wash down with a garden hose and then go into the house for a shower. I'd eat breakfast and then hit the playground and later the beach to guard or teach or play games.

Friday evenings, I'd drive south of Grand Rapids to work on a cottage that Large Root Beer owned. The existence of the cottage was a wonder to me, as was much about Large Root Beer and his curious life. By 1979, I knew as much about him as I did when I first met him—practically nothing. When his parents died, just before he and my mom were married, they left him a house in Battle Creek, the cottage south of Grand Rapids and a lot on Mullet Lake in Northern Michigan.

My mom told me he sold his parents' house shortly after they died, but he'd held onto the cottage.

"Why didn't you tell me about it?" I asked.

She shrugged her shoulders and shook her head. Then she told me a story about a woman who had recently knocked on our front door and asked if Lawrence Ryan Backofen lived there.

My mom said, "Who are you?"

"Lawrence's aunt," she said.

The woman claimed that Lawrence had not responded to phone calls or letters from relatives for a decade. Since his parents died. The family wondered what had become of him. The aunt was taken aback to learn that Large Root Beer had married and even more surprised to learn that there were kids, Brian and me.

He wasn't home. The aunt left a message with my mom. Large Root Beer ignored it.

I thought it was strange that he'd turned his back on his family. And I thought it was even stranger that they'd come looking for him.

Large Root Beer seemed to treat my mom decently. He whined and pouted and bickered at times. But he wasn't threatening. I didn't love him. I liked him okay. He was odd but not embarrassing. And, if not for him, we might still be living in the city. His friends were interesting and apparently successful and they treated me like an adult. And they embraced Large Root Beer's queer and peculiar personality with gusto and affection. I tolerated him.

Large Root Beer told me he wanted to sell the cottage, so he offered me a deal. If I fixed it up and could find a buyer then he said he would give me ten percent of the selling price.

I said, "Done."

He sketched a map and handed me a key and money for paint and building supplies. Each weekend of July and August I loaded up my mom's old Buick and made the hour-and-a-half drive to an area thirty miles south of Grand Rapids. The cottage was in a remote part of the state with rolling hills and tree-lined two-lane roads and sprinkled with farms and not much else. Lakes were abundant but small, with modest cottages and row boats tied to docks or pulled onto spits of sand.

Large Root Beer's cottage was simple and unassuming. It sat at the end of a dirt road, high on a bluff and overlooking a small, weedy lake. I waved at a neighbor, one of a handful, as I drove in. He greeted me shortly after I arrived. I explained who I was and my purpose and he invited me to dinner with his wife and him. I accepted.

The neighbor helped me fix the water pump on my second day, without which I had no running water. He provided power tools to supplement my wrenches and screwdrivers and hammers and handsaws.

He and his wife explained, over gin and tonics and dozens of perch filets, that the cottage was an eyesore and that they, on occasion, bushwhacked weeds and hauled away limbs. They were pleased that I was there to "pretty it up" and, when I was done with my work, they wanted to make an offer on the place.

I could hardly believe my good fortune. The next week, I phoned a real estate agent from the area. I told her I was considering listing the cottage. I asked her for a history of comparable sales. A week later, I received a package from her in the mail.

It took me six weekends to complete the work. I replaced shingles and fascia and stairs and decking and gaskets and rubber washers and trimmed trees and bushes and painted the place from one end to the other.

On my next-to-last visit, I asked the neighbors to make an offer. They did, and I considered their proposal to be fair. So with just a little bit of dickering, we signed an agreement. I told them a lawyer would call them the next week and that I enjoyed meeting them and thanked them for the privilege and their help and that I'd return, hopefully the next weekend, if I was still confident our deal was binding.

I did return, the next Friday, to say goodbye and gather my tools and to enjoy the only break I had the entire summer in the company of Gail.

The warmth of our relationship had cooled since high school, with my studies at Hope and Gail at Ferris State. And then, of course, with Leanne in my life. But Gail and I had shared much together and our friendship was sincere. She was my first love. She'd been right for me, at a time and in a place. I hoped she felt the same.

For two days, we fished and guzzled icy beers and floated and splashed around on huge, black inner tubes. And mostly, we just laughed and played and rekindled the affinity that we'd shared for years. It had gone dormant, yet was inexorably running its course.

She helped me scrub the interior of the cottage with buckets of Pine Sol. The last item to be checked off my to-do list. It only took an hour as there was no bedroom. Just a half bath and a galley kitchen and a living room that did double duty as a sleeping room. The cottage was small, but well built and fronted with glass. The view of the lake and the woods was satisfying and comforting and relaxing.

Saturday night, we ate sautéed lake perch and buttered sweet corn and drank gin drinks with the neighbors. Afterwards, back at the cottage, we stretched out our sleeping bags on the musty hide-a-bed and savored the last of our Stroh's beers. We listened to the late innings of the Tiger game on a transistor radio. Then we dozed off, warmed by the glow of fireflies and serenaded by the chirping of crickets.

We slept late and ate toast and drank black coffee and paddled the neighbor's canoe and then splashed around again on the tubes. Sunday afternoon I drained the cottage of water, turned off the pump and poured anti-freeze into the toilet and locked down the place, hopefully for my last time. I handed the key to the neighbors, telling them that even if our deal fell through they'd need access to the place. They were appreciative of the trust and the practicality of the act.

I wheeled my mom's enormous, ancient white Buick down the dirt road and out to the two-lane and north toward Grand Rapids and Muskegon. Twenty minutes into our trip, the dashboard lit up with flashes of red and, before I could pull over, steam began pouring up from under the hood. I stopped and popped the bonnet. The engine hissed. And so did I.

We were nowhere and near nothing but for a white farmhouse with one lonely gable that sat a hundred feet from the road. As the steam spewed, a gentleman in his mid-seventies in overalls and with short white hair and walking with a limp approached the car from around the farmhouse. He leaned over the engine and gave me a quick assessment.

"You gotta broken water hose. Nearest garage is twenty miles from here but it ain't open 'cause it's Sunday and there ain't no wreckers around here, either. But sit tight. I reckon I'll be right back."

"You reckon?"

"I don't reckon that. I will be right back."

"Okay. Thanks."

I looked at Gail and shrugged my shoulders. She smiled and gave me a wide-eyed stare and then she shrugged her shoulders, too. After five minutes, the farmer re-appeared from around his house. This time pushing a wheelbarrow with a toolbox, teetering on top.

He rolled up to the still-simmering Buick. With a small socket wrench, he unfastened a bracket holding the remnants of a broken hose. Then he compared that hose to what could only be described as an epic collection of engine hoses in myriad sizes, lengths, thicknesses and construction. As he picked through the pile, he explained that he'd been farming for more than forty years and in that time he'd had all kinds of pumps and machines and vehicles and "whenever somethin' died" he'd reclaim parts and pieces, because "you never know," he said, when someone's car will break down in front of your house and you can lend a hand. "You never know."

After a chatty ten-minute repair, the hood of the Buick came crashing down. With a neighborly smile and a firm handshake as remittance, we were paid in full.

As we pulled away, he said, "You're one lucky boy, you know?"

———◆◦●◦◆———

I'D CONSIDERED GIVING up baseball for good after my dad was stricken. I didn't play that spring at Hope or that summer in Muskegon. I had no time, working three jobs and fixing up the cottage. But I received a call at the end of August from the coach of a local team asking if I'd play during a Labor Day tournament at Marsh Field. I said, "Sure, what the heck?" I thought it might be fun.

Under the lights and late during our second game, I hit a high-bounding ground ball between the shortstop and third base. "Deep in the hole," as radio announcers would say. The shortstop back-handed the ball and made a long, weak, off-balance throw to first base. I had a decent chance of beating the throw because the shortstop had to go far to his right and I had good foot speed. I was digging hard, an inch inside the chalk line. I should have expected the throw to be down the line, toward home plate. At the exact moment that my cleated right foot hit the canvas bag, the big kid playing first base made direct and violent contact with my left shoulder as he lunged for the ball.

The next day, the surgeon told me that the snapping sound that reverberated through the stadium was not my fibula breaking, but the severing of the ligaments that connected the fibula to the talus, the bone that formed the lower part of the ankle joint in the tarsus of the foot. He said, "You were lucky that you didn't break the tibia, too."

I said, "Funny, I don't feel so lucky."

I landed on my back. When I raised my head to look, my right foot was at a ninety degree angle to my right leg, effectively disconnected. The crowd was hushed. Then I heard my first base coach say, "Oh, Jesus Christ." He'd figured out what I already knew. My baseball days were over.

The next morning, a trusted orthopedic surgeon sliced me open on each side of my leg, from just above where my ankle used to be to an inch above the sole of my foot. He ran a rod along my fibula and re-attached the two-inch piece that had broken off. The doctor bent the rod at the bottom to help secure the reassembled bone and he added screws and surgically

repaired the ligaments. Then boxed me into a cast.
    Some luck.

Thirty-six

Saying Goodbye

THE SURGEON TOLD me the operation "went well" and that within a few days "you'll be on your way," and we shook hands. He gave me a cock-sure smirk and jutted his chin in the air, pivoting and sashaying away so that he could spread his God-like magic onto other undeserving souls.

By midnight, the swelling in my foot and toes was such that, if a kielbasa had feelings, I knew what it felt like to be one. I'd become a living, breathing meat extrusion. After the surgery my right leg, from just below my knee to halfway up my toes, had been snugly wrapped in a plaster cast. The trauma from the injury and surgery caused a copious accumulation of fluids in the tissue of my leg and foot and ankle. With nowhere to go, the fluids migrated toward my toes which, most unfortunately, had doubled in size and turned a purplish-crimson color. Ice provided no relief. Neither did drugs. Calmly I explained to the nurses on three occasions that it felt like my toes were being squeezed in a vise. The pain had become unbearable. Perhaps I should have thrown a bed pan and bawled my eyes out, but instead I logically made my case. To no avail. So I gave up on the nurses. I called a friend who brought a screwdriver and pliers. In five minutes I had chopped and peeled away the cast and freed my toes.

Relief was immediate and I fell asleep in seconds. In the middle of the night, I was roused by an obese and threatening red-faced nurse asking, "What happened to your cast?" I told her a giant, large woodpecker flew in through the window and pecked it to pieces. She snarled and barked and returned to her box of doughnuts.

The next morning the surgeon returned for damage assessment. He said the nurses were "dumb-asses." The pot may have been calling the kettle black, but I felt the best course of action was to concur with his majesty. So I did. He re-wrapped the cast. But this time with space for my toes.

I called my new roommate, Jim Van Vliet, from my Muskegon hospital bed. I advised him that I'd miss the first few days of classes, but not to worry. I'd be in Holland before the end of the week. And sporting the latest in plastered fashion.

Jim and I played baseball together as freshmen and sophomores and, like me, he'd grown bored with the college game. He was big and soft and Dutch and was cursed with the additional physical challenge of being born without an ass. He had a steady girlfriend who visited our apartment often. Curiously, he liked to listen to her pee. When she went into the bathroom, he would sneak to the door and put his ear to it and giggle and rub his hands together and say, "I can hear you." I told him I thought he was weird and sick and needed counseling, but otherwise we got along fine.

We lived upstairs in a one and a half story rental on Fourteenth Street, just a few blocks from campus and Columbia One Stop, Hope students' favorite party store. The doctor put me in a walking cast after three weeks that facilitated getting up and down the stairs to our apartment and meant I no longer had to carry crutches on my bike as I peddled to and from classes. With crutches secured across the handlebars of my ten-speed, I took on the characteristics of a low-flying pterodactyl as I swept through campus and the Pine Grove. I'd shout, "Coming through!" and students would scatter and clear the walkways for me. Without any obvious rancor.

Leanne and I were able to regain the momentum of our relationship, but not without challenges. I wasn't the easiest person to be with—increasingly anxious about what would come after college. My dad was still in a coma and not enough time had passed since losing Charlie and Molly and Woody and Mark and Bessie. But Leanne had the patience of Job. She could have cast me aside and I wouldn't have blamed her. But we held on together, and to each other.

In late September, a week before The Pull, Bompi called and asked that I visit my dad. He said, "He's getting better, he really is. Being in the nursing home has been good for him. Please come see your dad."

I told him about my baseball accident and the surgery on my leg and that I had only one more week of Pull practice. He was adamant. Which was unusual. He said that he needed me there. "You'll see," he said. "You'll see."

━━━━━◆◆◆━━━━━

MY FAMILY HAD a prominent profile in Jackson. But not for reasons that would make one proud. Great-grandpa Patrick Henry O'Sullivan was a veteran of three wars and a local hero, a nurse and medic and a notable athlete. It was baseball, the semi-pro Jaxons, that brought him to town. When he was too old to play, he was a popular coach. But his drunken death in a sewer trench in 1939 was headline news, and an embarrassment that shook the family and the community.

Uncle Emmett O'Sullivan, the World War II sniper, also returned a proud veteran and hero, and he too was influential and popular. But the haunting, latent stress of battles fought and lives taken led to boozy self-medication and a violent and bloody suicide in 1947. And more distress and shame was heaped on the family.

My grandfather, both ridiculously and understandably, blamed himself for my dad's broken life.

"Both the Tigers and the Cubs wanted him. I insisted he go to the U of M and play football, too. I made him do it."

And then he broke his leg.

"It was my fault," Bompi would say.

"None of us went to college," he said. "I thought the pros could wait."

Many hopes had been hung on my dad, with his beaming smile and silver tongue and uncommon good looks. His successes on the ball field and in the classroom further inflated expectations. It was unspoken but understood that he, single-handedly, would overcome generations of shame. On his shoulders, he would lift the family out of a pit of indignity.

But, alas, he failed, too. And he left a trail of broken hearts and shattered promises. For twenty years he tortured himself and his family and his city and then, miracle of miracles, he found himself re-born. But, in the cruelest of ironies, he was stricken again before he could finish his greatest comeback. From hero to loser to hero again. Almost.

And Bompi's faith in God ran deep. He read from his devotional prayer book each morning. He worshipped every day. He said his "Hail Marys" and "Our Fathers." He would kiss his rosary and hold it next to his heart with the genuine belief that God was listening. A compassionate, kind, benevolent God. It was my desire to honor his faith. And, for that righteous reason, I agreed to visit my dad. I did it for Bompi.

ON A CRISP, bright, colorful Saturday afternoon in late September of 1979, I drove two hours southeast to Jackson to see my dad. This time I didn't take Leanne.

Bompi had been visiting him three times a day, at least, since he'd been moved to Jackson from Ann Arbor. After Bessie died in late June and was buried in July, he'd been able to spend more time with him. I'd receive periodic reports over the phone and Bompi would tell me how my dad was responding to his voice and that he was "looking better all the time." He said, "His condition is improving."

It had been four months since I'd been there. Gigi had stopped going. I wasn't sure about Mickey or my brother. If they did visit, I wasn't aware. I was pretty sure Mickey went, on occasion. But that was a guess. We found it too painful to discuss. It was better to pretend he was dead.

I drove straight to Medical Care and walked by the long, gray bench and the wet, smelly ashtrays and to the reception desk for directions to my dad's room. The door was cracked and Bompi was inside, talking to my dad and rubbing his arm. He smiled when he saw me at the door. "Come here. Come see Bub."

He continued to pat his arm, but my dad's body may as well have been disconnected. He was making small movements. Spasms and contortions. With no teeth, his lips had been reflexively sucked into his mouth, thus collapsing his face and drastically altering his appearance. But it was him. He still had curly hair. Bompi had fluffed it. But again, it was his eyes that spoke to me. They were open and dead. There was a nothingness to them that was haunting and empty. And the same filmy, white layer was still there, a dense milkiness that wasn't human. It was unnerving.

"He had a normal bowel movement this morning," Bompi said. He was almost giddy.

"Pardon me?"

"His bowel movement looked as normal as one you or I might have."

My dad's condition hadn't changed. The hemorrhage had expunged what was once viable. There would be no miracle recovery. His brain was not going to magically regenerate. I wanted to be upset with Bompi. We should have allowed him a dignified death in March.

But Bompi's faith in God prevailed.

And it had come down to shit.

Maybe that was appropriate.

Unfinished business would remain unfinished. There would be no reconciliation. We wouldn't take the fishing trip to Beaver Island. We would never talk about what it felt like to be abandoned and ashamed and humiliated and embarrassed. What it was like to grow up without a dad on hard streets.

There had been no reason to rush. A year ago we had a lifetime to mend our fences.

And now Bompi was celebrating the texture and consistency of his bowel movements.

That's where it was going to end for me.

"Bompi, thank you for asking me to come down." I meant it.

I was saying goodbye to my dad, but I wasn't going to say it. And I wasn't going to look at him again. So sad and pitiful. "How do people work here?" I whispered to myself. What a charade. A mockery. It was undignified and humiliating and rude. How many poor souls were in the building, pickling in their own shit?

Bompi was such a sweet old guy. He couldn't help himself. His heart was large. And in charge.

"I think I'm going to head back to school."

"Would you like to get something to eat?"

"I don't think so. I have a long drive. And I'm not really hungry right now. Tell Gigi I love her. And Mickey, too, if you see her. I gotta go."

We embraced. His whiskers scratched my face when we hugged. By noon each day he previewed his five o'clock shadow. His beard had a green tint that mystified me. He'd say, "It's because I'm Irish."

Bompi was a great, loving man. He deserved a better fate. But it was what it was.

⁙⸺⸺⸺✦⸺⸺⸺⁙

I WAS FORTUNATE, again, to be chosen to lead the signal calling. Thirty minutes into The Pull of 1979, it was time to throw our first airborne off-the-rope heave. Eighteen Pullers had their eyes trained on me. Their hips firmly against the rope. Feet leveraged on the boards in the front of their pits. Hands gripping the rope, between their legs and ready to throw their hips up and heads back. At the same vicious moment. And eighteen Morale Girls had their eyes on me, too. And hundreds of students and parents and alumni. All waiting for my hands to be raised toward the sky. The signal to heave.

Before the first hour was out, we knew that the Pull Team of 1982 would be undefeated as freshmen and sophomores. We tore down the sheets shortly into the second hour. A signal to our team that we had the utmost confidence in them. And a message to the class of 1983, on the other side of the river, that their time might come, but not on our watch.

An hour and fifty-five minutes into The Pull, the rope went slack and Freddie began to reel the beast across the Black River. Two minutes later, the knot reached our first pit. We'd won again. A decisive victory and validation and enough justice to suck some sting from the impulsive, quixotic ending of the 1977 Pull that had been called a draw. When it wasn't.

<hr>

HE DIED THE day after Thanksgiving.

I was on break from Hope and in Muskegon. It'd been a year since our mutual friend, Woody, launched his Blazer off the snowy sand dunes and into the unforgiving trees of Scenic Drive, and eight months after a cerebral hemorrhage left my dad diminished and comatose. He was preceded in death, by forty years, by his grandfather Patrick Henry O'Sullivan. And by his grandmother Bessie by just five months. She was ninety-seven. My dad would have been forty-three in December. He was preceded by his stillborn baby girl, Molly, by barely more than a year. He left two former wives and three divorcées and one living wife, Mickey, who could reclaim her life again. He left two sons, Brian and me. And Bompi and Gigi, his dad and mom. He had no brothers or sisters. He left us with memories. Many good. Many not. And a thousand regrets.

I felt at home in a funeral home. Bompi had worked in them since I was born, and he'd been retired only a year. As a kid I'd prowl through the basement, where they did embalming, and in the casket loft above the garage and, better yet, the casket showroom, where—if I took my shoes off—Bompi would let me lie in a coffin and pretend I was dead. But best was to be last to turn off the lights at night. It was a thrill I cherished. I'd say "goodnight" to the dead person nearest the stairs. Then I'd turn off the last torchiere and scramble up the stairway, into Bompi's arms. He'd laugh and so would I. He'd boil water and make Sanka and we'd eat soft, sugary Archway cookies, and by then my heartbeat would have slowed and I could go to bed, or sometimes I'd stay up late and watch cowboy movies until "The Star Spangled Banner" played. And the television stations went off the air.

I'd seen hundreds of dead people over twenty years. Perhaps it was the peace in their faces that appealed to me. No tension. No pain. No worries. Asleep on their satin pillows. Dressed for church. But not going. Often-times, the Catholics would have rosary beads wrapped in their clasped hands, across their chests, with the tiny cross on display for mourners. I loved the heavy perfume of the gladiolas, thick in the air, and thick in tiered vases stacked around the caskets. When I was little, I'd get my face down close to theirs and search for the work of the mortician. And always I'd look for a flare in the nose or the rise or fall of the chest. Just in case. But I never touched. Bompi told me that I should never touch the dead.

My dad was in an open casket. And in a sweater, not a suit. And that was good. A sweater was more his style. He wouldn't have looked natural in a suit.

He was, again, the same man I'd fished with the summer the year before. No longer were his lips sucked into his mouth or his face twisted and contorted. His curly hair was fluffy and perfect. His mustache had been trimmed and combed and his skin had color. Gone was the demeaning hospital gown. And the shit and the stench.

His eyelids, of course, were shut, covering the dead eyes that sent me cowering months before.

I'd never touched one. I'd watched other people touch death before. But my dad looked so good. He had come far. He was at peace. And I had to finish my goodbye.

I reached into the casket with both of my hands and I grasped his arm. He was cold and hard. Stiff as frozen meat. I flinched when I touched him. Surprised at how death felt. I wanted to pull away. But I didn't. I held onto him.

He made one hell of a comeback. I was glad he looked handsome in his shirt and sweater and slacks. The last time I'd seen him dressed so nicely was Thanksgiving three years before, when I dragged him from the backseat of his car and his bucket of chicken and thermos of whiskey and dressed up in his blazer and boots. All wrapped up and too drunk to go. He'd come a long way from playing Russian roulette with a bottle of booze to a new wife and a good job and a baby girl, almost.

It wasn't fair. But that didn't matter.

Finally, I said, "Goodbye, Daddy. I love you. And I miss you. And I forgive you. I forgive you, all right?"

I let go of his arm, but the cold didn't leave my fingertips.

And I was okay with that.

Thirty-seven

Promises Kept
(1980)

AS IT IS for most college seniors, my final semester seemed to end just days after it began.

And, for me, my dad's death meant more relief than grief. To be able to lie in bed at night and no longer wonder what might or might not be happening inside his battered brain was a burden removed.

I looked forward to leaving Hope, but I didn't. It was a place that didn't fit me well. And it fit me perfectly. Ironically, The Pull was the most consequential part of my college experience. I'm not sure I would have felt the same about the place were it not for that unexplainable annual endeavor.

And at Hope, it was instructive and added texture to be around kids who weren't like me: rich kids, preppy kids and preacher's kids, too. And to think I'd fallen in love with one of those preacher's kids. And she would comfort me. The glow of her affection guided me through some of my darkest and most turbulent days. I kept Leanne close to me my last few months at Hope. She was good for me. I hoped I was good for her. She changed me. She made me better because she was better.

But I'd decided to run away, sort of. There were few good jobs near where I lived in Michigan. The area was limping along in a torpid and deep and dreary recession, and big-toothed Jimmy Carter was threatening to dismantle the student loan program. So I decided to continue my schooling while borrowing money was still possible.

I was ready to see and live in a different part of the country. To breathe new air. To escape heartache. Distance was needed. Literally and metaphorically. I welcomed the chance to go someplace I'd never been. To start afresh.

For reasons I didn't fully understand, there was a mysteriousness about North Carolina that was appealing and provocative, almost titillating. I'd never been there, but I'd heard of the beautiful and remote Outer Banks, and I'd seen images of the ribbony highway they called the Blue Ridge Parkway. Anyone who had ever held onto a golf club knew of Pinehurst, a mecca for golf and surrounded by sand hills. I imagined the state smelling of pine and magnolia and to be evergreen and rolling, as far as the eye could see.

And, like most guys my age, I was a college basketball fan. On television, the announcers spoke of the state's "Tobacco Road" like it was a sacred passageway. They worshipped "The Big Four" schools that lined the mystical highway: Duke, Carolina, NC State and Wake Forest. I easily convinced myself it would be fun to spend a couple years eating slaw and pork barbecue and hush puppies that weren't shoes.

I selected Wake Forest. Admittedly, the sorority girls in the brochures reminded me of Catherine in Paris, delicate and light in her cheery sundress and strapped sandals. The images of the leafy campus were not unlike Hope's, and neither was the school's size, though Hope was not in Wake's league in terms of athletics or prestige.

Fortuitously, the design of Wake's master's in business program seemed to match my desires. It was icing on sour cream pound cake that Arnold Palmer, "The King" of golf, went to Wake. And who didn't think that Wake football star, Brian Piccolo, wasn't everyone's hero in the heart-wrenching movie *Brian's Song*?

So Wake it would be.

———◦—◦•◦—◦———

VISCONTI'S WAS A decidedly dingy dumpy downtown Muskegon pub, but in demand and across from the courthouse and jail. The tavern was my primary source of income the summer of 1980. My broken leg and shattered ankle had healed properly, more or less. I sported two hand-some Frankenstein scars that formed a decorative stirrup on my right leg. A permanent conversation piece. I lived at home on Bear Lake Road with my mother and Large Root Beer. I painted houses during the cool Michigan mornings and reported to the bar by four o'clock to help the owners during the raucous happy hour. Then I'd run the place by myself and close with a waitress named Lynn at two in the morning.

Tending bar was interesting, entertaining and sometimes dangerous. The proximity to the jail and courthouse and county building meant I was as likely to sling drinks to a judge or thug or attorney or social worker or cop or court reporter as anyone else. Lawyers were easy to identify because they were loud and in a rush to get drunk. They wore ill-fitting suits and last year's ties, loose around their sagging necks. Uniformed cops didn't come in, but detectives did. They were indistinguishable from the other good guys, or the bad ones, until one flashed a gun, handcuffs or a badge. The judges were arrogant and pompous and patronizing and would approach the bar and demand obscure brands of beer or mixed drinks that required a blender. But I'd put the blender away as soon as the owners left.

The weekday happy hour crowd drank dangerously fast and furious, slamming three or four or more drinks in an hour to get home, pre-medicated, to their waiting husbands or wives or parole officers. Fridays were different. By 4:30 in the afternoon the crowd would begin to swell and, by 5:30, boozers would be elbow to elbow. Ordering a drink required a forceful voice and full-body contact, leaning over and between other patrons and the sticky wooden bar. Folks would splash their drinks and cigarette ashes on each other, but they were toasted and roasted and didn't give a shit. Eventually, the happy hour crowd would flame out and turnover, but on Fridays there were a few hours of overlap with the evening throng, and the transition was seamless and the party went on, unabated, until after midnight.

At nine in the evening, a you-could-drink-him-good guitar player would set up and sing folks songs by Jim Croce and James Taylor and Paul Simon. He was largely ignored until eleven, when liquor transformed the musician into an unappreciated star and the crowd began to sway and sing along to familiar songs. Horny patrons slow-danced between tables and dropped dollar bills into his guitar case.

Lynn, the barmaid, was twenty-ish and redneck-cute. She had perky boobs and a nice butt and bad teeth and an alcoholic boyfriend with a record, a penchant for peril and a poor sense of humor. So I kept my hands and eyes off of Lynn. But Lynn liked danger and make-up sex with her boyfriend, and when he was in the tavern work was transformed into a contact endeavor. She would spend more time near me, and everything she did behind the bar had to come through me. If I was reaching down into the beer cooler, she'd come up behind me and put her hips against my backside and lean across me, with her boobs pressing into my back, when should could have just as easily stepped around.

"He hates you, you know?"

"Why?"

"He's jealous because you're a college boy and 'cause I told him you were cute. And he thinks you flirt with me.

"I think it's the other way around."

"He don't have to know that."

"Does he carry a gun?"

"Not any more, I don't think."

"Get back out there. You two scare me."

On most nights, there were three or four rode-hard-and-put-up-wet types that camped at the end of the bar, near the under-counter wine cooler and on the way to the skanky john. They chain-smoked Salems and drank bad vodka or gin and then switched to house chablis or chardonnay. They were women who never made homecoming court or prom queen, and they'd spent the last decade propping up or bailing out their poor choices in first husbands. Work didn't scare them, but getting old did. Years of cigarette smoke and hard living had yellowed their teeth and sucked life from their skin. But they fought back with discount store cosmetics and slinky tops and big hair and come-fuck-me attitudes that they telegraphed with too-tight jeans and loud, dirty talk and come-hither eyes.

My favorite Visconti's barfly was a lonesome soul named Rita. Like all the rode-hards, she had a decent body and quick tongue and when she inhaled her white wine she made out with the glass while she drank from it. She flirted big and tipped bigger and her generosity kept my attention. I made sure her glass was never empty and I laughed at her stories and I touched her shoulder when I walked by to deliver a tray of drinks for Lynn or bus a table.

Late one Saturday night, Rita slipped off her bar stool and gave me a wink and slid a finger across my hand and said, "Thanks, I'll see you soon."

"Sounds good. Bye, Rita."

Lynn and I made last call at 1:30 a.m. and we had everyone out the door in forty minutes. I sent Lynn home to her jealous boyfriend and I finished washing the dirty glasses and wiped down the tables and the bar. I pulled the cash drawer from the register and locked it in the walk-in cooler in the back, because that's what the owners told me to do. I checked the restrooms in case someone had passed out and I killed the lights and bolted the door behind me.

I stepped away from the building and toward my car on the street. Parked in front of me was a white Chevy van. When I approached my car, the back doors of the van swung open and revealed Rita on her knees, holding a box of pizza. She was wearing jeans, no blouse and spilling over the top of a lacy white bra. "Hotel California" played from speakers mounted inside the rear doors of the van.

"Come on, Patrick. Let's have some pizza."

"Rita, I'm sorry. I'm not hungry. I gotta get home."

"Come on, Patrick. Let's have some pizza. I drove across town to buy this thing. Just you and me. Let's have some pizza."

"Rita, I think you've had too much to drink."

"Have not."

"Yes, you have."

"How about you come on in here and just hold me for a while and we'll listen to the Eagles and then we'll have some pizza?"

"Rita."

"Yes, Patrick?"

"Rita, I gotta tell you, I'm flattered that you want to share your pizza with me. I have to say you look beautiful in your bra and jeans. If I wasn't in a committed relationship, I'm positive we'd be eating pizza. Together. You really look great."

"Fuck you, asshole." She pulled shut the back doors of her van, jumped in the driver's seat, goosed the accelerator while making a U-turn and squealed past the courthouse and police station and me. Where to I didn't know, but she flipped me the bird and shouted "fuck you!" one more time as she roared by.

———

ONE OF MY best friends from Hope was Ralph Skaio. He was tall and awkward and friendly and born and raised in New Jersey, but he lacked the expected abrasive edge. Ralph was short on street smarts and comfortably naïve, but he had an uncommon sensitivity to the human condition. He was empathetic. Someone I could talk to about stuff that most guys would rather avoid. He was one of the few kids at Hope aware of my dad's coma and death. He was a true friend. And Ralph and Leanne got along fine as well.

Ralph knew of my unrealized pacts, promised trips to Beaver Island with Uncle Charlie and my dad. Whether he felt sorry for me or was just curious, I didn't know. But he told me he wanted to share in my adventure.

Beaver's history intrigued me. Uncle Charlie told me that around 1850 James Strang, a polygamist Mormon, proclaimed himself King of Beaver Island and the island a Mormon state. After a couple of years as king, Strang was assassinated by a cadre of his followers and, shortly thereafter, off-island mobs drove Strang's two thousand Mormons from the island. They were quickly replaced by Irish fisherman immigrating from the mainland of Michigan and from Ireland directly. When he recounted the story, Charlie put extra emphasis on "Irish" and "Ireland," as if the gleam in his eyes didn't say enough.

The island's isolation appealed to me. As well as the Irish heritage. It was a destination for folks who loved water and wildlife and the solitude that came with the buffer of miles of deep, blue water in each direction. In addition to sailors and outdoorsmen, the island attracted authors and artists and musicians and anyone who needed to recharge or refresh. Or just get away.

In early August of 1980, Ralph and I packed a borrowed car and left Muskegon before sunset and reached the slumbering village of Charlevoix around eleven. But a hotel room wasn't in our pauper's budget, so we crossed over the whiny drawbridge and the Pine River and drove to a campground just northeast of town. There was no vacancy. The campsites were filled. Down the road we pulled off the two-lane, between Charlevoix and Petoskey, and we rolled out our sleeping bags on a mixture of sand and pebbles along the shore of Lake Michigan's Little Traverse Bay. We reclined under a clear sky, milky white with stars, and hoped that mosquitos wouldn't carry us away.

I slept remarkably well. We woke at daybreak to a sea of glass and common terns catching insects in flight. A pair of piping plovers picked along the water's edge. A lone gull coasted above the tree line, warmly lit by the rising sun, invisible to us but evident by the glowing breast of the bird soaring above.

We shook out our bags, rolled them and packed them away and headed southwest down the two-lane to the ferry dock in Charlevoix, only twenty minutes away. We secured passage on the Beaver Islander and bought a map of the island and went in search of coffee and bagels and orange juice. I used a pay phone to call Leanne to confirm that she and a friend would be arriving in Charlevoix, and then Beaver Island, the next day.

Ralph punched me in the shoulder and said, "So who's my date?"

"It's a surprise."

"I don't like surprises."

I reminded him that I'd never let him down before, and neither had Leanne. He needed to relax and enjoy the Northern Michigan water and air and sun. Everything would be okay.

We boarded the Monday morning ferry just before eight o'clock and sailed out of Round Lake and through the Pine River channel. In minutes, we were in Lake Michigan with a bearing to the northwest. The skies were still clear, but morning haze obscured the island for the first thirty minutes of the three-hour voyage.

The ferry was a hundred feet long with room for ten cars in her hold and at least two hundred passengers. Her belly was full of vehicles, but this morning only a few dozen people were making the trek to America's Emerald Isle. The Big Lake was no longer glass, but the freshening breeze raised mere ripples across the vast expanse of blue. As Charlevoix's pier and lighthouse shrank behind us, so did the weight of misfortune that had plagued me. And I reminisced that finally, some eighteen years after Uncle Charlie first told me about magical Beaver Island and two years since my dad and I made our pact floating in a johnboat on Moon Lake, I was going.

Two hours into our journey we neared the south end of the island and Iron Ore Bay. Then we cruised off her eastern shore for thirty minutes and approached miles-long and crescent-shaped Sand Bay. As we did, in the distance I could see stakes and buoys marking fishing nets in which Indians caught whitefish. Then after passing another mile of mostly wooded and rocky shoreline, we turned to port at a huge floating can marking safe passage into Paradise Bay and the settlement of Saint James.

We could have been arriving at a New England fishing village. A dozen sailboats were tied to white floats on the north side of the harbor. Cruisers and fishing tugs were beached or secured to docks and piers. There was a public beach to the left of our mooring and a neat, white clapboard church, Holy Cross, on a bluff above the shore. Across from the dock, flying the flag of Ireland, was the Shamrock Bar. A dozen vehicles and their drivers stood along Main Street and the pier, waiting for passengers to disembark.

Mail bags and produce were unloaded for the post office and the grocery store. And then friends began to greet friends. The flurry of activity ended almost as quickly as it began. Ralph and I grabbed our tent and cooler and sleeping bags and backpacks and began to walk south looking for Donegal Bay Road that, according to our map, would eventually take us to the township campground on the island's north shore.

Three hundred feet down the road, a farmer in a battered, dusty blue Ford pickup pulled over and said that the cooler and tent looked "mighty heavy" and that he'd be honored to give us a ride. He knew where we were headed.

We loaded the cooler and our gear onto the truck bed and we jumped into the cab. The farmer said the campground was just a mile up the road and that he often gave folks a ride, but that the walk was not bad if we weren't "hauling all that stuff." We asked him what he farmed, and he said that he didn't grow much of anything any longer. It was too costly to try to compete with farmers on the mainland. He just grew enough to sell locally and feed himself and his wife and their animals. We asked if we'd have any problem finding a spot to pitch our tent "because the campground near Charlevoix was full." He chuckled and said, "Shouldn't be a problem."

He dropped us off at the head of a two-track trail. A wooden sign said, "Saint James Township Campground." He told us he went into town every day and to look for him and say hello, and to let him know if we needed anything. We said, "Thanks." And he drove away.

We lugged our stuff a hundred feet down the trail and paused at the edge of a thirty-foot bluff, overlooking Lake Michigan and nearby Garden Island. To the northwest, we could see Squaw and Whiskey Islands. Beyond the islands and the shipping lanes, the Upper Peninsula of Michigan was represented by a ragged, bluish-gray line twenty miles to the north. As though on cue, a freighter, possibly a thousand feet long, appeared beyond Garden Island. Her hull was incomplete. The sun and waves made the great ship look as though she was floating on cotton just above the water line and then, like magic, the cotton disappeared and she steamed onward, to Milwaukee or Chicago or both.

Ralph said, "This is righteous."

I agreed.

A dozen primitive campsites were scattered along the bluff. There was a hand pump for water and a pit toilet, but no electricity. At that moment, we understood the farmer's chuckle. There were no other campers. We had our pick of sites. We chose the spot flattest and nearest the bluff's edge and assembled our green canvas Army surplus tent, which was no easy task.

After making camp, we walked to town and rented a 1969 Ford Galaxy sedan that lacked seat belts, radio, windshield wipers, a taillight and the right rear window. But she was cheap and would be inconspicuous on the island, as most every vehicle we'd seen was a rambling wreck.

We drove a half-mile up Main Street to McDonough's Market and bought beer and food and ice and returned to the campsite. We scavenged kindling and dry wood from the forest. We built a mighty fire before dark and ate cheese sandwiches and drank beer and shared stories and crawled into our tent, after I doused the fire. I told Ralph how much I appreciated his friendship. He said, "likewise," but that he'd hold off final judgment until he met his camping date the next day.

In the middle of night, I woke with my bladder bloated with beer and aching for relief. I untied the tent flaps and stepped into the Michigan evening and nearly soiled my pants. I couldn't see my hand in front of my face.

"Ralph, come here... Ralph, come here, dammit."

I couldn't see Ralph's head, but I knew from his voice that he was out of the tent and he was seeing what I was seeing. Nothing.

"For God's sake, Ralph, I can't see a thing. And I gotta pee."

Clouds had rolled in and obscured the moon and stars. There wasn't a light of any kind for miles. We laughed because he had to pee, too. We'd forgotten a flashlight and we couldn't see to find the matches, so we just stood next to the tent and relieved ourselves and hoped we weren't drowning anything important. We laughed out loud for minutes, with our peckers in our hands and not a worry in the world. Then we crawled back into our tent and giggled ourselves to sleep.

We woke to the jabbering of birds and chipmunks and squirrels and a distant screeching gull. A fresh breeze had pushed the late-night clouds south, and white paws of cats dotted the azure lake. With our noses, we selfishly drank in the smell of the watery world that surrounded us. We built a new fire and boiled water for coffee and ate stale French bread, slathered with crunchy peanut butter and raspberry jam. Life was good.

THE FERRY BUMPED to a final stop at the dock and I spotted delightful and delicious Leanne leaning over the rail on the top level, waving at Ralph and me.

I elbowed Ralph in the side. "Hey, Ralph," I said, "Do you know the words to 'Free Ride'?"

He said, "Is she cute? I don't see her. Tell me she's cute."

I said, "Ralph, old buddy, old pal, she looks like Edgar Winter."

"Are you shittin' me?"

"It'll be all right."

She wasn't unattractive. She was cute, very cute. Leanne's friend had long, fine, white hair, parted in the middle of her head. And white eyebrows. From a distance, she was a dead ringer for Edgar Winter on the 1972 *Free Ride* album cover, seemingly flying through the air, bare-chested and wearing costume jewelry. And bright red lipstick.

In jest, I said, "Ralph, I don't know if there's enough beer on Beaver Island to drink her pretty, but we can try. Come on, buddy. Let's go meet 'em."

The girls had disappeared from the railing and were making their way across the gang plank. Leanne ran to me and jumped into my arms and I started to laugh.

"What?" she said.

"Nothing," I said.

WE TOOK THE Galaxy out on rutted and bumpy Donegal Bay Road and to the bluff-side campsite where the girls marveled at that the panoramic view. They unpacked their gear and the four of us went off to explore.

At Font Lake we first heard a bird's wild laughter and then we saw the lone troubadour, a Common Loon, cruising the far shore of the small, shallow lake. We hiked up a dune the Mormons named Mt. Pisgah. Then we raced down her sandy face, all the way to the shore, and refreshed ourselves by splashing in Donegal Bay. We strolled down the Keebler Trail, once a railroad bed used to move harvested lumber, and we walked

through a meadow where we picked and ate wild raspberries. We passed
Barney's Lake, where the trail turned briefly to sand and then led us back
into the hardwoods and up a path that eventually intersected with a dirt
road where, at the junction, was what looked to be a monument or tomb.

We stood within the walls of the sarcophagus under a canopy of soaring
trees. It was a simple stone-and-mortar rectangle with a gate at one end
and open at the top. The end opposite the opening was slightly higher and
arched. Inside was an imbedded plaque honoring Feodora Protar.

> *To our Heaven sent friend in need*
> *FEODORA PROTAR who never failed us*
> *In imperishable gratitude and adoration*
> *His People of Beaver Island*

In the greenish, copper plate and above the inscription was the engraved
face of an old balding man with long, unruly hair and a scraggly beard.
Without warning, the wind picked up and birds began to sing, and through
the leaves above, the sun danced about the tomb. We decided it felt creepy.
Edgar said she needed a beer.

Back at camp, Ralph and Edgar built another fire and Leanne and I
descended the bluff and made love on the beach between fallen trees as
Lake Michigan lapped at our feet. Then we swam and bathed in the clear,
tepid, shallow waters off the north shore.

Edgar and Ralph were chatting around the fire when Leanne and I
returned. We ate cheese sandwiches and apples and drove into town to
buy more beer at McDonough's Market. On our way back to camp, we
stopped to tip a couple jars at the Shamrock Bar.

The sticky old tavern smelled of sea and pee and was wrapped in dark
paneling. The bar was to the right. The main room had seating for dozens
of patrons. There was a pool table and bandstand at the rear near the
bathrooms. College pennants were tacked to beams above: Michigan, Ball
State, Northern Michigan, Michigan State, Central Michigan and even the
orange and blue of little Hope College. Leanne stood on a chair underneath
the Hope banner. She had on her Sigma Sigma hooded sweatshirt. Ralph
stood on the floor in front of her wearing his blue and white Hope t-shirt.
She put her hands on his shoulders and he gave the thumbs-up signal and I
snapped a picture of them with their beaming smiles, while Edgar urgently
ordered another pitcher of beer.

The next day, the wind switched to the south and we moved our camp in the same direction. We'd learned, in the bar, of a worthy camping site on the north arm of Lake Geneserath. We broke camp and packed the Galaxy and rumbled down ten miles of dirt road on the east side of the island. We set up our new camp among tall white birch trees and aspen whose leaves flashed like pieces of silver in the wind. We borrowed canoes and paddled through lily pads and eventually into the larger expanse of the lake. But the wind got aggressive, so we opted to be pushed back to the camp instead of exploring any further. We ate crackers and cheese and then made a short drive to Iron Ore Bay to get relief from the building heat and humidity. We bodysurfed in the growing waves and drank cold beer in the warm sand. Our only company was a pair of gulls windsurfing in the thickening haze.

We returned to camp and, to our wonder, a man in his thirties and his young son had pitched a tent nearby. He told us that they were about to make a run into town for more provisions. He asked us if we needed anything. Edgar said, "12-pack of Stroh's beer," and she handed the man a ten-dollar bill.

We built a fire and ate and drank and told stories until well after dark. There was no apparent spark between Ralph and Edgar, but they seemed to get along. And the girls were crack campers. They embraced the primitive conditions and the sense of freedom and detachment and rebirth and camaraderie that Beaver Island inherently inspired. And we were happy and relaxed and without a worry in the world. It all felt so good.

A series of noisy storms rolled through after midnight. Thunder exploded around us and sheets of rain soaked our old canvas home. I prayed that one of the tall birch trees wouldn't fall victim to the wind or lightening and come crashing down on us. I considered evacuating to the car, but my fellow campers were deep in beer-assisted sleep. The next morning we were treated to bluebird skies and winds out of the northwest. And no humidity to speak of.

We hiked from our camp across the Eastside Road and down a trail and over the bluff to another deserted Lake Michigan beach. Armed with bars of soap and shampoo, and in our swimsuits, we bathed together in the quieting lake. With the offshore breeze, hungry black flies emerged by the hundreds. We were protected from bites only when covered with soap and shampoo. So we lathered up our heads and faces and kept our bodies submerged and yakked about nothing until our fingertips began to shrivel. Then we rinsed and sprinted to our towels.

We broke camp one last time and tossed everything into the trunk of the Galaxy. We said farewell to the man and his boy and drove north toward town, parallel to the Lake Michigan shoreline. After we passed the cottages that dotted Sand Bay, the road peeled away from the water. A doe and two fawns scampered in front of us. We passed a ragged nine-hole golf course that had neither clubhouse nor players. Then we went by Welke's Airport, with its dirt and grass airstrip, where rabbits outnumbered planes. We returned the Ford to the cabin rental agency, that also rented cars, and we ate a late, hearty breakfast back at the Shamrock Bar, where we waited to take the Beaver Islander back across the Big Lake, to Charlevoix.

We devoured western omelets and hash browns and sausage links and drank drip coffee and orange juice, and we tried to calculate the number of beers we'd consumed since we'd arrived. As we settled our bill, horn blasts from the ferry announced her impending departure. We scurried across Main Street and boarded the green-and-white boat.

The Beaver Islander reversed, pivoted and pulled away from the village. Friends and family waved goodbye and we waved as well, to people we didn't know. But everybody was waving to everyone and it felt good, but sad, to say goodbye. The harbor was teeming with sailboats and motor yachts and industrious islanders readying their tugs and barges and fishing vessels. At the mouth of the harbor, an ancient lighthouse stood sentry near docks and the peeling Coast Guard station, long abandoned but still sturdy and proud with her red tile roof.

Edgar retreated to a bench and began to read a book. Ralph, sitting a few feet away, fell quickly asleep, with his head slung so far back it appeared disconnected from his shoulders. His mouth was gaping. My good buddy began to snore while the boat gently rocked him.

Leanne and I stood together on the ship's bow, side by side, with the wind in our faces, the water below, and the rest of our lives in front of us.

She lit a path for me when clouds of doom obscured the sun and moon.

She faced the unknown with uncommon faith and courage.

She was friend and companion and lover.

I considered perhaps that, in Leanne, I had found the best thing in my life. But too early.

She felt the same, I thought.

And while we were meant to be, we were not meant to be forever.

I was going to miss her. I already did.

Thirty-eight

Dixie

WHEN FRIENDS ASKED where I planned to attend graduate school, I'd say, "Wake Forest."

They'd respond, "Isn't that near Chicago?"

And I'd say, "Do I seem like the kind of pompous preppy that would go to a school for cake eaters?

The response would baffle and bemuse. My unapologetic intent.

Lake Forest, Illinois, was home to a college with the same name as the city. The school that I was to attend, in Winston-Salem, North Carolina, shared a confusingly similar name, and a demography of privilege and an air of prestige. But Lake Forest and Wake Forest were on different sides of the Mason-Dixon Line, and my destination was the Land of Dixie.

Making matters more muddled, Wake Forest College, as it was once called, wasn't originally established in Winston-Salem, but in Wake Forest—the city—just outside of Raleigh. But in the 1950s, tobacco money brought Wake Forest a hundred miles west to Winston-Salem. And a university was born.

On a bright, hot, late summer day in the middle of August of 1980, I lashed my ten-speed bike onto my battered, blue VW 411 wagon, hugged my mom goodbye, gave a nod to Large Root Beer and sputtered down our dirt drive and away from Bear Lake and Muskegon and Michigan— the places I knew so well—to turn over some rocks in the red clay of the piedmont of North Carolina and see what surprises laid underneath.

I felt little anxiety and for no good reason—confidence that escaping to the South would be good for me. I had to borrow as much money to attend my first year at Wake as for the full four years at Hope. But I was optimistic and looking for adventure. In my lifetime, I'd talked to just two people from the state of North Carolina. The first was a girl at Hope I met my junior year. She was from the eastern part of the state. The way she said, "y'all" made my knees buckle. The second was my roommate-to-be. A slow-talking, aw-shucks kid named Max.

Max's name was on a list I received by mail in early July of students looking to share housing. I gave him a call. With his undulating drawl, Max sounded like Gomer Pyle on Valium. But he was courteous and friendly. He told me he'd be happy to find a place near campus to live. He asked if I minded if he unearthed a third roommate. "It'll save us quite a bit of money. Boy howdy."

I said, "You go right ahead, Max."

I broke my trip into two segments, spending the first night in Cleveland with Leanne at her parents' house. Then the next morning, I pointed my car south, toward North Carolina. It was five o'clock in the afternoon when I reached Winston-Salem and my apartment building. As I opened the VW's door, the heat reached inside and nearly pulled the air right out of me. The possibility of suffocation crossed my mind. Or spontaneous combustion. The sun exploded across the blacktop. The stillness was endless. Heat seared my face and neck. In seconds, my t-shirt was wet with sweat and I could feel perspiration running down my legs, under my jeans and streaming down the valley in my back. The air didn't move. Nothing moved. I said to myself, "Everything is dead." And then I heard the buzzing cackle of a katydid. First one and then two. There was life after all.

Max was amiable, and a pothead. He must have been thoroughly stoned when he selected our third roommate. The guy, Brad, was best described as a whiny-ass who, I expected, had a tiny dick. Smaller than a chicken's. Brad pouted about anything and everything. He was the most miserable person I'd ever met. But I could live with anyone, even Brad. And then one evening, after I'd finished washing the dishes, Brad sauntered into the kitchen. Between the backsplash and the sink he noticed a two-inch tall, wind-up plastic penguin. To amuse myself, but mostly to humor perpetually-high Max, I would wind the toy and let it swim in the soapy water, while

I washed dinner dishes.

I had just opened my Advanced Corporate Finance book on the dining room table and Max was French kissing his bong when Brad proclaimed, "Patrick, there will be no more toys in the kitchen. The kitchen is no place for toys."

"Go fuck yourself with something sharp," were the words that sprung forth from my lips. I wasn't going taking Brad's crap any longer. For two months, I'd tolerated his sniveling and snarling. Life was too short. I told them I'd be gone by the weekend. Brad retreated to his bedroom and slammed the door. Max took a prolonged hit from his bong, uninterested in conflict and resigned to a dismal year.

·——————————·

ED FELTON WAS paunchy, but not obese. He looked sixty, but I expected he was fifty. He had pale, pulpy skin and slick, thinning black hair and a doctorate and MBA from Harvard and a degree in divinity from someplace southern, but he looked like a sloppy, underpaid undertaker in his cheap black suit. As dean of the graduate school of business, he was our intrepid leader, and our introduction to the school was his "Doomed to Fail" speech. A deficient and transparent attempt at motivation by intimidation, but both he and his sermon were dull and ineffectual.

Minutes into Ed's monologue, I tuned him out and surveyed my new classmates. It was evident that I had little in common with the hall of men uniformed in starched, long-sleeved, button-down oxford shirts and crisp khakis and tasseled loafers. Some wore navy or black blazers. Their faces were clean shaven and hair close cropped. They reeked of Greek life and country clubs and second homes at the beach and dances with debutantes at cotillion. They sat attentively with good posture and seemed to hang on Ed's every word. I scanned the room in search of heretics like me and when I found them—and there were a few—we'd communicate by rolling our eyes and smirking as Ed blathered on.

I stuck out in my Visconti's Tavern t-shirt and Levi's and rubber flip flops. But there were a handful of others who had missed the memo on dress code. And, for the most part, the kids at Wake were good and personable, as was the talented faculty and attentive staff. They seemed to appreciate having a kid from Michigan on the leafy campus. The majority of the business students were from the Carolinas and Virginia, and I felt like my

Midwestern character and perspective were instructive and constructive. Over time, I began to feel at home at Wake and in Winston-Salem.

———— ❖ ————

A CLASSMATE, Tony, lived in the basement of a house two blocks from campus. He invited me to sleep on a cot, until I found permanent housing. He rented from a pair of elderly ladies who lived upstairs. They were sweet and reminded me of Great-grandma Bessie. One was an invalid for whom I gladly ran errands and wiped tapioca pudding and oatmeal from her fuzzy chin when I went upstairs to deliver the groceries, or just visit for a while.

Tony hosted a party before a Pat Benatar concert and I met a girl named Minxy Bland. She was a townie and spoke with a warm, cultured southern accent, but with a raspy, redneck edge that seemed incongruous, but wasn't. She was tall and athletic and hard and lean and had shoulder-length, dark hair and darker eyes. There was something about her that was mysterious and dangerous. And ridiculously sexy.

"Hi. I'm Patrick."

"Hey. My name's Minxy."

"Minxy," I said. "I like that."

"Most people don't know what it means," she said.

"You mean your name?"

"Yep. My name."

"I know what it means."

"You don't. No one does."

I said, "Minxy is a derivative of the root word minx. Minx is a noun, often used in humorous or derogatory context, meaning cunning or boldly flirtation young woman or pert, playful female. Minxish is an acceptable derivative, an adjective. Technically speaking, minxy is an inappropriate derivative, but I'll make an exception in your case."

Minxy slammed her fist into my shoulder. Twice. "How the fuck did you do that?" Immediately followed by "excuse my French."

"I memorized the dictionary."

"You have a photographic memory?"

"No. I have a pornographic memory."

"What'd you say?"

"Yes, I have a photographic memory. The root word for your name appears on page 801 of the *American Heritage Dictionary* (published by Houghton Mifflin). Sometimes I get the page numbers confused, so don't hold me to that. Minxy, are you promiscuous?"

She punched me in the shoulder again. Even harder.

I sang, "Hit me with your best shot."

She said, "Hey, Pat Benatar. That's funny. You're funny."

We chuckled and chatted, then drifted apart, afloat in a sea of mirth and impaired by Kentucky Bourbon.

I laughed out loud when Pat Benatar belted out, "Hit Me With Your Best Shot" in Wait Chapel on Wake's campus. I hoped Minxy did, too.

I didn't have the opportunity, that night, to apprise Minxy that my mom and Large Root Beer owned a black Labrador named Minx.

I'd always thought the name was clever.

I KEPT MY promise to Tony and moved out of the basement apartment and away from the old ladies upstairs. After December exams, I moved in with a guy named Jack, whose real name was John.

Jack was in the same program as Tony and Brad and Max and me but, unlike us, he'd attended Wake as an undergrad. He was from Virginia and, apparently, a family of privilege. He had matching, store-bought bedroom furniture and dozens of starched, pinpoint oxford cloth shirts in every hue imaginable. And he had ten pairs of khakis and ten pairs of shoes. Jack was tall and handsome and he had a booming, deep voice and winner-take-all, master-of-the-universe, fuck-them-if-they-can't-take-a-joke ambition. He was singular in his focus. He was going to be to be a rich, Wall Street investment banker. Not so coincidently, one of his Sigma Chi fraternity brothers told me his undergraduate nickname was God.

SALEM COLLEGE WAS located in Old Salem. The school for women was established by the Moravians, an early Protestant denomination that settled the area. Moravians were famous for their Love Feasts. But if you showed up at one with a six-pack of Stroh's and a box of Trojans, you'd probably feel out of place and be asked to leave in a hurry.

Old Salem was just blocks from downtown Winston-Salem and a few miles south of Wake's campus. The college's buildings and the community's shops and squares and homes and gardens had been impeccably and authentically restored to historic perfection. Looking as it did when the Moravians founded a girls' school there, in 1772.

Salem College sponsored occasional mixers. There were just a handful of women in our program at Wake, and there were no men at Salem College, so the parties were a welcome opportunity to meet coeds and vice versa.

A favorite classmate at Wake was a guy who played football for Western Maryland, Dave Wahrhaftig. Dave was uncommonly brilliant and disturbingly neurotic and he knew the words to every Bruce Springsteen song. We became fast friends. He'd introduce me to Salem girls as "the future youngest Governor of Michigan." It was the size of the lie that made it believable. Salem girls were the progeny of diplomats and politicians and investment bankers. They'd met their share of high-profile business mavens and celebrity statesmen.

But I always came clean. They liked the lie. And they liked the truth. I was just a regular guy, from a foundry town in Michigan, tip-toeing my way through a garden of southern belles. Clueless as to how far south I could go.

I met Georgina Dobie at my first Salem soirée. She stood out, literally, because she was two yards long, barefooted. Initially I thought she was Australian but, as I learned, she was from South Africa. Georgina had been a runway model in Paris and London. She attended boarding school in England, but had matriculated at Salem at the insistence of her parents.

She was a spectacular beauty and a pleasure to talk to—personable and witty and seemingly with world in the palm of her hand. But I learned she was lonely and bored and missed London and Paris, and she said, "I've yet to be asked on a date."

Before I could think straight, I said, "Until now."

The next Saturday night, I rang the bell at South Hall (built in 1805) and was greeted by a proper and polite coed who invited me to register and have a seat. She told me that she'd go upstairs, to Georgina's room, and advise her that her escort awaited.

Georgina began her reveal at the top of the ancient, wooden stairway. I didn't anticipate a reprise of my mom's topless performance at the rental on Clarklake, but then again I wasn't sure what to expect. First I saw her feet, which were strapped into chunky, open-toed midnight pumps.

And then just two inches of alabaster skin that disappeared into black leggings that dissolved just below her rump beneath the creamy tail of a sheer blouse that was unbuttoned to the waist, open across her chest and revealing a black knit camisole that handsomely displayed her ample bosom. Her hair was the color of cinnamon and sugar and straight and long to the bottom of her back, and braided on the sides. Woven into each long braid were tawny feathers, punctuated with white and tan beads. The look was unexpected and delightful. I told her she was beautiful. A fact I knew she knew. She smiled and kissed me on the cheek and grabbed my arm and said, "We're off."

Georgina was humored but considerate when she became acquainted with my battered car. On the drive south, in August, the mountains of West Virginia were too much for the old girl. Something had gone terribly wrong with the steering mechanism. Just turning corners created a loud, annoying chatter. The car shimmied and shuttered so violently that people stared.

She said she knew something about cars. I said, "How's that?" Georgina told me her dad owned the distribution rights to Mercedes-Benz, as well as other brands, for the African continent. I told her my dad used to own a trailer full of empty whiskey bottles and that he controlled distribution rights in Ohio and Michigan. She laughed and said, "Where's Ohio?"

I told her my plan was to take her to my apartment where I would grill hamburgers and then we could go to a movie, or maybe a bar. She liked the idea with the condition that we picked up beer and a bag of Chips Ahoy cookies.

I cooked and we ate and drank beer on my patio. Afterwards she asked if I'd show her my bedroom. "Okay," I said. I had a mattress that sat directly on the floor and two cardboard boxes in which I kept the clothes that I couldn't hang in my closet. There was a lamp next to my mattress. On the wall, I'd pinned a roadmap of Michigan.

And then, I thought she asked me, "Do you have any photography?"

"I barely had enough room for my clothes in my car, so I didn't bring any photography."

"No, silly boy. Pornography. Do you have any pornography?"

"Uh, no."

"Okay. Well then, would you like to go to a dirty movie?"

I was flummoxed. She wasn't kidding.

"I've always wanted to see an American dirty movie, okay?"

She was aware, she said, from the newspaper, that there was a local "drive-in" that showed pornographic movies.

I pulled the newspaper out of the trash. She was right, there was a movie theater on the north side of town, only a few miles from my apartment. And they showed adult flicks.

"What the heck? Let's do it."

I packed a cooler with ice and beer and my suddenly giddy pornographic princess grabbed the cookies. In twenty minutes, I had my car positioned at the optimal viewing angle and the speaker secured in my window. As luck would have it, we were in time for the first feature.

In the opening scene, a reasonably attractive big-breasted blonde was semi-reclined on a brown leather couch. As she explored her personal nether regions, there was a "knock- knock-knock" at the door. She rolled off the divan and bounced to the door and said, "Who is it?"

"My name's Johnny Wadd. Open the door. I'm a detective."

The not-so-distressed woman said, "How do I know it's you?"

He said, "I'll show you my identification."

The blonde secured the safety chain on the door and then flipped the dead bolt and opened the door until the chain stopped it.

Johnny said, "Here's my ID." Through the crack in the door appeared his massive penis. Georgina gasped and said, "Oh, my God," speaking though her hand.

Forty minutes into the movie and almost through scene three, I felt a touch on my elbow. I looked at Georgina and she looked at me and I thought to myself, "This girl is going to blow cookies and beer all over my dashboard."

There were only crumbs left in the bag of cookies. She'd washed them down with too many Buds. The combination was toxic. She started to rub her tummy and wipe saliva from her mouth. I feared we'd never make it back to Old Salem in time.

She was feeling better when we reached campus. She apologized. I told her not to worry and that I still thought she was beautiful. She'd given me a night to remember. That no one would ever believe. I said, "Georgina, if I ever get the chance to write a book, you'll be in it." She smiled and kissed me on the cheek one last time.

Then disappeared.

⟡————⟡⬢⟡————⟡

MINXY AND I met again, at a luau. Two months after the Pat Benatar concert. She said she liked my grass skirt. I told her I liked her coconuts.

And one thing led to another.

⟡————⟡⬢⟡————⟡

JACK AND I were each asked to the Salem College spring formal. My date was smart and friendly, but she looked like Mr. Ed, the talking horse. I was home in my own stall alone and asleep by midnight. When I'd last seen Jack he was dancing the shag with someone else's date and singing for all to hear in his booming voice, "Carolina girls...best in the world" and spinning and grinning from one preppy ear to the other.

At 2:30 in the morning, a ringing phone interrupted my sleep. I answered and Officer Todd Brown asked if I knew John Lough. I said, "Yes, you must mean Jack." He gave me directions to the police station and emphasized that if I didn't fetch Jack, "He'll be spending the night."

At the jail, Brown told me that he'd observed Jack repeatedly back his car up and then pull forward, across the railroad tracks near the cemetery, called God's Acre, adjacent to Salem's campus. He administered a field sobriety test and Jack failed. He refused the breathalyzer, but the officer said that Jack and his date had been well-behaved and otherwise agreeable. So he told Jack he would let him go home, with a ticket, if released into somebody's custody—me.

The officer took my driver's license and disappeared. Jack was sitting alone with his head down in a row of plastic chairs and along a wicker-colored cinder block wall. He hadn't noticed me, but when he did he jumped to his feet at mock attention. His regimental striped tie was still knotted tightly, with one small dimple, and slightly off center, by design. His Brooks Brothers suit pants and crisp, white shirt looked like they'd just been picked up from the dry cleaner. His jacket lay neatly across the back of the chair next to him. He was wearing gaudy cufflinks and skinny, black wingtips. He looked remarkably together, given the late hour and the circumstances.

He was Mr. Perfect until he opened his mouth and what came out was indiscernible babble. He was annoyed and agitated and I asked him to sit down and to "try and relax." He said, "This is shit. Not fair. Damn him. Fucker."

I explained to Jack that Officer Brown said he'd been driving erratically and failed the field sobriety test. Jack said that he "wasn't" and "didn't." He abruptly jumped to his feet, cracked his knuckles, and proceeded to walk me through the arrest.

He'd calmed himself down, to a degree. He was more deliberate with his speech. Jack explained that his car had stalled while he was crossing the crown of the railroad tracks, and he had trouble getting the stick shift back into the correct gear. He was adamant that he did not repeatedly go back and forth across the tracks.

"Okay. How about the sobriety test?"

First he replayed the finger-to-nose drill. Jack said he passed it "with freakin' flying colors." Then he told me he was asked to walk a straight line, heel-to-toe.

Jack turned his back to me and walked twenty feet. Then he faced me again and squatted and put his hands out in front for balance. He looked like a well-dressed, preppy, Russian folk dancer as he walked in a crouch with his feet spread widely apart and with his weight on his haunches. He extended his right leg straight out in front of him and when his heel hit the floor he said, "Heel." Then he rocked forward on the same foot. And when he was up on his toes he said, "Toe." He repeated the drill with the left leg, and then the right, and then the left. Eventually finishing in front of me.

I struggled to contain my laughter.

"Well, you definitely went straight, more or less. And you clearly walked from heel to toe. But I think you misinterpreted the instructions."

He looked at me like I was from Mars. When we got outside I walked heel-to-toe down a line painted on the parking lot. Jack recognized his error and yelled, "Fuck!" He snatched his keys from my hands and jumped into the car and sped away.

Thirty-nine

Curly

THE VW DIDN'T survive my first year in Winston-Salem. It died shortly after my date with the runway model and porn fanatic, Georgina. I got a hundred bucks for it. And the salvage yard owner agreed to haul it away.

My ride north in May was in the seatless back of a Ford Bronco next to a cooler of thawing shrimp. Fortuitously, my mom and three of her derelict girlfriends were returning to Michigan after a week of too-much-sun and too-much-fun in Florida. They made a slight but appreciated detour to provide a ride.

Minxy volunteered to store my bike and a couple of cardboard boxes filled with text books and clothes for the summer. She stopped at my place to say goodbye, and I loaded my stuff into her trunk. I hugged her and I said, "Thanks, girl. See you in a few months." She left after a long kiss and a short wave.

During the spring, by working the phone and writing letters, I was able to secure an internship with Herman Miller, the furniture company Wally's dad worked for. The job wasn't at their headquarters in Zeeland, near Holland and Hope, but in Grand Rapids. I'd have an hour commute each way.

I needed reliable transportation. Large Root Beer told me he couldn't lend me the cash. I called my mom's brother, Uncle John Sweetland, and made my case. He mailed me a check and I paid him back by the end of the summer. I bought a 1977 Pontiac Catalina with eighteen thousand miles on it. The car was beige and brown and plain and perfect.

On a Monday night in late May the phone rang. It was my high school buddy Ted Edsall.

"Hey, what's up?"

"What's up with you?"

"Nothing. Just trying to sell radio ads, you know. Hey, me and Roger, Tim and Jake and some of the guys, we're going over to JC's tomorrow night. It's Two-fer Tuesday. Come on out."

"I gotta drive to GR at seven every morning. I'm working for Herman Miller. I just started. I can't do it."

"Carrie will be there."

"I'll try and make it."

"See ya."

"See ya. Bye."

Ted had introduced me to Carrie the previous summer. He'd invited me to play beach volleyball at Pere Marquette Park on the south side of town, the same stretch of sand on Lake Michigan that I'd visited as a kid with Woody and Mik.

Between sets, I noticed a girl with a tangled mop of curls in a black bikini, sunning on a white sheet. I asked Ted who she was and he said, "Carrie Kloap." He introduced us. She was there with her kid sister, Sue, who was also cute. But Carrie gave me goose bumps. The good kind. I told Ted, "I'm gonna marry that girl someday."

I didn't talk to her again that summer, but I happened upon her at a party on the north side at Jennifer Tuttle's house on New Year's Eve, 1980. I was there with Gail. Carrie said she remembered me from the beach. I told her she looked better with her clothes off, in her little black bikini. She punched me in the shoulder. Hard.

"Are you in school?"

"When we met, I'd just graduated from Hope. Now I'm at Wake. In North Carolina. Business school. How 'bout you?"

"I'm at Western now. Five-year plan. Started at Central. Design major."

"Are you here with her?" She tilted her curls in the direction of Gail.

"Kind of. We used to date."

When I arrived at the bar she was there with her friends and my buddies. She greeted me with an affectionate hug and toothy smile, like we were long lost friends. Maybe we were. For the next two hours, for me, she was the only other person in the club. Everything around her faded, and fell away. It was thunderously loud and to talk we had to be in each other's ear, with our mouths. A simple conversation became a wondrous exploration of her neck and nape. Her hair tickled my lips and nose. She smelled of jasmine powdered with sugar. We continued to talk. And occasionally danced. At eleven I told her I had to leave because of work in the morning. She said, "hold on" and wrote her name and number on the back of a bar napkin. She folded and then pressed the paper into the palm of my hand, and said, "Call me."

CARRIE LIVED ON Forest Park Road, on the north shore of Mona Lake, down a long, serpentine drive befitting the daughter of the president of the largest gray iron foundry in town. I pulled up to her house, white and magnificent, the first Saturday of June, 1981. Her mom, Nancy, was pretending to sweep out an already pristine garage while wearing heels. She greeted me with cold, military efficiency. I felt as welcome as a gigolo in a nunnery.

"Park there. Carrie will be right out."

"Yes, ma'am. Thank you."

I didn't wait long. We rode to a dive bar in the Lakeside neighborhood next to a dollar movie theater that was playing *The Postman Always Rings Twice*. We drank beers in the bar and I excused myself to go to the restroom, where I was welcomed by a plastic garbage bag over the urinal and a junkie shooting up dope in the only stall. I used the ladies' room instead. And told Carrie we should go.

We drank cheap white wine, in red Solo cups, poured from a bottle we'd smuggled in Carrie's purse. We watched Jack Nicholson ravage an eager and seductive and luscious Jessica Lang on a kitchen table in a scene that was so real I thought I smelled sex. I hoped that Carrie wasn't offended. I put my hand on her arm and she put her other hand on mine. Then I knew that she was okay.

After the movie, we drove to my side of town, to the Bear Lake Tavern, a neighborhood restaurant and bar that was small, but iconic. She said she'd heard of the pub before but "never been."

The bar was festive and the owner, Jimmy Moyes, was holding court and pouring drinks for patrons. We shared a pitcher of beer and ate taco salads topped with shredded cheddar cheese and sour cream and olives. We were lifted by the energy of friends and neighbors and strangers celebrating, around us.

"How about a walk?" I said.

"Sure. Where to?"

"Across the street. To the boatyard. On Muskegon Lake."

We crossed Ruddiman Drive and walked, holding hands, along the west side of the narrow channel that connected Bear Lake to Muskegon Lake. We followed the channel to its end, a point of land that was home to a dozen sailboats in dry dock and each on its own massive, wooden cradle. Next to us was a single-masted thirty-two foot Morgan, with a ladder propped against her stern.

I pointed to the Morgan. "Would you like to go for a sail?"

"Sure. I'd love to."

I led up the ladder and then I turned and offered her my hand and welcomed her onboard with our first kiss. We sat together, on the cushioned bridge, with our feet up and Muskegon Lake below and beyond. The moonlit waters were framed by silhouetted sand dunes to the west and the lights of the city to the south. And as if satisfied with the setting, the fluttering halyards of the airborne regatta chattered against their masts in restrained applause while the wind blew us closer together, in search of warmth and comfort in the freshening breeze.

Our colloquy was uncommonly easy and natural and relaxed. We shared highlights of our life stories and glimpses into our souls and we grew increasingly comfortable with each other as our conversation sailed along. She aspired to be a graphic designer and intended to move to Dallas later in the summer. "Maybe I'll meet a dentist there," she said. I told her that I wanted to work in marketing or for an ad agency. I wasn't sure where I would live, but not New York or Chicago, and that I was growing to enjoy the South. Maybe I'd live there.

We weren't looking for love, we told each other, but maybe we were and we just didn't know it. On that boat, I fell in love. I'd been in love before. I knew how it felt. And this was it, only better. It was improbable and odd and beautiful and real.

A week after our first date, I introduced Carrie to my mom and Large

Root Beer. She came to my house. And it happened again. I felt chills and got goose bumps when I saw her. I think my mom did, too.

Her hair was dark brown and nothing but curls. The unruliness was exciting and irreverent. She carried herself with the confidence of a beautiful woman. And she was. She had broad shoulders atop a fashion model's body that blended to a sexy athleticism that was yummy to see and touch. Her Eastern European nose was not perfect, which made it exactly so. Her cheeks were subtle and did not detract from the harmony of her eyes and chin and mouth. Her upper lip was thin, almost invisible when her mouth was closed, and the ideal complement to her nose and almond eyes of blue and narrow eyebrows that framed a picture of prettiness and grace. I was implausibly proud for my mom to meet her. I'd never felt like that before. The instant of their meeting was indelible and singular and meaningful and entirely unanticipated. And welcome validation.

We dated just weeks. Then she left me for Texas.

Over the short summer, I spent time with her mom and dad and sisters. I was certain her mom didn't like me. But I wasn't sure she cared for anyone. I believed her sisters were fond of me. And I didn't know if that mattered. Her dad and I got along fine. He was fighting a vain and painful campaign with cancer and heart disease. I didn't feel like I'd met the real John Kloap. Not the whole man, anyway. But he treated me kindly and with respect and I thought perhaps that, at one time, we could have become great friends and that he would have been a mentor to me. I could see in his long, gray face that his fate had been sealed. I was saddened to see the great man diminished and dying.

Just before departing for North Carolina for my second and last year of graduate school, I received a letter from Carrie postmarked August 12, 1981.

Dearest Patrick,

…I said earlier that…I could not conceive myself getting married for a while. To be honest, I don't know if at this time I am ready to walk down the…aisle. However, I do believe I have found someone I could walk down that aisle with and spend the rest of my life trying to make happy. I am going to miss you more than you could possibly imagine (well, maybe you could) and I can't wait 'till the time…I won't have to miss you anymore.

I love you,

Carrie

Forty

No More Beer

BACK IN WINSTON-SALEM, I met Minxy for cold longnecks. And I told her about Carrie.

She said, "I understand. People fall in love. But we had some fun. You and me."

"I want us to stay friends," I said. "I'll come by and pick up my bike and boxes. I don't want my things to be in your way."

Minxy said that she was happy for me. She'd drop off my things over the weekend. I didn't have to come get them. It wouldn't be a problem.

We kissed. Just a peck. "I gotta go," she said. With a wink and a smile, she turned and swung her little boy's butt back and forth as she exited the bar.

The next Sunday morning, sometime between last call and first light, Minxy kept her promise and pulled into the driveway of my rental. She palmed her horn with both arms extended. Lamps popped on around the neighborhood. Curtains were pulled back and heads were exposed of those curious and concerned. I watched and listened from inside the house and through my open bedroom window, not eager to engage a woman full of scorn and beer and bourbon. She screamed my name and made sure everyone in earshot knew that I was a "selfish son-of-a-bitch," and that she never really liked me anyway, and that "fuckin' Yankees" couldn't be trusted.

She was all legs, in a denim mini and a black knit top, when she pulled two boxes from her backseat and turned them upside down, at the foot of my porch, first one box and then the other. Then she stomped on my clothes and books and screamed "fuck" and "fucker" and "fucking bastard."

Crying, she got back into her car and slammed the door shut and then yelled "fuck!" again. She pounded a fist on her dashboard and got out of her car and opened the trunk and dragged out my bike and dropped it to the ground. Then she reached back into the trunk one more time and heaved my front wheel across the yard. Finally in her car again, and with the door shut, it lurched backward into the street and then forward, spinning tires and spitting gravel down the road.

When the coast was clear, my new roommates, Tim and Rob, stoned and shaken, respectively, helped pick up my belongings from in front of our house. The night returned to calm and lights were dimmed. The neighborhood went back to sleep.

I thanked my roommates and went to bed and hoped that Minxy would be safe. I had no previous experience with her to think that she could be twisted so tightly, and that the unwinding would be crazy and frightening and dangerous. And just a little bit sexy, too.

<hr />

I WAS SITTING in my Advanced Operations class, actually paying attention to the lecturer, Bill Berry, when the dean came into the hall and asked that I step outside. The grim look on his face foreshadowed woe. He got straight to the point.

"I just got off the phone with one of your mom's friends. I hate to tell you this, but your stepfather has had a devastating stroke and is unresponsive. And on a ventilator. Your mom is not up to talking to you right now but you're to get on a plane, as soon as possible, and be by her side."

I stared back at him, trying to process what I'd just heard.

God. Not again.

"My office is checking on flights. Go home and pack and call back here and we'll discuss your options. We'll get you a ride to the airport. We'll call your mom's friend and give them your itinerary and someone will pick you up at the airport in Muskegon and take you directly to the hospital."

"Okay," I said. "Thanks."

"Patrick, I'm sorry."

"I know. Me, too."

On October 1, 1981, a tall, thin man greeted me at the airport gate in

Muskegon. He shook my hand with a sturdy grip and told me how sorry he
was. He was a friend and associate of my mom's brother, John Sweetland.
He'd relocated to town recently to run a company that built commercial
docks and piers in the tributaries to the Great Lakes. We chatted about his
business and the small talk filled time while he drove me to the hospital.
Rain pelted the windshield. The heartbeat of the wipers kept time with
mine. It was cold and wet outside. Dark and foreboding. I missed North
Carolina and dreaded what I expected was next.

In twenty minutes, we were at Hackley Hospital. The same place my
mom finished nursing school eleven years earlier. A block south across
Laketon Avenue and the railroad tracks was Marsh Field, where I played
summer baseball and fractured my leg and splintered my ankle. Less than
a football field to the west was the simple house where Harold and Billy
Woodard raised five kids, including my buddy Woody, dead three years.

My uncle's friend parked his car and led me to a waiting room somewhere upstairs in the hospital. We shook hands, again, and I said, "Thanks
for the ride and good luck." He nodded his head and turned and disappeared. My mom's rumpled buddies were there, a collective mess, with
their sagging shoulders and bloodshot eyes and runny noses and long,
sullen faces. One by one, I hugged them. And thanked them. They were
there for her.

He was thirty-eight years old and six years younger than my mom. She
and Large Root Beer had been married ten years. I honestly didn't know
who he was. For half of that time, I was away at Hope and Wake. He never
took much interest in me. But he didn't marry me either.

When they tied the knot, I didn't see it coming. They did it in secret
while I was away in Jackson, visiting my drunken dad. The first five years
he was in my life, I was dealing with Daddy's self-destruction and navigating the perils of adolescence. I was absorbed in sports and searching for
something to anesthetize me from the painful realities of life.

Large Root Beer struck me as odd the first time I met him. And that
feeling never subsided. There was no connection between us. No love
or hate. He was just there—for my mom. He was on the sidelines, with
respect to my life, and never really in my game until now.

When I first saw my mom, she looked tired and older and shorter and
beaten down. She shuffled her feet across the floor toward me. I met her.
And we held each other.

"We waited for you," she said.

She led me into his hospital room. The blinds were drawn and the lights off. It was dark, but for casts of blue and gray projected from monitors. He was dead, and still alive. The clacking and wheezing ventilator blew life into his lungs. His head was tilted and his visage, thankfully, shielded by a mask and tubes and tape and facing away, as though locked in a stare with the machine that sustained him. My mom asked if I wanted to go around the bed to see him. I shook my head, "No."

Our conversation with the doctor was brief. There was vast brain damage. The doctor was clear and concise. Papers had been prepared in anticipation of the decision.

My mom asked if I would stay with her in the room. I said, "No, I'm sorry. I can't."

I'd decided, on the flight north, that I'd rather imagine how he died than to be there. I'd had my fill of death and dying. I knew my mom would want me there. But I expected she'd understand. And I think she did. After all, he was already dead, really. Just like my dad.

The decision to terminate was not difficult. Reason trumped hope. Reality overruled superstition. She stayed to watch and be at his side when his chest rose and fell one last time.

We went back to the house on Bear Lake Road, relieved and in shock from the suddenness. And deeply saddened. Neighbors and friends responded and delivered food and bottles of wine. I excused myself to my bedroom to unpack and shower and change. The doorbell rang. I answered it and received a bouquet of roses from my classmates at Wake Forest.

I proudly walked them into the kitchen to show to my mom and her friends and then I fell apart and began to sob until I gasped for air. I returned to my bedroom and my bed and, with my face in my pillow, I cried myself dry. And then I felt better. I knew what was happening. I had to reconcile myself to unforeseen tragedy, and unexpected pleasure. This wasn't new to me. It was life and life was a bitch sometimes. And crying helped.

Later that evening, my mom told me Large Root Beer suffered his stroke while making love to her. I squirmed when she told me. But she needed to talk.

Then she added, "I never saw him naked. Not once in ten years."

They made love in the dark. Always. Without exception. And he changed clothes in a different room from her. Every time. They were never in the bathroom together.

And there were more secrets.

Large Root Beer revealed to her "during pillow talk," and just days before his stroke, that he hadn't filed income taxes in four years. The IRS had seized their bank accounts. To pay off the back taxes, he'd borrowed $20,000, "a business loan," from local Lumberman's Bank. And, I learned, the loan was taken out under false pretenses. He lied about the intended use of funds on the application.

Did he kill himself fucking?

Or did he fucking kill himself?

Son of a bitch.

He'd sold the cottage on the lake, with my help, and his parent's house in Battle Creek. He'd inherited money from an uncle. He worked. He was a lawyer, for God's sake. And it was all gone.

Over ten years, we went on just two family vacations. The house was in need of paint and new carpet. A basement renovation had been abandoned. The cars were in disrepair.

"Where'd the money go?"

"I don't know. I have no idea," my mom said.

It had been considerably more difficult for me to receive loans and grants and scholarships from Hope and Wake because Large Root Beer claimed that he didn't have time to provide financial information to the schools. It made sense. It finally made sense. And it made no sense at all.

"Did he use drugs?"

"I don't think so."

"Could he have made a bad investment or got caught up in a scam?"

"Not that I know of."

"How about a mistress, a girlfriend?"

"No. I'm sure not."

"How about gambling?"

"I don't know," she said. "I don't know."

He went from the hospital to the crematorium and into a generic brown, plastic box that I put in a closet, off the front entryway. I slid the container into a dark corner, on a shelf. Out of sight.

The crazy son of a bitch.

No money. No more Large Root Beer.

Gee thanks, God.

CARRIE'S MOM AND sisters joined the reception at the funeral home. I appreciated their presence and sincere condolences. Carrie was toiling as a junior graphic designer for a small studio in the University Park area of Dallas and, understandably, was unable to attend. We spoke by phone. She said she would come back. I insisted that she stay in Texas. I told her we'd be fine.

I spent a week at home and away from school. While I didn't want to leave my mom alone, I had no choice but to return to North Carolina and Wake. And finish what I'd started.

Back in Winston-Salem, I was able to secure interviews with Frito-Lay and Tracey Locke, an ad agency in Dallas. They financed a November trip for me to speak with them and, more importantly, see Carrie.

During our short summer together, we'd dated just six weeks. I couldn't explain the speed in which we'd fallen in love or the reasons it felt so deep and real. But while I was in Dallas, I asked her to marry me. She said, "Yes," But I had to "make it official" by asking her father's permission. I said, "Okay, I'll do so when I get to Muskegon for Christmas break."

Before Carrie returned for the holidays, I went to the Kloap home and asked her dad, John, if I could speak with him in his library. Once inside, I requested his consent to marry his daughter. He said, "Yes, of course." He shook my hand with both of his, and John's smile was the first brightness I'd seen in his sunken, ashen face. I prayed that he'd live long enough to celebrate our marriage, the first for one of his five daughters.

My mom and Carrie and I enjoyed Christmas Eve dinner, just the three of us, at the house on Bear Lake Road. We ate deliberately and drank excessively and talked about wedding plans and toasted Large Root Beer. Before the night was over, I went to the closet and retrieved the brown plastic box holding his baked bones. I shook the vessel with two hands over my head, like maracas. It sounded like gravel. Not ash or dust. We laughed, sufficiently tight from the wine and nonplussed with the racket coming from the box.

"Is this what deep-fried chicken shit sounds like?" I said.

I put the box on an empty fourth chair and he sat in the container, undisturbed, as we lamented his death and contemplated the future. He left my mom with nothing tangible. He was her odd—but loving—companion for a decade. He provided shelter and a thousand fond memories. She believed he cared deeply for her, and I believed he did as well. But he had peculiar and mysterious flaws. He was unable to confront them and his own secrets, so he hid or suppressed or ignored them. And, I was convinced, his secrets killed him.

"It's not fair. It's just not fair. Your dad's issues or problems— whatever you want to call them—they were more obvious than Lawrence's. And with your dad, I really didn't have any choice."

Carrie and I sat motionless. My mom licked the tip of her right index finger and ran the pad of her finger around the top of her wine glass, until the combination of lubrication and friction generated a tiny squeak. Then, satisfied, she stopped and smiled.

"He was very good to me, you know? I thought we were doing everything right. It's like that crazy Pull you did your sophomore year. Almost four hours on a rope, doing everything right. We thought you were winning and won and everyone was hugging and crying and then someone said it was a draw. I remember how hollow I felt. How empty. The void in my heart and gut. I feel that way now, only worse. The Pull was one thing. Lawrence was a person. He was my love. My once-in-a-lifetime."

We sat. No one said anything, for a minute. We looked into our glasses of wine. Searching for the right thing to say.

"You're gonna be all right. We're all gonna be just fine," I said.

"I know," she said. "But it hurts like hell right now."

"Of course it does. It's supposed to."

I looked at Carrie. Her eyes swelled with tears. My mom excused herself. She said she had something to share with me, a gift.

"After all, this is Christmas Eve."

She reappeared a few minutes later, lugging what looked to be a three-foot by two-foot framed picture or painting, wrapped in white tissue paper.

"This is for you. Open it."

My mom dabbled in art, drawing and painting mostly. She had a flair.

I tore back the tissue. It fell away easily and exposed a pen-and-ink and watercolor image on a white canvas within a muted green matte and black frame. The subject was a forest with tall, barren deciduous trees in the foreground and confiners blurred on the horizon. The stark and naked trees cast shadows on the white blanket covering the ground. I could sense the stillness of the woods. The quiet of the snow.

In an otherwise somber and bleak setting, there was a single, defiant seedling, perhaps a foot tall. It cast a shadow as well, but small among the tall oaks. The seedling had long, green pine needles. The only color in the scene. In perfect, cursive handwriting, above my mother's signature, and in the lower right-hand corner of the framed picture, were the prophetic words, "a green one for Woody."

Poor Woody, I thought. And Harold and Billie and Buzz and Deb and Michael and Terry. His parents and siblings. He was just a kid. Like Cousin Marko. So young. And so dead.

One right after the other. Uncle Charlie. Woody. Baby Molly. Marko. Great Grandma Bessie. My dad. And then, Large Root Beer.

All gone.

I took as deep a breath as I could, a futile effort to control my emotions, but the tears surged from my eyes and down my face. I shivered as I hugged my mom. I didn't want to let her go.

God, I missed Woody. I missed them all.

But there was hope in that little green tree. There was hope.

Forty-one

Nancy's Wedding

IN APRIL 1982, I accepted a job with an ad agency, Long Haymes Carr, in Winston-Salem. They were a respected shop with a fine reputation. I looked forward to cutting my teeth with them. I planned to start in the middle of June, two weeks after Carrie and I were to marry.

She quit her job in Dallas and pulled a U-Haul behind her crippled Ford LTD and joined me in Winston-Salem in early May. Two days later, and forgoing Wake's graduation festivities, we drove fifteen hours north, to Muskegon, for final wedding preparations and to be married on June 5. The plan was for Carrie to find work, hopefully in graphic design, when we returned south.

Upon arriving home on Bear Lake Road, my mom's mental health was of notable concern. She tried to put on a happy face, but her reality was evident and weighed heavy. Divorced and widowed, she was in her mid-forties and more than ten years out of nursing and twenty years out of social work and, before long, out of money. The house was crumbling around her. She had no clear or obvious path. While pleased for Carrie and me, she was moody and, at times, despondent. I feared what would happen to her alone in her decaying nest.

Early on, during the planning process, I learned that the wedding was not Carrie's or mine. It was for Nancy—Carrie's mom. I stayed clear of her majesty's way, and just as well. The ceremony at majestic St. Paul's was dreamy and spectacular. The reception, for two hundred guests, was held at Muskegon Country Club.

Built on virgin dunes overlooking Muskegon Lake and near Lake Michigan, the club was constructed generations earlier, when the city's industrialists were flush. Growing up, my exposure to the club was the modest entranceway on Lakeshore Drive on the way to Pere Marquette Park and the Lake Michigan beaches. I never aspired to be a member. That would have been inconceivable. Instead my buddies and I dreamed of caddying on the venerable course, designed by proficient and prolific Donald Ross and opened in 1908. The club was for members only. The exclusive haven of local elite, like Carrie's dad. And he was beyond proud to be the tuxedoed patriarch and lauded host of our wedding celebration.

It was another bluebird day. Perfect. Bright and sunny in the early evening with indiscernible humidity and the occasional cotton-ball cloud adding texture and depth to an azure sky. Sailboats sliced across blue and beautiful Muskegon Lake, visible from the veranda and the reception hall of the club. The sit-down dinner crowd overflowed into the bar, the result of a conspiracy among a dozen uninvited classmates from Hope. I shrugged my shoulders and smiled. Carrie and her mother were irritated. My new father-in-law, John, took it in stride. Much to my relief.

Leanne was on the invitation list, and among the expected constituents in the gang from Hope. Carrie had agreed to meet her a week before our wedding. The three of us lunched at the Bear Lake Tavern. Leanne was witty and gracious and charming. Carrie was magnanimous and greeted Leanne warmly, as a friend. I was thankful for their depth and maturity, and that they were both selfless and thoughtful. How was it that I had such strong, beautiful women in my life?

Late during the reception, my mom led a conga march while the band played "Beer Barrel Polka." The line ceded to pairs of polka dancers, Carrie's polish aunts and uncles, wildly spinning around the hall and crashing into each other. All in great fun.

The party was festive and fantastic. As dazzling as the day.

There was an announcement that dances with the bride were for sale. A hat was placed, upside down, on the floor. For thirty minutes, Carrie boogied with starry-eyed cousins and uncles and friends. My best man and freshman roommate, Dave Stevens, consolidated the money from the hat and stashed the cash in an envelope and handed the loot to me. I slipped the swag into my breast pocket. I hoped the bestowals were sufficient to fund the honeymoon and our return to Winston-Salem.

Finally the cake was cut and toasts were made.

Carrie and I slipped away to change. On our way to my car, we were showered with birdseed and good wishes. Then we drove an hour north to the Ludington Holiday Inn.

On our honeymoon bed, we counted and stacked fives, tens and twenties. Thankfully, enough cash to finance a few days up north and buy enough gas to get us back to Dixie.

Forty-two

A Beaver Island Miracle

WE WERE NEARLY alone on the boat when the South Shore reversed from her Charlevoix mooring in Round Lake. The ship then made her way under the unbuckled draw bridge and through the Pine River channel and out into vast and glorious Lake Michigan, toward the Beaver Archipelago.

The skies were clear. The winds were brisk from the north. The South Shore was the smaller of the two island ferries, so we rolled and bounced for most of the thirty-two miles. We were, at times, unsteady and uncomfortable, but after three hours we turned to port and slipped into placid, sheltered Paradise Bay at Beaver Island.

Carrie tolerated my role as tour guide as I pointed out the red-roofed Coast Guard station, at the harbor's mouth, and McDonough's market and the tricolor Irish flag flying next to the Shamrock bar. And, above the public beach, Holy Cross Church, where seagulls, coasting on a vortex of air, had formed a feathered, rotating halo over the white, clapboard sanctuary.

We watched the village of St. James sputter to life as our boat approached the pier. Family and friends walked and drove and biked to the ferry dock for the ceremonial unloading of people and provisions.

We were greeted by a handsome, slender and graying woman in her fifties. Her hair was cropped short and she wore simple, wire-framed glasses and khakis and a denim blouse. Behind her stood a van with the words "Beaver Island Lodge" rendered on its side.

"You must be Patrick and Carrie."

"And you must be Slim."

I'd spoken to Slim, by phone, on a couple of occasions. She knew of my late uncle Charlie and others in the Dunigan clan and, of course, Dr. Ludwig, Charlie's friend and a prior owner of the Lodge. The inn was close to town, a five- or ten-minute walk, and on the north shore and less than a mile east of the township campground where Ralph and Edgar Winter and Leanne and I overnighted.

The building was made of cinder block and brown, stained cedar and was understated and neat. On the lower level, overlooking Lake Michigan, was a small bar and restaurant, and on the forested side of the building, the living quarters for the owners. Ten guest rooms were upstairs, each with a view of the Big Lake.

Slim explained that the summer season didn't begin until late June and that the business wound down at the end of August. They were closed for most of the year, every year, and we would be the only guests in the Lodge for the nights of our stay.

Our room cost $35 per night, including morning toast and juice and coffee and fresh fruit, when available. Each day, Slim refreshed a vase of lilacs in our room. We drank their bouquet through our noses, as well as the scent of cedar from the woods that blew in through an open window. Our view of the lake was unobstructed but for one lonely arm of a single white pine that stood sentry over two Adirondack chairs that sat atop the bluff. The setting was pure and natural and unrefined and without pretense and comfortable and approachable and welcoming. There was something true and honest and real about Beaver Island that had pulled on me from the time I was a kid. It was a place of wonder and natural abundance. A source of renewal.

We rented mopeds and bundled up in jackets, spending hours scooting down dirt roads and hiking trails and walking empty beaches of sand and stone. We crawled up the spiraling stairs of the grand Beaver Head lighthouse. We scratched the nose of an old gray mare that stood in a doddering apple orchard along McCaulley's Road. We picked lilacs for Slim, and us, at a tumbledown farmhouse overlooking Barney's Lake. Late in the day, mosquitos chased us to the Shamrock bar where we drank beer and ate hoagies and chatted with boaters and went home and made love and showered in time to watch the sunset and enjoy a nightcap before bed. And then we made love again.

On our second day the winds were calm, so we rented a skiff and motored out of Paradise Bay and by Horseshoe Reef and two miles across Lake Michigan into Indian Harbor at Garden Island. We pulled the aluminum boat up on the beach and walked the trails until we found a cemetery where Indians once maintained spirit houses, and untold numbers were buried in unmarked graves.

Garden Island was without elevated bluffs like Beaver. It was low and peppered with ponds and wetlands, where we saw star flower and gold-thread and bog rosemary. Back on the beach, we noticed hoof prints from a pair of deer, apparently a doe and a fawn. A gull sat on semi-submerged rock and watched, as we poked and picked our way along the shore.

On our return, the afternoon breeze freshened out of the southwest, and we bumped our way back until Beaver sheltered us from the wind and we cruised smoothly along the rocky shore of Gull Harbor, by and around the Coast Guard dock and into Paradise Bay.

After returning our boat, we walked across Main Street to the Shamrock. Again we rumbled longnecks across the bar and toasted to our love and lifted the beers to the sky and poured them down our thirsty throats. After a few beers, we convinced ourselves that a swim was in order. We inquired as to the location of the best swimming beach. The bartender said, "Little Sand Bay, but it's too damn cold."

We fired up our mopeds. Picked up swimwear from the Lodge and then buzzed out of town, past the island's only school on what the locals called the Back Highway. We took a left where Barney's Lake Road became East Side Drive. The dirt and gravel lane led us past a century-old stone rectory and cemetery and angled to the right and by Welke Airport where we were told, by the bartender, we'd find an unmarked trail off the left side of the road.

We walked the mopeds down a sandy path that cut through an open field of orchard grass and dozens of juniper bushes. After a quarter of a mile, we were saluted by stands of cedar guarding a conifer swamp—a mushy, mossy bog. Down a meandering trail, we inched our way toward the lake. Locals had built footbridges and laid planks that bridged mounds of peat decorated with sedge. Beavers complicated the trip with their dams and ponds but we could smell the lake and, eventually, we saw bits of blue through the trees. Then, finally, we traversed the last of the ponds and mounds.

On the back side of the cedar bog, we were treated to a half-mile of sugar sand adorning a crescent beach that sloped gently into the gin-clear lake. The graduated aquamarine water telegraphed that the bay was shallow, and hopefully warm enough for an early season swim. We were overheated from the hike through the swamp, but Lake Michigan's water was bone-rattling cold. After crashing in, we lasted only seconds before escaping back to shore, shivering and shaking and laughing. We wrapped up in towels and sat on the cushion of white and watched a fishing trawler work northward with the bluffs of Good Hart on the mainland, just a sliver in the distance. I kissed my purple-lipped wife and I professed my young love for her. We held each other and counted our blessings on an afternoon unvarnished and beyond compare.

For dinner, at the Lodge, we shared dishes of sautéed morels and pecan-crusted Walleye and escargot in white wine and butter. We moved from our table, with a bottle of wine and glasses, to the Adirondack chairs and watched as Lake Michigan dined on the sun in the western sky. Once swallowed, the invisible sphere continued to redden the underbellies of clouds in a show that lasted considerably longer than expected, as though resisting the inexorable ending of our day. But light did give way to night and to the north we saw a lamp atop a single mast, at sheltered anchor in Indian Harbor, where we'd begun the day's adventures.

We lay in our bed under down covers, enjoying one more night of lilac and cedar carried by a cool and gentle late spring breeze. We listened to the Big Lake's waves nibble at the shore as we contemplated our life together.

An agitated blue jay served as our morning alarm, and Slim fixed us bowls of fruit and toasted muffins and coffee and orange juice at the same table we'd eaten breakfast and dinner the day before.

We told her how much we appreciated her hospitality. Carrie admitted she'd been apprehensive about visiting a place so remote, but her perspective had changed. We asked Slim to sit down with us. She did. Eventually, the conversation led to my mom's sad story and the heavy heart that she carried and the unanswered questions about her future. Her needs were complex. Carrie and I were befuddled, betwixt and bemused as to what to do.

Slim was not. She was direct and resolute. When we got back downstate, we were to send my mom to Beaver Island and the Lodge. Slim needed summer help and my mom could work in the kitchen or dining room, perhaps waiting tables. Slim would find her a place to stay. My mom needed a heavy dose of Beaver Island.

Two days later, we were back in Muskegon on Bear Lake Road.

"Mother, this might sound half insane, and maybe it is. But please, hear me out. Okay?"

"Okay."

"Well, Slim, the innkeeper, from the Lodge, she'll give you a job and a place to stay on the island for the summer. Carrie and I have talked about this. And you know what? We think you should do it. You need to get away. To escape."

<hr>

WE NEARLY MADE Winston-Salem in one day, but succumbed to fatigue less than an hour from town. We pulled into the Best Western near Pilot Mountain. For the first time in a week, we were too weary to make love. We slept in our clothes.

Late the next morning, we checked in at our apartment complex in Winston-Salem. The assistant manager insisted on a tour of the clubhouse and pool area. We begrudgingly acquiesced.

Seconds after stepping onto the deck from across the pool, I heard a female shout "Patrick!"—somehow finding five syllables in my two syllable name. She wore a black one-piece bathing suit, cut high above her hips, making her legs look even longer and more delicious than they already were. She jogged toward us, on her toes, with her boobs a-bobbing.

Minxy gave me an indulgent hug and a wet kiss. She said, "I didn't think I'd ever see you again."

"Hey, Minxy, great to see you. I wanna introduce you to my wife, Carrie.

"I figured that's who you were."

"Y'all movin' in here?"

I nodded my head, wondering if Carrie had changed her mind.

"Good. Well, I lifeguard out here once in a while, so maybe I'll see ya 'round. Carrie, it was nice to meet you. You got ya a good one, right here."

Minxy turned and, with her tight little butt on a swivel, made her way back across the pool deck to the lifeguard stand, but not without looking over her shoulder and waving goodbye.

Carrie asked, "How many Minxys will I meet down here?"

I shrugged my shoulders.

◇────◦●◦────◇

SHE SAID SHE'D go and she did. My mom packed her bags and drove three hours north to Charlevoix. She boarded the ferry to Beaver Island. Slim met her at the dock. She gave her a job and a place to hang her hat. After two weeks, someone suggested my mom attend a concert at the parish hall across from Holy Cross Catholic Church.

As an ensemble of talented islanders entertained the crowd, she noticed a handsome man a few years her senior dressed in the local uniform of denim and flannel, his hands stuffed deeply into his pants and nervously shuffling his feet.

She introduced herself to Joe Williams. His eyes were small and blue and kind and sincere and uncomplicated. He asked what brought her to the island. She told him her story.

"Why are you here? Are you running away from something, too?"

He was from Detroit. He'd served in the military during the Korean War and worked three decades for Chrysler as a tool-and-die man. He'd been coming to the island for many years and, with the help of friends, built a small cottage on the north shore near the Lodge.

"Nothin' more than a hunting cabin," he said.

He was uncomfortable telling her the rest. And he didn't right away. They stood next to each other, in awkward silence, for several minutes. Then Joe spoke again.

"My wife cheated on me."

"I'm sorry. I really am."

"Worse than that. She was sleeping with my sister's husband."

"Oh, God. Your wife was screwing your brother-in-law?"

"Yup. And my sister and me, we were the only ones that didn't know. Everyone knew what was going on. Everyone. Right under our noses."

"Oh, God."

"Yup."

My mom asked Joe to dance.

He said, "Okay."

And they did.

They spun slowly in a small circle of life. And that night, serenaded by friends, they fell in love—honest, sincere and real.

Not long after that fateful evening, they stood together, arm in arm, in a sugary bowl of sand on the north shore of Beaver Island just down the lake from the Lodge. Among family and friends, Slim the innkeeper—an ordained minister—asked Lois and Joe if they would love each other forever. They said "Yes" and "I will."

In the brilliant blue sky, rising on a vortex of air and rotating in a feathered halo of love, the white seagulls of Holy Cross rejoiced in a chorus of affirmation. Waves clapped their approval at the water's stony edge. A soothing breeze bathed the beach in an organic cologne of pine, cedar and juniper.

And they lived happily, ever after.

They really did.

Epilogue
(Summer 2012)

AS I WRITE this note on Sunday, August 5, an implausibly aquamarine Lake Michigan is striped with foaming whitecaps. It's seventy-one degrees and gray-rimmed cotton balls dot a mid-afternoon, powder-blue sky. A ragged line of treetops, twenty miles north on the Upper Peninsula of Michigan, is clearly visible beyond Whisky and Squaw islands. The Tigers are playing the Indians on the television—tied 4–4 in the sixth inning. Poppa Joe has just dozed off, the remote teetering on his right thigh.

Carrie and my mother, Lois, are on the back deck reading and occasionally chatting and chuckling, their sounds sometimes obscured by an agitated blue jay and the wind whipping through the oak and birch that stand astride Lois and Joe's tiny Beaver Island home.

My daughter, Caitlin, will be twenty-one this month. She flew out of North Carolina this afternoon; we'll pick her up at Welke Airport at 7:45 tonight. Kelly, our twenty-two-year-old son, just left Winston-Salem within the past hour and will spend the night at his aunt Kathy's house tonight in Charlotte. He'll catch a plane in the morning and join us here in paradise tomorrow.

Today, life is good.

Author's Note

A memoir, by definition, is a collection of memories. And for the most part, my memory is pretty darn good. Ironically, my recollections have been aided by the fact that, as an accidental gypsy, I made beds in almost a dozen places as a kid, thus enabling me to connect whatever happened, good or bad, with where I was at the time.

If I did mistakenly recall events in this book, I'm sorry. Luckily, I was aided by Great-grandma Bessie's plentiful journal, boxes of annotated family photographs, school yearbooks and the best single-source for "anything O'Sullivan," my cousin Phyllis Corona.

Phyllis, now in her eighties, is the daughter of my late uncle Emmet (my grandfather's brother) who took his own life in the opening chapter. She'd been sent to the movies on that dismal day. Phyllis's beauty is unequalled, and her selflessness is without reproach. The year Carrie and I were married, 1982, her brother P. Michael O'Sullivan, the gifted photojournalist from Chicago, suffered debilitating brain damage from a motorcycle mishap. For more than two decades, Phyllis and her late husband, Carl, cared for my diminished cousin until cancer did what concrete and metal couldn't.

Like my long-dead great-grandmother Bessie, Phyllis deserves the moniker of "Family Treasure."

The names, dates and places mentioned in this book are intended to be accurate, with a couple of exceptions. I changed or disguised the names of a handful of people in the book. I saw no advantage in sullying their present-day lives by highlighting past indiscretions.

Patrick O'Sullivan

Made in the USA
Charleston, SC
11 November 2013